# must-see

D0539926

CONTENTS

Published by Thomas Cook Publishing
A division of Thomas Cook Holdings Ltd
PO Box 227, Thorpe Wood
Peterborough PE3 6PU
United Kingdom

Telephone: 01733 503571
E-mail: books@thomascook.com

Text: © 2000 Thomas Cook Holdings Ltd
Maps prepared by Polly Senior Cartography
Maps © 2000 Thomas Cook Holdings Ltd

ISBN 1 841570 71 0

Distributed in the United States of America by the Globe Pequot Press,
PO Box 480, Guilford, Connecticut 06437, USA.

Distributed in Canada by Whitecap Books, 351 Lynn Avenue,
North Vancouver, British Columbia, Canada V7J 2C4.

Distributed in Australia and New Zealand by Peribo Pty Limited,
58 Beaumont Road, Mt Kuring-Gai, NSW, 2080, Australia.

Publisher: Donald Greig
Commissioning Editor: Deborah Parker
Map Editor: Bernard Horton

Series Editor: Christopher Catling

Written and researched by: Christopher Catling, Adele Evans, Teresa Fisher and
Brent Gregston.

Although every care has been taken in compiling this publication, and the
contents are believed to be correct at the time of printing, Thomas Cook
Holdings Ltd cannot accept responsibility for errors or omissions, however
caused, or for changes in details given in the guidebook, or for the consequences
of any reliance on the information provided.

The opinions and assessments expressed in this book do not necessarily
represent those of Thomas Cook Holdings Ltd.

Readers are asked to remember that attractions and establishments may open,
close or change owners or circumstances during the lifetime of this edition.
Descriptions and assessments are given in good faith but are based on the
author's views and experience at the time of writing and therefore contain
an element of subjective opinion which may not accord with the reader's
subsequent experience. We would be grateful to be told of any changes or
inaccuracies in order to update future editions. Please notify them to the
Commissioning Editor at the above address.

Cover photograph: John Heseltine

# must-see ITALY

## Edited by
## CHRISTOPHER
## CATLING

# Getting
# to know
# Italy

# Discovering Italy

*A glance at a map of Italy shows that it is a land crafted in the form of a long, tapering boot. From top to toe and heel of that elegant boot, this country is, for many, the most beautiful and varied in the world. Birthplace of the pizza, home to superlative cities, sparkling lakes, mountains, sun-drenched rivieras, treasure troves of antiquities, capitals of romance, hedonism and style, Italy has it all.*

## La terra

Italy's great variety is due, in part, to its enviable geographical location. Bordered on all sides in the north – by Switzerland, Austria, Slovenia and France – lapped by the **four seas** of the Mediterranean from the Ligurian, Tyrrhenian, Adriatic and to the Ionian Sea of the deep south, the coastline covers 7 500km (4 660 miles). Yet it is only just over half the size of France or Spain. From the highest peak of Monte Rosa, at 4 634m (15,203ft), in the Italian Alps to the Apennines, the 'backbone' of Italy running from Genoa into Sicily, 75 per cent of the terrain is covered by mountains and hills. In the south between Sicily and Naples the **volcanoes of Vesuvius**, **Etna** and **Stromboli** continue to smoulder and occasionally erupt and earthquakes here and in central Italy are not uncommon.

Plains cover 21 per cent of the land; the largest is the **Po valley**, following the course of the Po, Italy's longest river at 650km (404 miles).

## Italian warmth

The Latin temperament is noted above all for its warmth, but the Italian climate varies dramatically over the length and breadth of the peninsula. The sizzling summers and mild winters of the south are matched by equally hot, humid summers in the plains, where the winters are cold and damp. In the Alpine north, the snows never leave the highest peaks, but, although chilly in winter, it is usually bright and the summers are warm. The northern lakes have their own microclimate, where lemon trees and sub-tropical plants flourish, all the more exotic given the proximity of the Swiss–Austrian borders.

## Food and style

In Italy, food is a sensuous celebration of life to be shared and enjoyed by everyone. Each region has its own specialities – from the gourmet 'fat' lands of Emilia-Romagna to the less rich terrain of the south, where inventiveness has triumphed over poverty. The Mediterranean diet, rich in olive oil, tomatoes, fresh fish, meat and vegetables, washed down with sun-filled wines, is not only highly nutritious, but also utterly delicious.

**Presentation of the self** is an art form in which the Italians excel, learned at their mothers' knee. *La bella figura* – the art of being seen to look one's best – is on show every day in the early-evening *passeggiata*, when families, friends and couples take a stroll out on the streets to see, be seen and preen. The style of Italy, from the glories of Michelangelo and Leonardo to **modern-day designers** such as Prada and Gucci, never fails to seduce visitors to this beautiful and richly varied country.

# Life in Italy

*There is no such thing as a typical day in the life of a typical Italian. Venetian, Roman, Tuscan, Milanesi – in fact, 20 different regional tribes – all have their own characteristics.*

The **diversity** of Italy is its special appeal, yet all Italians are united in their love of the family, even though their country has one of the lowest birth rates in the whole of Europe. Although it is the **centre of Roman Catholicism**, less than 10 per cent go regularly to Mass, and birth control, abortion and divorce have all been on offer since the 1970s. Tax avoidance is a way of life and the tentacles of the **Mafia** still exert a stranglehold.

## Back to the roots

Although essentially an agricultural land, nowadays only just under 7 per cent of the whole population of around 57 million people is employed in agriculture. Italy is now an **important industrial power** and is among the world's seven most industrialised countries. Some believe that the industrial north subsidises the poor south, and there is growing support for the political parties that want to create a more partitioned Italy. At the beginning of the 20th century there was a **mass emigration** from the south to the USA, and elsewhere, and the 1950s and 1960s saw significant migration to the north, notably Turin. The north is now experiencing yet more prosperity, but fewer Italians are willing to take up factory work and the country is experiencing a huge influx of both legal and illegal immigrants who are all too grateful for the jobs.

## Speaking in tongues

Charles V, the Holy Roman Emperor, famously said that he spoke Spanish with God, French to the court, German to his horse and Italian to women. Today, the beautiful Italian language has around 1 500 different dialects, at a conservative estimate. Only three newspapers are circulated nationally, Rome's *La Repubblica*, *La Stampa* from Turin and Milan's *Corriere della Sera*; all other papers are regional apart from sports publications. Food is a major topic of conversation everywhere – so much so that you wonder sometimes how so many Italians manage to stay thin.

## Fit for life

In the 1980s a fitness and health boom resulted in a rash of centres and clubs devoted to the body beautiful. Motor racing and cycling are popular spectator sports, but **football** (*calcio*) has the most fanatical following, with clubs competing to sign up the world's most expensive and flamboyant players. Italians love the sybaritic pleasures of the **seaside** and escape there as often as possible. The **mountains** are popular in the summer for hiking and climbing and later become a winter-sports playground.

## Life's rich pattern

In Italy a red traffic light is just a light, sunglasses are used 24 hours a day in winter and summer, but rarely to block the sun's rays, a mobile phone is an indispensable fashion accessory, and smoking is endemic, but drunkenness is taboo. Enjoy *la bella Italia!*

# Yesterday and tomorrow

*The united kingdom of 'Italy' was created only in 1861, but the Italian peninsula has evidence of some of the oldest human habitations anywhere; some finds date back 70,000 years. By the 8th and 7th centuries BC, the Etruscans had enjoyed their age of glory and the Greeks had established settlements along the southern coast and Sicily.*

## The Roman empire

According to legend, Italy's capital was founded by **Romulus** in 753 BC, when he killed his twin brother **Remus**, and declared himself the first King of Rome. After the final overthrow of the Etruscans, the first **Republic of Rome** was born in 509 BC; the 'Roman Code' gave rights to its citizens and proved to be an important contribution to future civilisations. Under **Julius Caesar** and **Augustus**, Roman civilisation flowered, but by the 5th century AD, the empire was under attack from Teutonic tribes from the north and from Arab forces in the Mediterranean. Corruption, laziness and decadence all contributed to Rome's **decline and ultimate fall**, in AD 476.

## Towards unification

The Barbarians were followed to power by Byzantines, Lombards and Franks and, in the north, powerful city states flourished. In the 1350s, the **Italian Renaissance** was born in Florence, and transformed the whole of Europe. In the 15th century northern Italy was the most cultured and prosperous region in western Europe. After Spanish and Austrian domination, Italy fell to **Napoleon** in 1796. In

1861 the **Kingdom of Italy** was proclaimed under Victor Emanuele II, although it was not until 1870 that Italy was **finally unified**, following the efforts of **Cavour**, **Garibaldi** and **Mazzini**.

# Into the 21st century

By 1919 Benito **Mussolini**'s Fascist party had become a symbol of aggressive nationalism; with the coming of the Second World War, Mussolini formed an alliance with Hitler, and led Italy into the conflict in 1940. In 1946, the monarchy was disbanded and Italy became a **republic**. Since that time there have been 55 governments – few of which have escaped corruption.

Italy was a founding member of the European Economic Community and has been a part of the growing political and economic unification of western Europe, including the introduction of the **euro** in January 1999. Yet, today, there seems to be an increasing **move away from unification**. The political right wing has made important gains in recent local elections, defeating councils and left-wing mayors, even in traditionally liberal areas of Italy. The right-wing alliance has promised to take a hard line on immigration, and as a result is tipped to win the next general election.

The new century has brought a wave of optimism, and the **restoration of many sites**. The 7 000-m (22,966-ft) façade

of St Peter's in Rome has been cleaned to a state of renewed splendour, and millennium funds are being extensively used for restoration in the south. **Pedestrianisation** and new traffic-calming schemes are a huge bonus to visitors' enjoyment of many cities; in Rome's Piazza del Popolo, the only vehicles now are children's tricycles.

# People and places

*'Don't go with an itinerary, go with an open heart,' is the advice from Sicilian Domenico Dolce of the world-famous fashion design duo, Dolce e Gabbana.*

Galaxies of writers, artists, celebrities and travellers have always flocked to this beautiful country, including **Shakespeare**, who set countless plays here. In the 18th century, many who came on the 'Grand Tour' took up residence in exile from their own grey lands, allowing themselves to be dazzled and inspired by Italy's voluptuousness. Rome and Naples were the last ports of call on the **Grand Tour**.

## Glitterati

*It Started in Naples* was one of the many films of the gorgeous Italian actress **Sophia Loren**, but one of Italy's earliest international stars was **Rudolph Valentino**, a migrant from Puglia who during his brief career was the undisputed heart-throb of the silent movies. Sicily was the setting for *The Godfather* series of Mafia films, and of **Visconti**'s *The Leopard*, adapted from Tomasi de Lampedusa's powerful work. The decadence of Rome in the late 1950s is remembered forever in Federico **Fellini**'s *La Dolce Vita* (*The Sweet Life*), made in 1960 – who can forget the scene of starlet Anita Ekberg frolicking in the Trevi Fountain?

The great director Fellini and best-loved actor **Marcello Mastroianni**, who starred in *La Dolce Vita*, both died in the 1990s, and are still much lamented, but new talent is emerging. In 1999, **Roberto Benigni**'s film *La Vita è Bella* was awarded three Oscars. It was cause for great celebration after a number of years of relative obscurity for the Italian film industry – with the notable exceptions of *Il Postino* and the warmly nostalgic *Cinema Paradiso*. Released in 2000, **Anthony Minghella**'s film *The Talented Mr Ripley*, starring Jude Law and Gwyneth Paltrow, is a homage to the glories of Italy and gave a huge boost to tourism – if one were needed!

It is now possible to visit the sets of some of the 'sandal and toga' epics and other great Italian films at Rome's famed *Cinecittà* studios ( *by appointment, tel: 06 722 86257* ).

## Movers and shakers

Turin is the home of one of the country's most powerful men, **Giovanni Agnelli** of the Fiat dynasty fame, who owns the Juventus football team. **Vittorio Cecchi Gori** is a media magnate and centrist politician – chairman of Fiorentina football club and owner of a huge film production company. Former prime minister **Silvio Berlusconi** is another multi-millionaire tycoon. He was handed a suspended sentence for fraud in 1997 but, as well as retaining his media empire and the chairmanship of the football team AC Milan, he is still allowed to head a political party – the right-wing Forza Italia.

## The world's a stage

Italy is responsible for **Enrico Caruso** and his *O Sole Mio*, the **birth of opera** in 14th-century Florence, **Farinelli the *castrato***, whose unbroken angelic voice caused 18th-century ladies to faint with excitement, and today's most famous opera singer, the equally 'swoon-making' but richly deep-toned **Luciano Pavarotti**. The Italians are a drama themselves – they are experts because they live life on the fabulous, glittering stage of Italy.

# Getting around

## Air

The national Italian airline, **Alitalia** ( *central reservations, UK tel: 0870 544 8259; Rome tel: 06 65 641* ), serves 20 airports, using the main hub centres of Milan and Rome as onward departure points. **British Airways** flies to nine cities in Italy ( *reservations tel: 020 8759 5511* ). As well as the major airlines, several 'no-frills' operators fly direct from the UK to destinations all over Italy. **Ryanair** ( *reservations tel: 0870 156 9569, or online: www.Ryanair. com* ) has nine routes from London Stansted. **Go**, British Airways' low-cost airline ( *reservations tel: 0845 605 4321, or online: www.go-fly.com* ), has four routes from Stansted. For domestic flights, contact **ATI**, **Alitalia**'s domestic service ( *Rome, tel: 06 65 641* ), or **Meridiana** ( *tel: 020 7839 2222* ), which has a new direct daily service from London Gatwick to Turin and Catania (Sicily).

## Bus

There is no national bus company in Italy, but there is a fairly good network of services throughout the country; as a general rule, the further south you go the more erratic they become. Buses usually depart from a terminal next to a railway station or from a town's main squares; tickets must be bought before travelling, either from the depot, station kiosk or tobacconists (look for the white 'T' on a blue or black background). Major Italian bus companies include **SITA** ( *Florence, tel: 055 483 651* ) and **Autostradale** ( *Milan, tel: 02 801 161* ).

# Car

Whether you take your own car, or decide to hire one locally, remember that the reputation of the crazy Italian boy racer behind the wheel is, on the whole, well deserved. The main cities are very congested, and driving on their streets is best avoided by visitors. However, a car can give you the greatest freedom for discovering the Italian countryside and less touristy areas.

If you are planning to cross the Channel from the UK and then drive south to Italy, Calais and Boulogne are the best French arrival ports. The route through the mountains has been made more difficult by the fact that the **Mont Blanc tunnel** remains closed after the tragic fire of March 1999. The official re-opening date for the Mont Blanc tunnel has been set for March 2001, although local residents say that the work is unlikely to be completed by then.

All the major **car-rental companies** have offices at airports and in the larger cities. If you need to pick up a car from a city centre office, do check on opening times; the majority will be closed during the sacrosanct hours of lunchtime.

As well as your driving licence, you need an **international green card of insurance** and, if resident outside the EU, you are required to have an **international driving permit**. Drivers must be over 18 years old and have had a driving licence for at least two years. It is compulsory to carry your documents with you so that you can present them if stopped by the police. **Speed limits** are as follows: 130km/h on the motorway ( *autostrada* ); 90–110km/h on main roads; 50km/h in urban areas. **Seat belts** in both front and rear are now compulsory – you may even see enterprising Neapolitans wearing T-shirts printed with a belt! Drink-driving tests are now in regular use and the permitted legal limit for blood alcohol is 0.08 per cent. The *autostrada* network is good and the tolls are reasonable; payment is by cash or credit card. The cheapest petrol is usually found at supermarkets with their own petrol station.

The telephone line for 24-hour road assistance ( *tel: 116* ) is transferred to the **Automobile Club of Italy** (ACI) (*head office in Rome, tel: 06 499 8234*). For information in English on roads, weather conditions and tolls, *tel: 06 44 77*.

# Rail

It is possible to travel by train from the UK to Italy but, although scenic, it is a long journey (up to 20 hours from London to Milan), and the cost is not much less than flying. The state railway network (**FS**, or *Ferrovie dello Stato*) within Italy is, however, a convenient, easy and relatively cheap way of travelling around the country. Options range from the **Locali** services, which stop absolutely everywhere, to the **Diretto** and **Espresso** (also called **Regionali** and **Interregionale**), the long-distance fast trains which stop at larger stations. **Intercity** links the major Italian cities, while **Eurocity** services interconnect with other European capitals. Both the Intercity and Eurocity are around 30 per cent more expensive than the ordinary services and you need to reserve a seat in advance. The ultra-fast and luxurious **Pendolino** is the shining star of the network, offering first-class intercity travel, including a meal, newspapers and seat reservation.

The FS offers two main rail passes for visitors to Italy: the **BTLC** (*Biglietto Turistico Libera Circolazione*), a go-as-you-please ticket for different durations, and a **FlexiCard** allowing four pre-determined days' travel within nine days, and other variations. Both these cards represent good value and can be bought at the main Italian stations – be prepared to queue! Validate your ticket or pass in the yellow machine on the platform or in the ticket hall, otherwise you'll be liable to a hefty on-the-spot fine. For information in London, contact Italian State Railways (*tel: 020 7724 0011, www.fs-on-line.com*).

# Scooters and bikes

If you fancy joining the scooter crowd, there are plenty of places in major towns where you can hire a traditional buzzing **Vespa** (or 'Wasp'). The wearing of crash helmets is now compulsory and, even if others flout the law, the high

number of accidents may make you think twice about doing so. **Bicycles** are popular and easily hired and, in some towns, such as Ferrara, really are the best way to travel.

## Taxis

Taxis are difficult to hail on the streets, but you will usually find taxi ranks in main piazzas or outside railway stations. Always use a **licensed cab** and make sure that the meter is running;

supplements are charged for luggage and late-night or early-morning services and for airport transfers. If you've ever gazed longingly out from a marooned cab at scooters weaving deftly through the traffic, the new blue and yellow *Motobeep* service could be for you. The fleet of scooters, complete with on-board computer, rainproof hood and helmet fitted with a microphone (and, of course, driver!), are now available for hire service in Rome and Palermo.

# Don't miss

## 1 Amalfi coast

Named after its biggest town, Amalfi, this gloriously wild and rugged coastline studded with beautiful villages and lush vegetation is Italy's finest stretch of coast. **Pages 238-9**

## 2 Lake Como

Inspiration to Shelley and Wordsworth, among a galaxy of poets and artists, Lake Como is not only the most dramatically scenic of the northern lakes, but also the most romantically Italian. **Page 31**

## 3 Florence

One of the artistic capitals of the world, Florence was the birthplace of the Renaissance and is the jewel of the gently rolling, cypress- and olive-clad fabled Tuscan countryside. **Pages 124-47**

## 4 Le Cinque Terre, Liguria

Liguria's five little villages cling, as if in a time warp, to steeply terraced rocky cliffs in a remote and spectacular setting above sparkling azure seas. **Pages 26-7**

## 5 Naples

Capital of the 'Mezzogiorno', the land of the midday sun, Naples is beautiful, chaotic, colourful and noisy, lying in the fabulous setting of the Bay of Naples, dominated by the beautiful but terrible Mount Vesuvius. **Pages 246-9**

## 6 Ravenna

The sleeping beauty of Emilia-Romagna will awaken even the most jaded visitor's senses to the breathtaking glory and exuberance of its world-famous mosaics. **Pages 116-17**

## 7 Rome

The Eternal City of fountains, fabulous art treasures and monumental ruins is looking even more gorgeous after her face-lift for Jubilee Year in 2000. **Pages 180-211**

## 8 Sicily

Power struggles, corruption, smouldering volcanoes and a host of invaders have all given this, the largest island in the Mediterranean, a fascinating, unique and gloriously rich heritage. **Pages 252-5**

## 9 Siena

If there is such a thing as a perfect medieval city, Siena is it: the city is also the site of the spectacular and thrilling festival of the Palio horse race. **Pages 168-71**

## 10 Venice

Omar Sharif has called it 'the most romantic city in the world'. No other city seemingly floats on water and the magical sight of St Mark's at its pulsating heart never disappoints. **Pages 74-101**

# Turin, Milan and the Northwest

*From the plain of Lombardy and its fabled lakes, and maritime Mediterranean Liguria, to the foot of the mountains in Piedmont and the towering peaks encircling the Valle d'Aosta, this area is striking in its diversity of landscape. It also has the north's two major cities: elegant, yet often underestimated Turin and the business and fashion city of Milan, Europe's 'catwalk capital'.*

# BEST OF

# Turin, Milan and the Northwest

*Getting there: Milan's Malpensa airport handles mainly scheduled and long-haul flights, while Linate is served by European and charter flights. Turin airport is especially popular for the Gran Paradiso National Park and winter sports around the Valle d'Aosta. The airport at Genoa is well placed for the Cinque Terre and served by low-cost airlines, as well as Alitalia. The Italian railway has frequent services and a choice of trains, from the high-speed* Pendolino *to regional* Locali, *which stop at every station. The road system in the north is generally excellent, with good (toll-paying) motorways.*

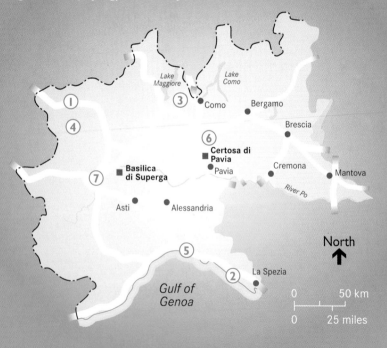

## (1) Aosta

The capital of the Valle d'Aosta, with Roman ruins set against the backdrop of Europe's highest mountain, Mont Blanc, is an excellent base for access to the eleven valleys of the area and to France and Switzerland. **Pages 24–5**

## (2) Le Cinque Terre

Five villages cling perilously and dramatically to the steep cliffs of the Ligurian coastline, fringed by terraced vineyards and azure seas. A great contrast to the more developed towns further up the coast, the Cinque Terre remain relatively untouched by Italian tourists. **Pages 26–7**

## (3) Italian Lakes

Lakes Como and Maggiore are beautiful, busy and justifiably popular, set in stunning landscapes. The Borromean Islands at the centre of Maggiore and Como's Bellagio are both jewels. Choose between them – if you can. **Pages 31–2**

## (4) Gran Paradiso

For walkers and nature-lovers, Italy's first national park, the Gran Paradiso, never fails to impress and inspire. **Page 30**

## (5) Genoa

Capital of the province of Liguria, this salty city is colourful and sleazy in parts, yet fascinating, with a fine medieval centre. **Pages 28–9**

## (6) Milan

Italy's top business city is also home to the spectacular Duomo, the world's largest Gothic cathedral. La Scala opera house is legendary, but Milan is best known as a capital of style and fashion. **Pages 34–9**

## (7) Turin

Café society is still very much alive in this surprising city where long boulevards and graceful colonnades reflect a heyday as the capital of Savoy, and of the whole of Italy from 1861 to 1865. **Pages 42–5**

## Travel information

The main access from France to the Aosta valley, the Mont Blanc tunnel, remains closed after the tragic fire in March 1999; although the official re-opening date is March 2001, it is by no means certain that this will be met.

## Tourist information

**Liguria**: *Agenzia Regionale di Promozione Turistica 'in Liguria', Palazzo Ducale, Piazza Matteotti, Genova. Tel: 010 530 31 76; www.regione.liguria.it/turismo.*
**Lombardy**: *Assessorato Regionale al Turismo Giunta Regionale, Via Sassetti 32, Milan. Tel: 02 67651; www.regione.lombardia.it/turismo.*
**Milan**: the main APT centre is at *Via Marconi 1 (corner of Piazza del Duomo). Tel: 02 725241.*
**Piedmont region**: *Assessorato Regionale al Turismo Direzione Turismo, Sport e Parchi, Via Magenta 12, Turin. Tel: 011 432 15 03; www.regione.piemonte.it/turismo,* or: *Agenzia regionale per la promozione turistica del Piemonte, Via Viotti 2, Turin. Tel: 011 554 11 11.*
**Valle d'Aosta**: *Assessorato Regionale del Turismo, Piazza Navarone 3, Aosta. Tel: 0165 272725; www.regione.vda.it/turismo.*

# Aosta

*Tourist information: Piazza E Chanoux 8. Tel: 0165 23 66 27. Open: daily 0900–1300 and 1500–2000; closed Sun pm out of winter and summer high seasons.*

Aosta is the capital of the Valle d'Aosta, Italy's smallest region, which has been an important passage between Italy, Switzerland and France since ancient times. Surrounded by the majestic peaks of Monte Bianco (Mont Blanc), Europe's highest mountain at 4 807m (15,770ft), Monte Rosa and Monte Cervino (the Matterhorn), the area's scenery is spectacular.

Founded in 24 BC by the emperor Augustus, Aosta has some well-preserved Roman remains, and the local nickname of 'Rome of the Alps'. Disregard the rambling, busy outskirts and enter the old town by the stone arches of **Porta Pretoria**, flanked by a medieval tower, originally the main gateway to the old Roman city. A few paces north along Via di Baillage take you to the **Teatro Romano** (*open: daily 0900–1900 in summer, 0930–1200 and 1430–1630 in winter; £*). Part of the façade still stands 22m (72ft) high, studded with arched windows, and a lower section of the auditorium remains intact; performances are held here in the summer. Heading west, you come to the remains of the old market place, the

## Tip

*Aosta is very popular on market day (Tuesday), when visitors from Switzerland and France come to buy delicious Italian gourmet specialities, including the crisp white Blanc de Morgex wine, which comes from the highest vineyards in Europe (up to 1100m, or 3 610ft) in the Valle d'Aosta.*

**Foro Romano** (*Piazza Giovanni XXIII; open: daily; £*); there is still much speculation as to the original use of the extraordinary colonnaded underground gallery, the **Criptoportico**. Next to the forum is the **Museo Archeologico Regionale** (regional archaeological museum) (*Piazza Giovanni XXIII; open: daily 0900–1900; £*), which has an interesting collection of Celtic and Roman artefacts found in the area.

# Brescia

*Tourist information: APT, Corso Zanardelli 34. Tel: 030 43 418. Open: Mon–Fri 0900–1230 and 1500–1800; Sat 0900–1230. Tourist information also at Piazza della Loggia 6. Tel: 030 240 0357. Open: Mon–Sat 0930–1830 Apr–Sept; Mon–Sat 0930–1230 and 1400–1700 Oct–Mar.*

After Milan, Brescia is Lombardy's second city. It is a mixture of art treasures, Roman remains, fine Renaissance buildings and pretty piazzas juxtaposed with harsh Fascist architecture.

The **Piazza della Loggia** is Brescia's prettiest square, dating back to the 15th century when the city invited Venice to protect it from Milan's all-powerful ruling Viscontis. The Venetian influence is clear both in the ornate **Loggia** (partly built by Palladio), which is now the town hall, and the **Torre dell'Orologio** (clock tower) opposite. The tower, modelled on the campanile in Venice's Piazza San Marco, is topped by two clockwork figures that strike the hours. The remains of the old Roman town, *Brixia*, are around the Piazza del Foro; the **Tempio Capitolino** (temple) (*Via Musei 57a; tel: 030 46031; open: Tue–Sun; £*) was built in AD 73. Another highlight is the main art gallery, the **Pinacoteca Civica Tosio-Martinengo** (*Via Martinengo da Barco; tel: 030 377 4999; open: Tue–Sun 1000–1700 June–Sept, Tue–Sun 0930–1300 and 1430–1700 Oct–May; £*), which houses richly coloured works of the Brescia school, as well as Tintorettos and masterpieces by Raphael, including his *Ecstasy of St Cecilia*.

# Le Cinque Terre

*Tourist information: Piazza Garibaldi, Monterosso. Tel: 0187 51 83 41. Open:*
*Mon–Sat 0930–1230 and 1530–1830.*

These five picturesque fishing villages, known as the Cinque Terre ('Five Lands'), are gloriously difficult to get to, except on foot, or by mule. However, the effort is well rewarded, with views of the rocky Ligurian coast, studded with inlets and coves lapped by turquoise waters, and its tiny villages.

*" You will see many marvels [on the Ligurian coast] which will be easier to admire than to describe with any human pen: wherever you turn you will see pleasant valleys, rushing streams and hills known for their steepness. "*

**Fourteenth-century poet Petrarch, in his guide for pilgrims**

The main source of income in these dramatic hideaways is still fishing, olive-growing and the production of some nationally renowned dry white and dessert wines from steeply terraced vineyards. It is possible to drive to all five villages, leaving cars at the entrances, but the best way to travel is by the ancient 14-km (9-mile) coastal footpath, the **Sentiero Azzurro**. The largest, most commercialised of the five villages is **Monterosso al Mare**, on the northwest edge, with a view down to a wide bay and lovely sandy beach.

**Vernazza** is perhaps the prettiest; its **Castello Doria** offers magnificent vistas. The stretch between **Vernazza** and **Corniglia**, the next village, perched high on a ridge, covers some fairly tough terrain; halfway between the two lies the splendidly isolated **Guvano** beach, ideal for a private dip. From **Manarola**, a fairly steep climb winds through vineyards to the top of the mountain, a great vantage point on a clear day from which to see all the villages. The end of the path is by the lemon-tree-scented **Via dell'Amore** at **Riomaggiore**, one of the larger villages, wedged into the tumbling hillside.

# Cremona

*Tourist information: APT, Piazza del Comune 5. Tel: 0372 23 233. Open: Mon–Sat 0930–1230 and 1500–1800; Sun 0945–1215.*

Cremona is famous, above all, as a centre for music. Its famous sons include the composer Claudio Monteverdi and Antonio Stradivari, who developed the melodious Stradivarius violin. The town also has a lovely square, a fine cathedral and is the site of Italy's tallest medieval tower. The **Torrazzo** (*Piazza del Comune; tel: 0372 27 057; open: daily 1030–1200 and 1500–1800; £–££*) is 111m (364ft) high and, as well as providing superb views from the top, has a fascinating workshop on the first floor, the **Bottega della Torre**, where violins are still made. Linked to the tower by a Renaissance loggia is the Lombard-Gothic-style **Duomo** with its richly sculptured façade and huge 13th-century rose window. On the west of the piazza is the opulent **Palazzo del Commune** (town hall), which has an exhibition of historic violins, including a 1715 Stradivarius, in the **Sala dei Violini** (*open: Tue–Sat 0830–1800, Sun 0915–1215 and 1500–1800; £–££*). They are played occasionally, to keep them in working order – you may be lucky! The **Museo Stradivariano** (Stradivarius museum) inside the **Palazzo Affaitati** (*Via Palestro 17; open: Tue–Sat 0830–1800, Sun 0915–1215 and 1500–1800; £–££*) has models, drawings and violins made by the maestro, who produced more than 1 100 beautifully crafted musical instruments during his lifetime; some 400 still exist.

# Genoa

*The salty maritime capital of Liguria revels in the nickname of* La Superba *('The Proud'). Its famous natives include Christopher Columbus, Italian freedom fighter Giuseppe Mazzini, national hero Giuseppe Garibaldi – son of a Genoese from across the border in Nice – and great violin virtuoso, Niccolò Paganini. It is also the site of Europe's largest aquarium, has a street that some describe as the most beautiful in Italy and is the country's busiest and most important port.*

In Genoa's medieval centre, beautiful art treasures and marble palaces recalling the city's heyday of the 16th and 17th centuries contrast with characterful labyrinthine lanes (*caruggi*). (Watch out for 'colourful' characters, too, and hold on to your wallet.) 'Italy's most beautiful street', the **Via Garibaldi**, was created on the northern edge of the city between 1551 and 1558 for newly rich merchants anxious to escape the cramped medieval quarter. The magnificent **Palazzo Doria Tursi** (*Via Garibaldi 9; tel: 010 557 111*) is now the town hall, with a municipal art museum. The treasures within include three manuscripts by Christopher Columbus, and his ashes, and one of Paganini's favourite violins. **Palazzo Bianco** (*Via Garibaldi 11; tel: 010 557 34 99; open: Tue–Sun 0900–1300, Wed and Sat until 1900; £–££*) houses one of the city's finest art collections. Flemish, French, Spanish and Dutch, as well as Genoese artists and Italian masters such as Caravaggio and Veronese, are all represented. Of Genoa's many beautiful ancient churches, the **cathedral of San Lorenzo** (*Piazza San Lorenzo; tel: 010 247 18 63; open: daily; Museo del Tesoro, tel: 010 31*

" *The rapid passage from a street of stately edifices, into a maze of the vilest squalor ... make up, altogether, such a scene of wonder: so lively, and yet so dead: so noisy and yet so quiet.* "
**Charles Dickens, *Pictures from Italy* (1846)**

*12 69; open: Mon–Sat; £*) is especially fine. Its treasures include a glass chalice believed to have been used by the disciples at the Last Supper and to have caught drops of Christ's blood after the crucifixion.

Genoa was at the forefront of the cause for the unification of Italy, the *Risorgimento*. The **Museo del Risorgimento** (*Via Lomellini 11; open: Thu–Tue 0900–1300, closed Wed and second and fourth Sun each month; £–££*) gives a fascinating insight into the unification and the life and times of Giuseppe Mazzini, born here in 1805, a romantic figure permanently clad in black mourning after the abortive revolution in 1821.

At the port, the Piazza Caracamento has hosted a market since the 12th century and nearby the new **Marina Molo Vecchio** provides cafés, bistros and glittering yachts; originally, the Molo Vecchio was a place where condemned prisoners were hanged, after being blessed. The centrepiece is **Il Grande Bigo** (*open: daily 1100–1300 and 1400–1800; £*), which whisks people 200m (656ft) high in a circular lift to enjoy a bird's-eye view of the waterfront and city. Just north along the pier is the **Acquario di Genova** (aquarium) (*Ponte Spinola; open: Tue–Fri 0930–1830, weekends until 2000, also open: Mon in summer; ££–£££*), built in 1992 at the time of the great Columbus Exhibition; creatures of the deep can be seen up close in modern well-designed habitats.

*Tourist information: main office at Palazzina Santa Maria, Porto Antico (on the waterfront). Tel: 010 248 71. Open: daily 0900–1830.*

# Gran Paradiso National Park

*Tourist information: Cogne, Piazza Charnoux 36. Tel: 0165 74 040. Open: Mon–Sat 0900–1230 and 1500–1800; Sun am.*

Named after the Gran Paradiso massif towering above at 4 023m (13,200ft), this is Italy's first national park. Originally a hunting reserve for the Savoys, the land was donated by King Vittorio Emanuele II to the state in 1922 and now has fabulous flora and fauna, including the Alpine ibex goat – the king of the park – virtually extinct in the rest of Europe.

The three main valleys of the national park have spectacular views of tumbling waterfalls, vast blue-speckled glaciers and lofty snow-capped peaks set against deep green forests. It is a paradise for walkers and cross-country skiers during the winter. The most popular and dramatic section is the **Val di Cogne** and its main village of the same name, **Cogne**. A variety of walks are achievable from here, including leisurely scenic strolls along the Grand Eyvia River. To the southwest, the little village of **Valnontey** is the starting point of a popular walk up steep terrain to the **Rifugio V Sella** (refuge) (*tel: 0165 74 310 Easter–Sept*), at 2 559m (8 395ft). (Avoid Sundays in summer and August, when it can become seriously busy.) For strong walkers, the ascent of **Gran Paradiso** starts at the next valley west at **Valsavarenche**; it's a climb rather than a hike. If you are here just for the views, take the cable car from **Cogne** to 2 112m (6 929ft) at **Montseuc** and, for just a bit of exercise, walk to the summit at 2 346m (7 697ft), and admire the view.

# Lake Como

*Tourist information: APT, Piazza Cavour 16, Como. Tel: 031 269 712. Open: Mon–Sat 0900–1300 and 1430–1830; Sun 0930–1230.*

Shaped like an inverted 'Y', Lake Como is the deepest, most dramatic and most varied of all the northern lakes; some say it's also the most romantic, with its glorious setting, framed by mountains. The main town of **Como** is somewhat industrialised, but it remains Italian to its voluptuous (and sometimes frustratingly busy) core. Its **Duomo** ( *Via Plinio; open: daily apart from lunch, 1200–1500* ) was built from the 14th to the 18th centuries, and is Italy's finest example of a church in Gothic-Renaissance style. Nearby, the **Museo Alessandro Volta** ( *Piazza Cavour; open: daily except Mon; £* ) tells the story of the 19th-century discovery of the volt by Volta, a native of Como.

The main access point for ferries, hydrofoils and paddle steamers is **Navigazione Lago di Como** ( *Piazza Cavour; tel: 031 579 211; ££–£££* ). Take a boat to **Cernobbio** on the western leg of the lake, famous for the 16th-century Villa d'Este, now a palatial hotel. Virtually opposite, on the steeper and less touristy shore, beautifully situated **Torno** was the inspiration for Rossini and Shelley, among others. Further up on the western leg, the popular resort of **Menaggio** is dominated by Monte Bregagno at 2 107m (6 913ft). The jewel of the Lake, **Bellagio**, nestles between the two 'arms' of the 'Y'; it is utterly picturesque, with winding cobbled streets, seductive shops, lovely walks and cafés along the waterside.

" *The language of these enchanted spots, which have not their like in the world, restored to the Contessa the heart of a girl of 16.* "

**Stendhal on Como, *The Charterhouse of Parma* (1839)**

# Lake Maggiore

*Tourist information: Via Principe Tommaso 70/72, Stresa. Tel: 0323 301 50. Open: daily, am only at weekends; closed Sun in winter. International music festival held in Stresa in late Aug–early Sept.*

Known as *Lacus Verbanus* to the Romans, Maggiore is the second largest of the Italian lakes (after Lake Garda). Verbena, lemon trees and countless sub-tropical species flourish on its shores and the town of **Verbánia** on its western shore enjoys an extraordinarily mild winter climate. In the town, the **Villa Táranto** ( *Via Vittorio Veneto 111; tel: 0323 55 66 67; open: daily 0830–1830 Apr–Oct; ££* ) has a superb botanical collection, created in the 1930s by retired Scottish soldier, Captain Neil McEachern. It displays 20,000 different species, including some which are both rare and exotic, around pools and fountains.

> " *An enchanted palace, a work of the fairies in the midst of a lake encompassed with mountains, and far removed from the haunts of men.* "
>
> **Edward Gibbon on the Borromean Islands,** *Memoirs* (1764)

Further north, the charming old market town of **Cannobio**, just 5km (3 miles) from the Swiss border, has a tangle of narrow streets lined by pastel houses. The most popular site on the lake is **Stresa**, which lies halfway along the western shore. Although lacking in Italian character, it is the main departure point for cruising across the lakes and benefits from superb views across to the **Borromean Islands** (Isole Borromee). **Isola Bella** ( *open: daily mid-Mar–Oct; £££* ) has a beautiful **Palazzo**, extraordinary grottoes and glorious gardens with pure white peacocks. Little **Isola dei Pescatori** was the

writer Ernest Hemingway's favourite, and retains some of its character as a fishing island.

# Mantova

*Tourist information: Piazza Mantegna 6. Tel: 0376 32 16 01. Open: Mon–Sat 0830–1230 and 1500–1800; Sun 0930–1230.*

Known to the locals as *La Piccola Venezia* ('Little Venice'), the old city of Mantova lies in the plain of the River Po, on the southern edge of three lakes. For Charles Dickens it was 'a marshy town … so intensely dull and flat', yet for Aldous Huxley it was the most romantic city in the world. Outside the historic centre, the petrochemical works have contributed to the grime of the Fascist-era buildings but within the city walls there is a beautiful medieval centre. It is punctuated with lovely ancient towers and piazzas, and has a glorious centrepiece, the **Palazzo Ducale** (*Piazza Sordello; tel: 0376 32 02 83; open: 0900–1300 and 1430–1700, closed Sun and Mon pm; ££*). Formerly Europe's largest palace, and once the home of the Gonzaga family, the palace has some 500 rooms. The tiny **Camera degli Sposi** (the room where marriages were recorded) has richly lyrical Renaissance frescos by Mantegna.

Standing in parkland south of the old town, the **Palazzo del Tè** (*Viale Tè; tel: 0376 32 32 66; open: Tue–Fri 0900–1730, Mon 1300–1730; ££*) was built as a Renaissance pleasure dome for Federico Gonzaga and his mistress. The frescos and paintings in the **Sala di Psiche** are powerfully erotic. Next door, in the **Sala dei Giganti**, Jupiter's rage against the Titans is acted out in paintings of astonishing movement and destruction; the gasps of visitors reverberate in the room's echo chamber.

# Milan

*Although Rome is the capital of Italy, Milano (Milan) is the country's economic and financial heart and by far its most prosperous commercial and manufacturing city. Milan has risen to prominence since the unification of the Italian state in 1870 and many Milanesi (and others) believe that it should have become the country's capital.*

A traditional Milanese saying, in old dialect, suggests that a house should be *bella de denter, per i padrôn, brütta de foera, per i minciôn* ('beautiful inside for the owners, unattractive outside for the stupid'). This city of contrasts could not be described as beautiful on the outside; it was heavily bombed during the Second World War, and modern building has been indiscriminate and, at worst, ugly. Yet, under the surface of its understated charms lie treasures, beauty and great style. **Leonardo da Vinci** lived and worked here for 20 years, and Milan has inspired many others, including 19th-century writer **Stendhal**, who so loved the city that he wished to proclaim himself 'Milanese' in his epitaph.

## Tip

*Many sights, shops and restaurants in Milan are closed on Monday; the city's major market is on Saturday and there is a good flea market on Sunday morning at Navigli. Listings magazines include Mese Milano ( monthly, in Italian, with an English section ); HelloMILANO ( www.hellomilano.it ) is a smaller guide in English, available at information centres and also distributed in hotels and bars.*

The old Roman name for Milan, *Mediolanum*, meaning 'middle of the plain', reflected its key position between the trade routes of northwest Europe and Rome. In the 4th century AD, under the guidance of its bishop **Ambrogio** (St Ambrose), it rapidly became an important centre of Christianity. Centuries of rule by power-hungry Italian families followed – the Viscontis laid the first stone of the **Duomo** in 1386 – before it came first under Spanish rule, in 1535, and then Austrian, in 1713. Today, there are many remnants of significant 4th-century AD Christian sites. The Austrian Habsburgs built the **Palazzo Reale** (Royal Palace), in muted yellow tones, and the world-

famous **La Scala** opera house. More recent buildings reflect the architectural style of Mussolini, particularly the massive, chilling white megalith of the **Stazione Centrale** (central station). Nearby, on the Piazzale Loreto, is the spot where the body of the Fascist dictator was strung up in front of a baying crowd.

*Tourist information: main APT Centre, Via Marconi 1 (corner of Piazza del Duomo). Tel: 02 72 52 41. Open: Mon–Fri 0830–2000; Sat 0900–1300 and 1400–1900; Sun 0900–1300 and 1400–1700. Also at the Stazione Centrale, down a corridor on the main upper level, 'departures gallery'. Tel: 02 72 52 43 60. Open: Mon–Sat 0900–1900; Sun 0900–1230 and 1330–1800.*

## Tip

*The city's largest and most central park is the Parco Sempione, a good place to take time off from being a tourist and watch the Milanesi at play. In a city that has one of the lowest quotas of green area in Europe, Sempione is a very popular and welcome oasis by day, but at night it becomes the domain of drug dealers.*

# Milan: Piazza del Duomo

*The sign that greets visitors to the Piazza del Duomo, the city's central square, reads: 'It symbolises the city of Milan; please behave respectfully!'.*

The **Piazza del Duomo** is completely dominated by the huge white marble confection of the world's largest Gothic cathedral, the **Duomo** ( *Piazza del Duomo; tel: 02 86 46 34 56; open: daily 0645–1845* ). The best vantage point from which to view the exterior is the Piazzetta Reale, adjacent to the cathedral. You can see most of its 135 spires and the highest, central one, from which the 4-m (13-ft) gilded statue of the Madonna soars almost 109m (358ft) above the ground.

The whole cathedral is a mix of Gothic and baroque styles covering an extraordinary 12,000 square metres (129,171 square feet). Begun in 1386 under the Viscontis, it was not completed until almost five centuries later. Nearly all the pinnacles and spires were added in the 19th century, and a bronze door was added as recently as 1960. The Duomo's style is not to everyone's taste – it has been called over-

elaborate, and the 19th-century writer Heinrich Heine described it as 'a playground for giant children'. Hewn from the finest white marble from Candoglia (near Lake Maggiore), it is certainly of extraordinary proportions, and is Europe's third-largest church, after St Peter's in Rome and the cathedral in Seville.

Inside in the nave is the world's largest sundial, where the time is shown by a beam of light that shines through a hole in the roof – it is no longer accurate. Other points of interest include a gruesome statue of St Bartholomew carrying his flayed skin and, most important of all, a huge crucifix containing a nail from Christ's cross, which is lowered for the Feast of the Cross on 14 September. But the highlight of a visit here is the climb via 250 steps (or the lift) to the **roof** ( *open: daily 0900–1730; £–££* ). From here, another 80 steps lead to the top, from where there are stunning views across the city and as far as the Alps on a clear day, as well as a close-up sight of the intricate detail on the marble statues and of the Madonna. You'll also be able to look down on Milanesi sunning themselves on oleander-covered roof terraces.

North of the Duomo, it is just a short sashay to the glass-domed arcade, **Galleria Vittorio Emanuele II** ( *enter from Piazza del Duomo or Piazza della Scala* ). Known as the **Salotto di Milano**, the 'salon' was designed by Giuseppe Mengoni, who tragically tumbled from the roof's scaffolding to his death in 1877, the year before it opened. This is a superb spot for people-watching, lingering over a long drink or quick shot of caffeine, perhaps at **Il Salotto**, reputed to serve Milan's best coffee, or for window-shopping in the smart shops. At **Prada**, look behind you to see a floor mosaic of the zodiac sign Taurus. Don't be alarmed if you see a crowd of people taking it in turns to stand on it; it is considered good luck to step on the bull's testicles, which are now virtually rubbed out!

# Milan: the city centre

Walk through the *galleria* from the Piazza del Duomo to find the world's most famous opera house, the **Teatro alla Scala** (*Piazza della Scala; tel: 02 72 00 37 44 for tickets; see*

*page 47*). If you can't secure tickets for a performance, you can still get a bird's-eye view of Europe's largest stage, and the theatre's opulent interior and massive glittering chandelier, at the **Museo Teatrale alla Scala** (*Piazza della Scala; tel: 02 805 34 18; open: Mon–Sat 0900–1200 and 1400–1700, Sun May–Oct; £*). The museum has a fascinating collection of theatrical items, some pre-dating La Scala's inauguration in 1778. There are plaster casts of the hands of great composers, busts and pictures of Verdi, and his passport, and sumptuous costumes from recent ballet productions such as *Swan Lake*, choreographed by Nureyev in 1990.

A short walk north leads to **Via Brera**, full of small galleries, art shops and a thriving (although touristy) night-time restaurant scene. It is also the site of Milan's best art gallery, the **Pinacoteca di Brera** (*Via Brera 28; tel: 02 72 26 31; open: Tue–Sun 0900–1745 (2000 on Sun), closed Mon; ££*), which houses particularly fine medieval and Italian Renaissance art, as well as works by some modern artists, including Modigliani. Highlights include Andrea Mantegna's masterpiece *Dead Christ*, Raphael's *Marriage of the Virgin* and, on a more secular theme, Francesco Hayez's *The Kiss*.

A ten-minute walk west brings you to the vast red-brick castle of **Castello Sforzesco** ( *Piazza Castello; tel: 02 62 08 39 40; open: Tue–Sun 0930–1930; free* ), whose interior is much more welcoming than its austere exterior might suggest. It was originally built as a fortress by the Viscontis, and new ruler Francesco Sforza had it reconstructed in the late 15th century as a Renaissance palace. The castle houses four museums; highlights include **Michelangelo**'s last work, the unfinished **Rondanini Pietà** sculpture (Room 15), and the **Sala delle Asse**, decorated with a little-known but lovely fresco of the same name (depicting tree foliage) by **Leonardo**.

" *All his* [Leonardo's] *actions seem inspired, and indeed everything he does clearly comes from God rather than human art.* "

**Giorgio Vasari,** *Lives of the Artists* **(1568)**

One of Milan's top attractions is **Leonardo**'s *Il Cenacolo* ( *The Last Supper* ), housed in the **Cenacolo Vinciano** (Vinci Refectory) next to the **Santa Maria delle Grazie** church ( *by metro, MM1 Conciliazione or MM2 Cadorna; Piazza Santa Maria delle Grazie 2; tel: 02 98 42 11 46; open: Tue–Sun 0900–1900 (2000 on Sun), closed Mon; £££* ). Booking is compulsory ( *tel: 199 199 100* ); if you don't get a booking, try joining the waiting-list queue in the piazza, where unused tickets are made available.

The restoration of one of the world's most famous works of art (1494–7) was completed in 1999 and continues to be the subject of much controversy. Leonardo chose oil in preference to the traditional fresco technique of painting on to wet plaster. Although oil gives richer colour and tone, it is more vulnerable to weathering. Bad restoration in previous centuries – and the wall having been used for target practice by Napoleonic troops – means that very little of the original colouring survives. However, the painting retains an extraordinary, even miraculous power; in 1943, a bomb destroyed the whole building, but the wall of *The Last Supper* remained standing.

# Pavia

*Medieval Pavia, on the banks of the Ticino river, was once known as the 'city of a hundred towers'. Most of these tall structures have fallen over the centuries, but it is still easy to see what this lovely town must have been like in the days when it was the capital city of the Lombards. Pavia lost its status to Milan in 1359.*

Founded in 1361, Pavia's **University**, on Corso Strada Nuova, is one of Europe's oldest, linked with an ancient law school that dates back to 825. Famous alumni include Christopher Columbus and physicist Alessandro Volta (*see Lake Como, page 31*). The prestigious first colleges of Borromeo and Ghislieri of the 16th century have, with later additions, made Pavia the Oxford of Italy.

The **Piazza della Vittoria** is the heart of town; the cobbled streets leading from it are lined with enticing ice-cream parlours, bars and restaurants. On the square is the **Duomo**, with its vast cupola (*Piazza della Vittoria and Piazza del Duomo*). Although it was begun in 1488 (with Leonardo da Vinci lending a hand), the cathedral was only finally completed in the early 20th century. Tragically, the 11th-century Civica tower, which used to stand alongside, collapsed in 1989 with a death toll of four.

*Getting there: 38km (24 miles) south of Milan – less than 30 mins by train. Tourist information: Via Fabio Filzi 2 (near Stazione Centrale). Tel: 0382 221 56. Open: Mon–Sat 0830–1230 and 1400–1800. Market days: Wed and Sat.*

## Certosa di Pavia

For many, the **Certosa di Pavia** is the most beautiful Carthusian monastery in Europe, intricately crafted from glorious Carrara marble. Originally begun in 1396 by Gian Galeazzo Visconti of Milan as the family mausoleum, it took some 200 years to build, by which time the Viscontis had been replaced in power by the Sforzas. The gloriously

frescoed tomb of Gian Galeazzo Visconti – the only Visconti to be buried here – is visible in the south transept.

The marble façade of the building was masterminded by architect and craftsman Giovanni Antonio Amadeo, who created fabulous friezes and lavish inlaid marble detail. Still home to the **Order of Carthusians**, who are subject to a strict vow of silence, the monastery may be visited on a guided tour led by a monk released from the vow. The Great Cloister is enclosed on three sides by the monks' cells, each of which has a small garden. In the refectory, the frescoed ceiling and readings from the Bible provide the only entertainment during meals. The old pharmacy has an excellent tasting room, where you can sample (and buy) the famous yellowy-green **Chartreuse liqueur** – it's sweet, strong and divinely delicious.

*Getting there: 9km (6 miles) north of Pavia. Bus from Piazza Piave, Pavia to Certosa, or train, then 15-minute walk; by car, A7 autostrada from Milan and exit at the Bereguardo or Gropello C. Viale Monumento. Tel: 0382 92 56 13. Open: Tue–Sun 0930–1130 and 1430–1630; usually to 1800 in summer. £ (donation).*

# Turin

*The capital of Piedmont, Torino (Turin) is all too often dismissed as an ugly, industrial powerhouse, second only to Milan as Italy's largest industrial city. Certainly, the sprawling outskirts and suburbs are far from beautiful, but the city itself is the gem in Piedmont's baroque crown containing some of Italy's finest treasures.*

Turin is an elegant city with a thriving café society and no less than 18km (11 miles) of colonnaded walkways serving as a wet-weather or heat refuge. It has 40 museums, some among the best in the world, and is home to the famous Juventus football team owned by Gianni Agnelli, the Fiat boss, whose family founded the vast empire of Fiat in 1899. It is the site of the controversial Turin Shroud, the birthplace of Italian cinema and was once the capital of Italy. It has also been chosen as host city for the 2006 Winter Olympics.

The centre of the city of Turin is very compact. The best starting point is the **Piazza Castello**, which is dominated by the 17th-century **Palazzo Reale** (Royal Palace) ( *Piazza Castello/Piazza Reale; tel: 011 436 1455; open: Tue–Sun 0900–1815, some Sats 2100–2400, Sun until 2000 during summer; £; gardens free* ).

<blockquote>
Here is the city of my heart. I would never have believed that a city, thanks to its light, could be so beautiful.
</blockquote>

**Philosopher** Friedrich Nietzsche**, who lived and worked in Turin from 1888 to 1889,** *Letters from Turin*

Behind an austere façade, a plethora of *chinoiserie*, frescos and elaborately carved ceilings testify to the palace's importance as the House of Savoy's principal seat from 1646 to 1865. The gilded wooden ceilings were designed by Michelangelo and Carlo Morello (1660–3). Outside, in the gardens, 17th-century statues decorate the fountains and the flowerbeds designed by French landscaper Le Nôtre, who also designed the gardens of Versailles, outside Paris.

A north wing of the *palazzo* houses the **Armeria Reale**, one of the world's most important and largest collections of armoury and arms, collected by the Savoys ( *opening times vary, but usually Tue–Sat am and Tue, Thu pm; admission included in entrance fee to* palazzo).

43

Behind the *palazzo* lies the **Duomo** ( *Piazza San Giovanni; open: daily; free* ). The cathedral was built in 1497–8 and is Turin's sole example of Renaissance architecture. Most famously, the chapel – the **Cappella della Santa Sindone** – houses an urn on top of its altar that contains the **Turin Shroud** ( *Sindone* ). Said to be the winding sheet in which Christ was wrapped after the crucifixion, it was pronounced a forgery after carbon dating in 1988. However, it is still an object of great reverence for believers and the curious alike; the 'genuine' article is rarely on display (most recently in summer 2000), but there is a good photographic reproduction. The magnificent chapel was badly damaged by fire in 1997 yet, miraculously, the *Sindone* was left totally unscathed.

## Tip

*Turin's major Grand Balôn antiques/flea market takes place every second Sunday of the month, in the area behind Porta Palazzo.*

*Tourist information: main centre at Piazza Castello 161. Tel: 39 011 535 181/ 011 535 901; www.comune.torino.it. Open: daily 0900–1930. Also at Stazione Porta Nuova. Tel: 39 011 531 327. Open: daily 0830–1930.*

# Turin: the city centre

Bypassing the ornate baroque façade of **Palazzo Madama** (*Piazza Castello; closed for restoration until 2002*), a stroll south down the city's main street, **Via Roma**, with its elegant colonnades, cafés and chic shops, brings you on the left-hand side to the famous **Museo Egizio** (Egyptian Museum) (*Via Accademia delle Scienze 6; tel: 011 56 17 776; open: Tue–Sat 0900–1900, Sun 0900–1400, closed Mon; ££*). Alongside Cairo and London, this is one of the world's most important collections of Egyptian art. On three floors, 30,000 artefacts are displayed, including the black granite statue of Ramses II and a papyrus topographical map that is reputed to be the world's oldest.

Just south of here is the beautiful **Piazza San Carlo**, considered by some to be the best square in Italy after St Mark's in Venice. Pick a café and try a *bicerin* – the *Torinese* speciality of coffee, chocolate and lashings of cream – mentioned by Alexandre Dumas as being 'among the good and pleasant things of the city' during his stay in Turin in 1852.

Turin's enduring tall city symbol, the 167-m (548-ft) **Mole Antonelliana** (*Via Montebello 20; tel: 011 817 04 96; closed at the time of writing*) stands to the east. It will house the **National Museum of Cinema** in an exhibition covering 3 200 square metres (34,445 square feet) over four floors, designed with the help of British film director Peter Greenaway. The Italian film industry began in Turin in 1904 and the museum will trace the history of the cinema, from magic lanterns to modern-day technology. The view from the lift of the *mole* is stunning.

This vibrant city has museums of everything, from marionettes to mountains, and its Museum of Unification is especially significant as Turin was Italy's first capital. Modern and contemporary art lovers will be fascinated by the **GAM-Galleria Civica d'Arte Moderna e Cotemporanea** (*Via Magenta 31; tel: 011 562 99 11; open: Tue–Sun 0900–1900*). It hosts superb visiting exhibitions and has a permanent collection that includes works by Picasso, Chagall and Modigliani. About 3km (2 miles) south of the city is Italy's only motor museum, the **Museo dell'Automobile** (*Corso Unità d'Italia 40; open: Tue–Sun 1000–1830; £*), which houses a remarkable collection of cars in a huge modern building. The collection includes the first Fiat, made by the Fabbrica Italiana Automobili Torino company, which was established in the city in 1899, and the gleaming Isotta Franchini driven by Gloria Swanson in *Sunset Boulevard*.

# Basilica di Superga

If you have time to explore further afield, take a trip to **Superga** for glorious views across the city, and as far as the Alps, from the great baroque **Basilica di Superga**. Built by 18th-century architect Filippo Juvarra, in gratitude for Turin's delivery from the French army in 1706, it is a magnificent sight. Below it lie the tombs of the princes, princesses and kings of Savoy. It is a site of popular pilgrimage for locals, too, who regularly visit the tomb of the Turin football team, who tragically all perished when their plane crashed into the hillside in 1949.

*Getting there: east of Turin on a hill. Take train or tram no 15. Strada di Superga 73. Tel: 011 898 0083. Open: daily 0900–1200 and 1500–1800 May–Sept; daily 1000–1200 and 1500–1700 Oct–Apr. £.*

# Eating and drinking

### Vecchia Aosta
*Piazza Porte Pretoriane 4, Aosta. Tel: 0165 36 11 86. Closed Wed. ££.* Set in the historic surroundings of the old Roman walls, this friendly restaurant specialises in regional specialities and excellent pasta: try perhaps the delicious *tagliatelle con funghi porcini* (with wild mushrooms) and one of their mouth-watering puddings, if you have room.

### Gambero Rosso
*Piazza G Marconi 7, Vernazza, Le Cinque Terre. Tel: 0187 81 22 65. Closed Mon in winter. ££–£££.* This little restaurant is set in a picturesque piazza where the speciality is the freshest seafood served with a good selection of wines, including excellent local ones. Outdoor tables.

## Genoa

### Caffeteria Le Corbusier
*Via San Donato 36. £.* Next to the church of the same name in the old town, this is a very popular spot with the 'young and beautiful'. It also does good snacks and cocktails.

### Cantine Squarciafico
*Piazza Invrea 3r. Tel: 010 247 0823. Closed Sun and lunch in summer. £–££.* Located between the port and the old town, the restored wine cellars of a lovely 15th-century building make this an atmospheric wine bar/restaurant. Wines from every region of Italy are on offer with good, local cheeses and salamis and more substantial meals.

### Gran Gotto
*Viale Brigate Bisagno 69r. Tel: 010 56 43 44. Closed Sun and Sat lunch. £££.* Proud bearers of a Michelin star, the Bertola brothers continue to strive for perfection. Widely considered to be Genoa's best restaurant, the Gran Gotto puts an emphasis on seafood, but caters for carnivores too … as well as chocoholics: the *flan di cioccolato con crema di cioccolato bianco* defies translation. Excellent wine list, including reasonably priced regional wines, and impeccable service.

## Lake Como

### Harry's Bar
*Piazza Risorgimento, Cernobbio. Tel: 031 51 26 47. Closed Tue. £££.* Smart watering hole (and restaurant) by the lake, especially popular for late-night drinks.

### Ristorante Belvedere
*Piazza Casartelli, Torno. Tel: 031 41 91 00. Open: daily in summer. ££.* Gloriously situated overlooking the lake, this friendly restaurant excels in good, unfussy cooking with lake fish (*lavarello*) and pasta specialities. Popular, yet not too touristy. Book ahead for a table alongside the lake on the lovely vine-covered terrace.

## Milan

### BICE
*Via Borgospesso 12. Tel: 02 760 025 72. Closed Mon. £££.* Very stylish and much loved by the chic fashion crowd, this restaurant was the late Gianni Versace's favourite. One of the dishes on the huge menu, *tagliate di pesce o carne* (thinly sliced grilled fish and meat) is very popular – ideal for the model figure!

### Trattoria Milanese
*Via Santa Marta 11. Tel: 02 8645 1991. Closed Tue. ££–£££.* A long-established family-run restaurant, this

temple to Milanese cooking is popular with everyone (including the Milanese). Friendly and very atmospheric, near the Biblioteca Ambrosiana.

## Turin

### Il Bicerin
*Piazza della Consolato 5. ££.* This is *the* place for heavenly *bicerin* – coffee with chocolate, cream and (optional) brandy.

### Caffè Torino
*Piazza San Carlo 204. £££.* Lovely *caffè* with finely embossed wooden panelling and gilded mirrors, which have changed little since it opened in 1903. Great for a cocktail or vermouth – another Torinese invention.

### Tre Galline
*Via Bellezia 37d. Tel: 011 436 6553. Closed Mon. £££.* In the historic centre, this restaurant dating back three centuries is Turin's oldest. Each evening brings a different Piedmontese speciality: Wed and Thu are *bollito* (succulent boiled meat) nights.

# Nightlife

## Genoa

### Louisiana Jazz Club
*Via San Sebastiano. £–££.* Live music every night – mostly trad jazz – from 2200.

### Teatro Carlo Felice
(opera house) *Piazza de Ferrari. Tel: 010 58 93 29.* Offers a year-round programme, but do book in advance.

## Milan
The most lively bars and discos are around the canal-side Navigli area and the Brera gallery. **Bar Magenta** (*Via Carducci 13*) is *the* happening place for the young and beautiful.

**Propoganda** (*Via Castelbarco 11–13; tel: 02 5831 0682*) in the Navigli area has themed disco nights in summer and live rock in winter.

### Teatro alla Scala
*Piazza della Scala. Tel: 02 72 00 37 44 for ticket availability. Office open: daily 0900–1800.* Tickets can be bought in person from the office on the left-hand side of the theatre, *Via Filodrammatici (open: daily 1200–1800).* Tickets bought with a credit card (*tel: 02 86 07 75*) or online (*www.lascala.milano.it*) are subject to a 20 per cent surcharge (*£££*). Half an hour before a performance, 200 tickets for standing places are put on sale outside the theatre at the entrance to the Theatre Museum – one ticket per person (*£*). The season opens on 7 December, the feast day of Milan's patron saint, Sant'Ambrogio.

### Football in Milan
Get tickets for one or both rival teams, AC Milan and Inter, from **San Siro Stadium** (*tel: 02 48707 123*).

## Turin
Turin hosts a **jazz festival** in July (*tel: 011 561 3926*) and a music festival, **Settembre Musica**, in September (*tel: 011 442 4715*). Year-round, the city's nightlife centres around the area known as the **Murazzi**, the riverside strip between the bridges of Umberto I and Vittorio Emanuele I. For listings, pick up a free copy of *News Spettacolo* at the APT information centre.

# Milan – 'Catwalk Capital'

*Italian style is famous worldwide and the capital for chic and designer clothes is undoubtedly Milan. Legendary names such as Prada, Versace (the late Gianni and his sister Donatella), Dolce e Gabbana, Armani, Gianfranco Ferre and Moschino all began their careers here.*

Today, their glamorous showrooms jostle together in the designer district around the *Quadrilatero* or 'Golden Triangle'. Four streets around Via Montenapoleone make up this oasis

of 'drop-dead gorgeous' style, where you'll need to be much more than a lire millionaire if you fancy kitting out yourself – and the family – from head to toe; a designer baby's pram (*carrozzina*), complete with little parasol, will set you back a couple of million. However, smaller items, such as **leather goods** or **sunglasses** – every Italian's favourite designer accessory – are often cheaper than the equivalent back home, and are stylish souvenirs. If the price tags of the Golden Triangle are just a little out of range, you'll find good, high-quality clothing in shops on the streets around the **Corso Vittorio Emanuele II**.

Department stores do not feature as high on the chic scale, but the oldest, La Rinascente, on the Piazza del Duomo, is still regarded as the classiest. If you seek the Italian goal of *la bella figura*, but are on a strict budget, there are some excellent 'factory outlets' within the Milan area, selling designer clothing at a fraction of the normal retail price. Wherever you see it, the sign *Spaccio* will lead to a designer outlet, most of which tend to be on the outskirts of Milan, around Como and across the border. Foxtown in Switzerland is an enormous store, with items from Gianfranco Ferre, Versace, Gucci, Prada, Iceberg and many other luminaries of the fashion world, at savings of up to 70 per cent.

One false economy is a fake designer handbag of the kind that is sold on the streets in all major Italian cities. As soon as you show the slightest flicker of interest the seller's attentions become extremely urgent and you may well think you're getting a superb bargain. Inevitably, the bag will fall apart in as many days as the minutes it took to make your deal. If you don't mind the temporary nature of these items, there is a huge market every Wednesday in Luino on Lake Maggiore specialising in fake designer goods.

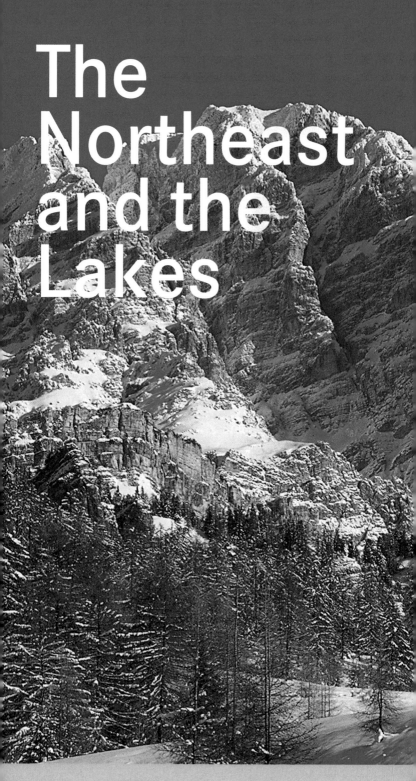

# The Northeast and the Lakes

*The three distinctive areas of Trentino-Alto Adige, Friuli-Venezia Giulia and the Veneto give this area a fascinating diversity of rich culture and landscape. Bordered in the north by Switzerland, Austria and Slovenia and in the south by the lovely cities of Verona and Vicenza, it is also the region of the Dolomites – Italy's most dramatically beautiful mountain range – and of its largest lake, Lake Garda.*

# The Northeast and the Lakes

*Getting there:* the main airports serving the region are Venice and Treviso (30km (19 miles) inland from Venice). The state rail network has good connections between Venice, Trieste, Udine, Padua, Treviso and Vicenza. The roads in general are good, although busy during high season. The road from Verona north to the Trentino-Alto Adige region runs through Trento and Bolzano up towards the main entry of the Brenner Pass. In the Dolomites, care should be taken during the winter on the winding roads; snow chains are mandatory on many higher routes.

### ① *Aquileia*

Once one of the most important bastions of the Roman empire, the town today has reminders of its ancient heyday in fabulous 4th-century AD floor mosaics and two fascinating archaeological museums. **Page 54**

### ② *Cortina d'Ampezzo*

Stunningly located in the heart of the glorious pink-tinged craggy Dolomites, this famous mountain town is popular in both summer and winter, but best known as a top ski resort. **Page 56**

### ③ *Lake Garda*

Italy's largest lake is also the most popular, benefiting from a warm and gentle climate. As well as water-based pleasures, it also offers good opportunities for walking in the nearby mountains. **Page 57**

### ④ *Padua*

This old university town has wonderful frescos by Giotto and is one of Italy's most popular places of pilgrimage. Thousands come every year to see the Basilica of St Anthony, one of the country's most highly revered saints. **Page 58**

### ⑤ *Trento*

Capital of the Trentino region, this lovely medieval town is a good staging post on the way to the Dolomites. The cathedral was the setting for some of the meetings of the Sixteenth Council of Trent, set up to counter the Reformation. **Page 60**

### ⑥ *Trieste*

Capital of the Friuli-Venezia Giulia region, Trieste's fascinating history is based upon its former status as the port for the Austro-Hungarian empire. Its prominent position on the Adriatic means that it is well placed today for exploring nearby Slovenia or Croatia. **Page 62**

### ⑦ *Verona*

One of Italy's most beautiful cities, known in Roman times as 'Little Rome', with a fabulously well-preserved amphitheatre. The famous opera festival in July and August remains eternally and deservedly popular. **Pages 64–7**

### ⑧ *Vicenza*

Everywhere in this elegant Renaissance city you will see reminders of its most famous son, Andrea Palladio, whose glorious buildings give it such great distinction. **Pages 68–9**

53

# Wine

*The area produces some very good wines. Try a glass of prosecco, the Veneto's own deliciously crisp sparkling white wine, as an apéritif. The best white wines come from the Friuli, while Trentino (Teroldego and Rovareto in particular) produces some excellent reds. One of Italy's most famous reds, Bardolino, comes from the eastern shore of Lake Garda.*

# Aquileia

*Tourist information: Piazza Capitolo 4. Tel: 0431 91 94 91. Open: Fri–Wed 0830–1800 in summer; weekends 1000–1200 in winter.*

Fourth in the hierarchy of great towns of the Roman empire, after Rome, Milan and Capua, Aquileia's population has dwindled to just over 3 000. The little town is often bypassed by visitors on their way to the popular Adriatic seaside resort of **Grado** (11km (6.8 miles) south), but it is rich in sights. The most important is the **Basilica** (*Piazza Capitolo; tel: 0431 910 67; open: daily 0730–1830 summer, closed at lunchtime in winter; free*), founded in AD 313. The exterior is largely 14th century but, inside, the richly coloured original mosaic pavement remains, stretching the entire length of the nave. Parts of the original church can also be seen underground in the **Cripta degli Scavi**, while the **Cripta degli Affreschi** ripples with fine 12th-century frescos (*£ for both crypts*). Close by is the **Museo Archeologico Nazionale** (*Via Roma 1; tel: 0431 910 16; open: daily in summer, am only in winter; £*), which has more beautiful examples of mosaics excavated from the old city, together with fine carvings.

## Food

*The strong Austrian influence in the north of the region is reflected in its gastronomy, where the hearty local dishes include dumplings, speck (the equivalent of Italian prosciutto, or cured ham), goulash, black bread and bowls of steaming yellow polenta (made from maize). Seafood and fish are particularly good further south and at Lake Garda.*

# Bolzano (Bozen)

*Tourist information: Piazza Walther 8. Tel: 0471 307 001. Open: Mon–Fri 0900–1830; Sat 0900–1230.*

The main town of the Alto Adige (or Südtirol) is distinctively Tyrolean. Always a pawn in the power struggle between Trento and the Tyrol, it was finally passed to Italy after the First World War in 1919. The old town's 15th-century Gothic **Duomo** (*Piazza Walther; open: daily; free*) has an ornate spire and a yellow and green mosaic roof. Inside there is a 'wine door', carved with figures toiling among the vines; the grape has always been important to the local economy, and a wine trail, the **Strada di Vino** (Südtiroler Weinstrasse), runs from Bolzano south to Trentino. On the western side of

## Sense of Italy

the old town is the **Museo Archeologico** (*Via Museo 43; tel: 0471 98 20 98; open: Tue–Sun 1000–1800 in summer, 0900–1700 in winter, closed Mon; £–££*). The museum's most famous exhibit, preserved in a refrigerator, is the Ötzi mummy, discovered in the Ötzaler Alps in 1991, and reputed to be over 5 000 years old.

# Cividale del Friuli

*Tourist information: Corso Paolino Aquileia 10. Tel: 0432 73 13 98. Open: Mon–Fri 0900–1300 and 1500–1800 (closes 1700 in winter). Market day: Sat.*

Close to the border with Slovenia, this picturesque little town, founded by Julius Caesar in 50 BC, was the former capital of Friuli. The dramatic ravine of the River Natisone is spanned by the **Devil's Bridge** (Ponte del Diabolo), accessed by a gate in the medieval walls. Through the cobbled streets above the river's north bank you come to the lovely 8th-century church, **Tempietto Longobardo** (*Piazzetta San Biagio; open: daily 0900–1300 and 1500–1830 in summer, 1000–1300 and 1530–1730 in winter; £*), also known as the **Oratorio di Santa Maria in Valle**. It has an exquisite 8th-century stucco arch of female (saintly or human) figures and fine 14th-century frescos.

# Cortina d'Ampezzo

*Tourist information: Piazzetta San Francesco 8. Tel: 0436 3231; www.sunrise.it/dolomiti. Open: Mon–Fri 0900–1230 and 1500–1900; Sat 0930–1230 and 1600–1900; Sun am.*

## Tip

**Overheard on a Cortina ski lift: 'How would you describe your skiing?' 'I'd call it "syncopation" – musically speaking – the irregular progression from bar to bar.'**

Set in the heart of the dramatic towers, lonely pinnacles and giddily steep faces of the pink-tinged Dolomites, Cortina, the 'Queen of the Dolomites', is arguably Europe's most beautiful alpine resort.

From the town, a series of three cable cars takes visitors up to **Tofana** (*£££*) at 3 243m (10,640ft), where there is a variety of walking trails linked by over 50 *rifugios* or mountain refuge huts. The **Gruppo Guide Alpine** ( *Piazzetta San Francesco 5; tel: 0436 47 40; open: daily 0800–1200 and 1600–2000 in summer* ) offers guided treks in summer. In winter, the Dolomites Superski pass covers a huge skiing area, where gold-medallist Alberto Tomba learnt to ski. Since 1956, when Cortina hosted the Winter Olympics, the town has changed little; no new buildings have been allowed. The resort has over 25 sunny mountain restaurants – the Italians know that lunch is just as important as the skiing – as well as 250 shops. Post-skiing, at around 1700, the evening *passeggiata* parades up and down Cortina's **Corso Italia**.

# Gorizia

*Tourist information: Via Roma 9. Tel: 0481 38 62 24. Open: Mon–Fri 0900–1300 and 1500–1800; closes 1700 in winter.*

The 'Nice' of the Austrian Habsburgs in the 16th century, Gorizia finally came under Italian control after the First World War. Today, it is a major shopping centre, whose customers are mainly Slovenes. The town's highlight is the medieval castle, **Castello** (*Borgo Castello; open: Tue–Sun 0930–1300 and 1500–1930 in summer; 0930–1230 and 1400–1700 in winter; £*), which suffered severe damage during the First World War but offers superb views. Nearby is the museum of the Great War, **Museo della Grande Guerra** (*open: Tue–Sun 1000–1800; £*). A trip across the border to **Nova Gorica** in Slovenia (no formalities except a passport) is worthwhile.

# Lake Garda

*Tourist information: Via Repubblica 3, Gardone Riviera. Tel: 0365 20 347. Open: daily 0900–1230 and 1600–1900 in summer, closed Sun pm; Mon–Sat in winter, closed Thu pm.*

A round trip by road around Garda, Italy's largest lake, covers 144km (90 miles). The countryside varies from gentle plains in the south and lush vines, olives and citrus trees on the west shore, to the more untamed north, dramatically ringed by snow-capped peaks.

The spa town of **Sirmione** in the south is Garda's most popular resort, with a lovely medieval castle, the **Rocca Scaligera** (*open: Tue–Sun 0900–1800 in summer, 0900–1300 in winter; £–££*). The much-visited highlight of the lake is at **Gardone Riviera** on the west bank. Here, the exotic **Villa Il Vittoriale** (*open: daily 0800–2030 in summer, 0900–1230 and 1400–1730 in winter; ££–£££*) was home to the controversial fascist sympathiser, soldier, womaniser and poet **Gabriele d'Annunzio**, who lived here from 1922 to 1938. It is crammed with objects reflecting his own powerful conception of himself.

**“** *The terraces of the garden are held up to the sun, the sun falls upon them, they are like a vessel slanted up, to catch the superb, heavy light.* **”**

**D H Lawrence on Lake Garda, *Twilight in Italy* (1916)**

# Padua

*Wealthy Padua (Padova) has been a flourishing university town since the Middle Ages. During the Second World War it suffered extensive bombing, but the bulk of the medieval centre escaped, as did the city's two greatest treasures: the Cappella degli Scrovegni and the Basilica di Sant'Antonio.*

## Basilica di Sant'Antonio

*Piazza del Santo. Tel: 049 824 28 11. Open: daily 0630–2000 Mar–Oct; daily 0630–1900 Nov–Feb.*

This monumental multi-domed basilica, known locally as **Il Santo**, was built in the 14th century to house the body of **St Anthony**, patron saint of Padua. Devotees still flock to the **Cappella dell'Arca** in the north transept to pay their respects at his tomb. The surrounding walls are adorned with marble reliefs depicting scenes from his life. The high altar has a magnificent series of St Anthony reliefs by **Donatello**

## Cappella degli Scrovegni

*Part of the Museo Civico Eremitani. Piazza Eremitani 8. Tel: 049 820 45 50. Open: Tue–Sun 0900–1800. £££ (including entry to the Museo Civico Eremitani).*

Paduan nobleman **Enrico Scrovegni** built this small chapel to atone for the sins of his father, commissioning **Giotto** to decorate it between 1303 and 1305. The resulting fresco cycle is one of the greatest achievements in the history of art, marking a decisive break with the Byzantine tradition of the preceding 1 000 years.

The chapel is bathed in a cool blue light. The *Story of Mary and Jesus* is portrayed in 38 square panels on the altar and both side walls, connected within a group of geometric marble designs. The blues, reds and golds are brilliant. The entire west wall of the chapel is taken up with a formal presentation of *The Last Judgement*

# Central Padua

Stroll around the tightly knit medieval heart of the town, with its narrow arcaded streets, ancient town hall and surrounding squares, until you find the legendary **Caffè Pedrocchi**, in Piazza Cavour. When it first opened in 1831, this was the largest café in Europe, and it remains *the* coffee stop in which to see and be seen in Padua.

Nearby, the medieval **Palazzo Municipale** (town hall) is disguised behind a contemporary façade. Opposite is the main university building. Head westwards to lively market squares of **Piazza delle Frutta** and **Piazza delle Erbe**, usually ablaze with colour. In between, the **Palazzo della Ragione** ('Palace of Reason') was Padua's medieval law court ( *tel: 049 820 50 06; open: Tue–Sun 0900–1800; £*). Its interior contains 333 frescos on an astrological theme.

Bounded by charming arcades, **Piazza dei Signori** contains the **Loggia del Consiglio**, an elegant Renaissance building which once housed the ruling body of the city, and the **Palazzo del Capitanio**, formerly the seat of the Venetian governor. To the southwest, the interior of the tiny brick-built **Baptistery** ( *Piazza del Duomo; tel: 049 65 69 14; open: 0730–1300 and 1500–1800; £*) is smothered in beautiful 14th-century frescos.

# Prato della Valle

This oval piazza, or *Prato* ('field'), with its verdant lawns and gently trickling water, claims to be the largest public square in Italy. It has been restored to its Renaissance glory, and is encircled by a newly dredged canal and **78 statues of celebrated Paduans**.

*Getting there: accessible in summer from Venice along the Brenta Canal; boats depart San Marco around 0900 and arrive in Padua around 1800; return journey by bus or train; advance booking essential. Tourist information: Riviera dei Mugnai 8. Tel: 049 875 06 55.*

59

# Trento

*Information centre for the region: Via Romagnosi 11. Tel: 0461 83 90 00; www.trentino.to. Open: Mon–Fri 0840–1220 and 1430–1700. For fabulous views, take the cable car from Ponte San Lorenzo (near the bus station) to Sardagna on Monte Bondone (££).*

Capital of the Trentino region, Trento's pretty main square, **Piazza Duomo**, was first laid out by the Romans. Against the lovely backdrop of Monte Bondone, the old town is very attractive, with frescoed palaces, arcades, cafés and restaurants. Piazza Duomo is overlooked by the Romanesque **Duomo** ( *medieval crypt and foundations of early church open: daily 1000–1200 and 1430–1800; £*), the site of some of the meetings of the Council of Trent (1545–63), precursor to the Counter-Reformation.

A short walk north is the **Castello del Buonconsiglio** ( *Via Bernardo Clesio; tel: 0461 23 37 70; open: Tue–Sun 0900–1200 and 1400–1700; £–££*). This 13th-century castle was once the seat of the ruling bishop-princes of Trento and now houses a good collection of paintings and sculpture.

## Tip

*During the annual festival, 'Sounds of the Dolomites', which takes place in July and August, concerts are held in the mountains at some of Trentino's loveliest Alpine lodges. Each year, festivals of Vinum Bonum – eating and drinking well – are organised for the whole Trentino region, reflecting the area's strong gourmet and wine traditions.*

Drive northwest to the **Adamello Brenta Nature Park**, the largest in the province of Trentino, with 612 square kilometres (236 miles) of glorious terrain, from high, rocky mountains to wooded valleys with streams and rivers that swell to become raging torrents in late spring. It is also home to the shy brown bear.

# Treviso

*Tourist information: Piazza Monte di Pietà 8. Tel: 0422 547 632. Open: Mon–Sat 0900–1200 and 1500–1800.*

Treviso is often overlooked by visitors to nearby Venice, but it is a pleasing town, with canals where willows weep, attractive frescoed houses and Gothic churches, all enclosed by 16th-century walls.

Fashion-industry giant Luciano Benetton is the town's most famous son, but Treviso is also known as the **Città Dipinta** ('City of Frescos'). The **Duomo** (*Calmaggiore; open: daily 0730–1200 and 1530–1900, until 1300 and 1900 Sun*) has its origins in the 12th century and is famous for Titian's *Annunciation* and for Il Pordenone's fresco, *The Adoration of the Magi*. At the Dominican church of **San Nicolò** (*Via San Nicolò; open: Mon–Fri 0800–1230 and 1530–1900*), there are fine frescos from the 13th to 16th centuries. Especially remarkable are those on the church's columns inside, by the 14th-century north Italian artist **Tommaso da Modena**. The adjoining monastery, the **Seminario** (*open: daily 0800–1800 in summer, 0800–1230 and 1500–1730 in winter; free*) has some 40 of da Modena's frescos, depicting famous Dominicans, while the tiny chapel of the church of **Santa Lucia** (*Piazza San Vito*) has more fine examples of his work.

# Trieste

*Tourist information: Via San Nicolò 20. Tel: 040 36 98 81. Open: Mon–Fri 0900–1900; Sat 0900–1300.*

This cosmopolitan Adriatic town on the frontier between Italian-, Slav- and German-speaking lands first became an important commercial centre in the 18th century, when it provided the Austrian empire with its only significant access to the sea. It was held under Allied occupation from 1945 to 1954, before finally being attached to Italy. Today it is the capital of the Friuli-Venezia Giulia region and the Adriatic's largest seaport.

Overlooking the harbour, **Colle de San Giusto** was the site of the ancient city; the Piazza della Cattedrale has the ruins of a Roman basilica, a castle and the Basilica of St Justus. The 15th-century **Castello di San Giusto** (*Piazza Cattedrale 3; tel: 040 31 36 36; open: Tue–Sun 0800–sunset; £, including admission to museum, open: am*) was built by the Venetians and has superb views over the town and sea. The **Cattedrale di San Giusto** (*Piazza Cattedrale; tel: 040 30 96 66; open: daily*) stands on the site of an Augustan temple and, unusually, has two thrones and two apses, which have fine Venetian-style mosaics.

At the harbour, near the fish market, the marine theme continues in one of the city's most popular attractions, the **Acquario Marino** (aquarium) (*Riva Nazario Sauro 1; tel: 040 30 62 01; open: Tue–Sun in summer, am only Nov–Mar; ££*).

# Udine

*Tourist information: Piazza 1 Maggio 7. Tel: 0432 29 59 72. Open: Mon–Fri 0900–1300 and 1500–1700; Sat 0900–1200.*

Udine, the second city of Friuli-Venezia Giulia, survived the Second World War unscathed, but a major earthquake in 1976 did much damage and claimed hundreds of lives. One of the casualties, now restored, was the 16th-century castle, **Castello**, which houses the **Museo di Storia e d'Arte** (*Castello di Udine, through the Arco Bollani; tel: 0432 50 28 72; open: Tue–Sat 0930–1230 and 1500–1800, Sun am; £*). This museum has a superb collection of works by Caravaggio, Bronzino, Carpaccio and the great Renaissance painter **Giambattista Tiepolo**, who lived in Udine for many years.

From the castle's watchtower there are wonderful views of the Alps, and of the city and its Renaissance, distinctively Venetian central square, **Piazza della Libertà**. The square is dominated by the lovely **Palazzo del Commune** (also known as **Loggia del Lionello**, from the name of its architect), built in rose-coloured stone in the style of the Doge's Palace in Venice, and is lined with elegant and pleasingly proportioned buildings. Northeast of here is the **Palazzo Arcivescovile**, which houses the **Gallerie del Tiepolo** (*Piazza Patriarcato 1; tel: 0432 250 03; open: Wed–Sun 1000–1200 and 1530–1830; £–££*), where there are wonderful examples of Tiepolo's frescos.

## Trieste dialect

*Irish writer James Joyce lived in Trieste between 1905 and 1915, and was apparently particularly taken with the dialect:* 'the residents of Trieste, who had congregated there from Greece, Austria, Hungary and Italy, all spoke the dialect with special pronunciations. The puns and international jokes that resulted delighted Joyce.'

**Richard Ellmann, Joyce's biographer**

# Verona

*Verona is one of the most prosperous cities in northern Italy, a vibrant commercial place that is also rich in history, art and architecture. Located west of Vicenza and near Lake Garda, it is best known as the setting of Shakespeare's* Romeo and Juliet, *and for its Roman remains, notably a magnificent amphitheatre – the venue of a world-famous opera festival.*

The prehistoric settlement of Verona became a Roman colony in 89 BC, and soon developed into a town of considerable importance, as the size and grandeur of its classical remains testify. Later, Charlemagne's son **Pepin** ruled here as King of Italy, then it was controlled in turn by the Saxon and Hohenstaufen emperors, the Venetian Republic, France and then Austria. Finally, in 1866, Verona joined the newly united kingdom of Italy.

The provincial city has survived its chequered history with most of its Roman, medieval and Renaissance monuments intact. Contained within massive 16th-century walls, and clustered around the swift Adige river, the picturesque streets and squares of its compact historic core are still laid out according to the grid pattern decreed by the **emperor Augustus**, and many of its ancient *palazzi* stand on Roman foundations.

*Tourist information: Piazza Erbe 38. Tel: 045 59 28 28. The centre is largely pedestrianised, and most of the sights are within easy walking distance.*

# The Arena

*Piazza Brà. Tel: 045 8003204. Open: Tue–Sun 0800–1900 (0815–1500 during the opera season). ££.*

The interior of Verona's massive **amphitheatre** has survived virtually intact. Built around AD 30, with seating for 14,000, in its heyday it could hold the entire population of the city, as well as visitors from the far corners of the Veneto. They came to watch combats to the death between men and wild beasts, or between pairs of gladiators, butchering one another to cries of '*Jugula!*' ('Slit his throat!').

From the **44 tiers** of the arena, you can see the maze of dungeons and underground passages where the animals were kept in cages, before being winched up to arena level. After the slaughter, attendants dressed as Charon (the mythical ferryman of the dead) would carry off the bodies and rake sand over the blood.

Nowadays, the arena is used for plays, pop concerts and dazzling opera performances.

## Castelvecchio

*Corso Castelvecchio 2. Tel: 045 59 47 34. Open: Tue–Sun 0900–1830. ££.*

This graceful castle was once the home of the **Scaligeri family**, one-time powerful medieval rulers of Verona, and is now the **Museo Civico d'Arte**, one of the finest galleries in the Veneto. Its maze of courtyards, chambers and an overhead walkway affords sensational views of Verona and the surrounding countryside. Inside, the displays include important canvases by **Mantegna**, **Giovanni Bellini**, **Veronese**, **Tintoretto**, **Tiepolo** and **Canaletto**.

# Verona: the old town

## Casa di Giulietta

*Via Cappello 23. Tel: 045 8034303. Open: Tue–Sun 0800–1900. ££.*

The 'House of Juliet' looks the part, with its quaint marble balcony and romantic courtyard setting at the heart of the old town, but there is no reliable evidence linking it with the **legend of Romeo and Juliet**. Even so, half a million visitors come here each year, eager to have their picture taken on Juliet's balcony or outside the beautiful red-brick Gothic **Casa di Romeo** in nearby Via delle Arche Scaligeri.

The **Montague** and **Capulet** families of Shakespeare's play did exist, but, far from constantly feuding, they actually lived amicably in their castles near Vicenza. The first person to write the story of the star-crossed lovers was a Vicentine noble, **Luigi da Porto**, in 1530. Four centuries later, Verona started to exploit the Romeo and Juliet myth, turning the House of Juliet into one of the most popular tourist sights in the city.

## Churches

Verona has more than its fair share of beautiful churches. The largest – **Sant'Anastasia**, on the river – contains some striking frescos, including **Pisanello's** *St George* in the sacristy and faded 15th-century scenes from the life of St Peter in the Gothic portal. Near by, the **Duomo** (Cathedral) is known for its exterior carvings, the richly decorated altars of its magnificent interior, Romanesque cloisters and **Titian's** *Assumption* (in the first chapel on the left).

The beautiful **San Zeno Maggiore**, built between 1123 and 1135 to house the relics of Verona's patron saint, is northern Italy's most ornate Romanesque church, with a magnificent ship's-keel ceiling, an intricately carved marble façade and an altarpiece by **Mantegna**.

Tiny **Santa Maria Antica**, also Romanesque, is dominated by the **Scaligeri tombs**. As it was their parish church, this famous Veronese family chose to be buried here, and their graves are marked by elaborate Gothic tombs depicting them as soldiers – a permanent reminder of their military prowess.

## Piazza delle Erbe

The elongated main square of the old town is among the most lovely in all Italy, situated on the site of the old Roman forum. Named Piazza delle Erbe after the city's ancient herb market, it is now a colourful fruit and vegetable market. The **Lion of St Mark** atop the marble column at the northern end of the square is the symbol of Venetian authority (Verona was the principal city of La Serenissima's *terra firma* empire from 1405 until 1797). The Madonna statue on the fountain in the middle of the square dates from Roman times.

The market is an ideal place to purchase mouth-watering picnic fare to enjoy in the scenic countryside surrounding Verona, and there is also a tempting assortment of cafés, restaurants and shops around the square.

> " *There is no world without Verona's walls,*
> *But purgatory, torture, hell itself.*
> *Hence – banished is banish'd from the world –*
> *And world's exile is death …* "

**William Shakespeare, *Romeo and Juliet*, III.iii.17–20**

THE NORTHEAST AND THE LAKES

# Vicenza

*Wealthy Vicenza, the capital of the Veneto, is an elegant historic town on the edge of the fertile Po plain. Brilliant architect Andrea Palladio spent much of his life in Vicenza, and you can see here his beautifully preserved theatre, basilica and several palaces. His fine Palazzo Chiericati houses the civic museum and gallery. On a hill just outside the city, La Rotonda is the most famous of all Palladian villas.*

**Corso Palladio**, Vicenza's main street, provides a clear impression of the city's wealth and beauty. Among its handsome Palladian palaces are **Palazzo Bonin** (at No 13), **Palazzo Zilere dal Verme** (at No 42) and **Palazzo da Schio** (at No 147), also known as 'Ca' d'Oro' owing to its resemblance to Venice's 'House of Gold' (*see page 79*). Many of Vicenza's smartest shops and cafés are to be found under this street's arcades.

*Getting there: 50km (31 miles) from Venice. Tourist information: Piazza Duomo 5. Tel: 0444 32 08 54.*

## Palazzo Chiericati (Museo Civico)

*Piazza Matteotti 37–39. Tel: 0444 32 13 84. Open: Tue–Sun 1000–1900 Apr–Sept; Tue–Sun 0900–1700 Oct–Mar. £££ (combined entry with the Teatro Olimpico and Museo Naturale e Archeologico).*

On the ground floor of the civic museum are interesting local archaeological collections. But the museum's real appeal is the **impressive picture gallery** on the first floor, which contains major works by local painters (including **Montagna** and **Buonconsiglio**), alongside such familiar names as **Tintoretto**, **Tiepolo**, **Van Dyck** and **Bellini**.

# Piazza dei Signori

The massive, green-roofed Renaissance town hall – now called the **Basilica Palladiana** (*open: Tue–Sun 0900–1700*) – in Vicenza's lively main square was Palladio's first major triumph. Its revolutionary design encased the original Gothic

*palazzo* within a two-storey loggia. The square is surrounded by grand 15th-century residences, the slender, brick 82-m (269-ft) **Torre di Piazza** and a variety of shops and cafés. At the western end of the basilica is a **marble statue of Palladio**, usually surrounded by market stalls overflowing from Piazza delle Erbe. At the northwest corner of Piazza dei Signori, the **Loggia del Capitanio** (formerly the residence of the Venetian governor) was begun by Palladio in 1571.

69

# Teatro Olimpico

*Piazza Matteotti 11. Tel: 0444 32 37 81. Open: Tue–Sun 1000–1900 Apr–Sept; Tue–Sun 0900–1700 Oct–Mar. £££ (combined entry with the Museo Civico and Museo Naturale e Archeologico).*

The Teatro Olimpico is Palladio's last work, begun in 1580 and completed by **Scamozzi** five years later. Built of wood and stucco, this remarkable building is a Renaissance adaptation of the classical style of amphitheatre, and the **earliest surviving indoor theatre** of modern times. The auditorium, with seating for 1 000, rises in steep, semicircular wooden tiers, with an elaborate balustrade surmounted by ancient statues. The permanent stage-set, with its three openings and *trompe-l'œil* street scenes evoking Renaissance Vicenza, were painted in exaggerated perspective to give the illusion of great depth. The theatre's first production (and for many years its only one) was Sophocles' **Oedipus Rex** in 1585.

# Eating and drinking

### Colombara
*Via Zilli 41, Aquileia. Tel: 0431 91513. Closed Mon. ££.* Traditional restaurant with emphasis on seafood. Service is good and the wine list features many regional variations.

### Amadè
*Via Cavour/Vicolo Ca' de' Bezzi 8, Bolzano. Tel: 0471 97 12 78. Closed Sun. ££–£££.* Lovely setting in an old mill where the regional dishes combine the flavours of the Tyrol and the Veneto.

Eating is a serious business in **Cortina d'Ampezzo**, with more than 80 restaurants to choose from. The **Enoteca** wine bar (*off the Corso Italia*) has wines from all over the world and all of Italy's regional varieties too. In the mountains, the **Rifugio Averau** at **Cinque Torri** has stunning views and is one of the area's best bars/restaurants.

### Al Bersagliere
*Via Donatello 6, Padua. Tel: 049 8760314. Closed Wed. £££.* This small, rustic *trattoria* near the Prato serves traditional Paduan cuisine and a good selection of regional wines.

### Vecchia Riva
*Via Bastione 3, Riva del Garda. Tel: 0464 55 50 61. Closed lunch and Tue. ££–£££.* Here the speciality is lake fish, but there are plenty of other delicious offerings too in an intimate, pleasant restaurant.

### Al Tino
*Via Santissima Trinità 10, Trento. Tel: 0461 98 41 09. Closed Sun. £.* Good-value food and wine make this bustling *trattoria* in the historic centre very popular. Booking advised.

### Due Spade
*Via Don A Rizzi 11, Trento. Tel: 0461 23 43 43. Closed Sun and Mon lunch. £££.* This welcoming 16th-century *osteria* serves delicious traditional Trentino specialities. Discreet and attentive service and an excellent wine list.

### Caffè Pasticceria Pirona
*Largo Barriera Vecchia 12, Trieste. £.* Great for pastries (as well as coffee) and once a regular haunt of Irish writer James Joyce.

### Caffè San Marco
*Via Cesare Battisti 18, Trieste. ££.* Lovely art-nouveau-style café that is both famous and very popular.

### Olivo
*Piazza Brà 18, Verona. Tel: 045 8030598. Closed Mon, and Tue lunchtime. ££.* Sophisticated pizzeria overlooking the Arena, with smart, modern décor.

### Pampanin
*Via Garibaldi 24, Verona. Open: Wed–Mon 0730–0000, except Aug. £.* Riverside *gelateria* serving Verona's finest ice cream.

### Antica Casa della Malvasia
*Contrà Morette 5, Vicenza. Tel: 0444 54 37 04. Closed Sun evening, Mon and Aug. ££.* Hearty home-cooking in an ancient Veneto inn, with live music (jazz/blues) most Tuesday evenings.

### Tre Visi
*Corso Palladio 25, Vicenza. Tel: 0444 32 48 68. Closed Sun evening and Mon. ££.* A popular locals' haunt, serving traditional Vicentine dishes in a quiet courtyard near the historic town centre.

# Shopping

Every town in the Veneto boasts an excellent range of food shops, and many have seasonal speciality markets. In **country areas** you can buy wines, cheese and olive oil direct from the producers. **Verona** is also strong on fashion with Max Mara, Versace, Stefanel, Benetton, Gucci and Fiorucci, among others, in the main shopping street ( *Via Mazzini* ) alone.

### Rinascente
*Piazza Garibaldi, Padua*. Smart, affordable fashions and stylish household goods in a popular, national department store.

### Les Bonbons
*12a Via Garibaldi, Verona*. A tiny, old-fashioned sweet shop, chock-a-block with gorgeous sweets and chocolates.

### Città del Sole
*Via Cattaneo 8b, Verona*. Dreams are made of this! A toyshop selling everything imaginable, from dolls to dinosaurs and dumper trucks.

### Stecco
*Piazza dei Signori 57, Vicenza*. Jewellery made in Vicenza, the 'city of gold' – one of the main Italian centres for the working of this precious metal.

# Nightlife

The two main cultural venues in the Veneto are **Verona**'s **Arena** (staging everything from a spectacular summer opera festival to pop concerts) and the **Teatro Olimpico** in **Vicenza**. Tickets for Arena events are available from the official box office ( *Via Dietro Anfiteatro 6b; tel: 045 8005151; open: Mon–Fri 0900–1200 and 1515–1745, Sat 0900–1200 during the festival, 1000–2100 on performance days, 1000–1745 on days without performances, or book online at www.arena.it*). For details of the Teatro Olimpico's theatre season, contact the Vicenza tourist office.

## Vino from the Veneto

*The Veneto produces large quantities of red, white and rosé wines, with white the most popular with locals. Soave is the main 'big-name' white wine of the region, although the best-quality whites actually come from Friuli and Trentino-Alto Adige regions. If you get the chance, try Bianco di Custoza, an 'upmarket' Soave from the eastern shores of Lake Garda, and sweet Gambellara (made with Soave grapes), an exceptional white dessert wine. Popular light, fruity reds include Bardolino, also from Lake Garda, and Valpolicella, while rich Recioto della Valpolicella and fortified Recioto Amarone count among the best red dessert wines.*

# Palladio

*A recurring theme throughout the Veneto is the genius of Andrea di Palladio (1508–80). Born in Padua, he moved to Vicenza at the age of 16 to work in a stone-carving workshop. While working on the decorative details of a new villa here, he met powerful local aristocrat Count Trissino, the leader of a group of humanist intellectuals dedicated to the revival of classical culture. Impressed by the young stone-cutter, Trissino agreed to fund his studies of ancient architecture, and even financed several research trips to Rome.*

As a result, Palladio developed a new, unique architectural style by reinventing such classical features as porticoes, arcades, domes and pedimented pavilions, which all became hallmarks of his design style. His early patrons were mainly Vicentine nobles, for whom he designed country villas, and Venetian patricians, keen to acquire a newly fashionable estate on the mainland.

Palladio's first major break came in 1549 when his ingenious design for Vicenza's Gothic town hall (now called the Basilica Palladiana; *see page 69*) established him as the leading Italian architect of his day. From here to his last great triumph, the Teatro Olimpico (*see page 69*), he totally transformed the appearance of Vicenza – a city still celebrated the world over for its architecture.

Each of his designs, although always unmistakably 'Palladian', is surprisingly different, ranging from the ornate, statue-clad **Palazzo Chiericati** in Vicenza (*see page 68*) to the simple, unadorned **Villa Pisani Ferri** at Bagnolo di Lonigo. Palladio ideally liked to build near water, and would create classical gardens for each villa, believing the natural environment was vital to 'help conserve the health and strength of the villa's inhabitants, and restore their spirits, worn out by the agitation of city life, to peace and tranquillity' (*Quattro Libri dell'Architettura*, 1570).

**Villa Rotonda** near Vicenza – a dazzling white edifice, striking for its regular, symmetrical forms, its simple design and pleasing proportions, balanced by neat green lawns and terracotta roof tiles – is widely considered to be his greatest achievement. It has since inspired look-alikes as far afield as London, Delhi and St Petersburg. Today, Palladian designs continue to influence architects around the world.

THE NORTHEAST AND THE LAKES

# Venice

*Nothing can prepare you for your first sight of La Serenissima, this uniquely beautiful floating city built on 200 tiny islands. Ageing palazzi, flaking façades and tilting bell towers testify to its ephemeral nature, yet it remains a delicate miracle of survival, with an unrivalled artistic richness. St Mark's Basilica, the Doge's Palace, the Rialto Bridge and the Grand Canal are must-sees, but visitors will remember just as clearly pasta al fresco in a sun-splashed piazza, gondolas tied to striped poles, buildings reflected in still waters, the sights and scents of local markets, and shop windows brimming with carnival masks and dazzling glass.*

# BEST OF
## Venice

*Getting around:* in Venice, public transport is by water. Cheap **vaporetti**, **motoscafi** or **motonavi** *(water-buses)* go all over the city. Buy tickets (stamp them in the machine before boarding) at landing stages, at ACTV offices (tel: 041 5287886), or at bars, shops and tobacconists displaying the ACTV sign, or invest in a travel pass or a block of tickets. **Water-taxis** are much more expensive (hire from taxi ranks, or order one on 041 5229750 or 041 5222303). The **traghetto** *(gondola-ferry)* is a relatively cheap and entertaining way to cross the canal.

VENICE

## 1 Accademia

The glory that was once Venice lives on in this dazzling collection of paintings spanning the 13th to the 18th centuries. From Veneziano to Veronese, Tintoretto to Tiepolo, the city's main art gallery is absolutely unmissable. **Page 78**

## 2 Basilica di San Marco

The magnificent gilded interior and mosaics of St Mark's Basilica, the city's cathedral, the 'Church of Gold' and one of the world's most richly embellished churches, lingers long in one's memory. **Page 92**

## 3 Churches of Venice

Venice was a huge world power for centuries, and its immense wealth was celebrated in art and lavish construction. Although Napoleon destroyed over 50 of its churches, the city still has more than 200 ecclesiastical buildings left, designed by some of history's finest architects. Many churches are crammed with the most astonishing works of art, too. **Pages 80-1**

## 4 Grand Canal

The 'high street of Venice' is almost too good to be true. Sweeping graciously through the city, flanked by crumbling *palazzi* with distinctive Venetian windows and ground floors frequently awash, and bustling with all manner of boats, this most beautiful of waterways is like a life-sized stage-set. Admire it from the front seats of a *vaporetto* (water bus), and take plenty of film. **Pages 82-5**

## 5 Islands of the Lagoon

The outlying islands offer a taste of Venetian life off the main tourist drag. From the glamorous, lively beach resort of the Lido to the glassworks of Murano, the multi-coloured houses of Burano and the outlying oasis of the nearly deserted Torcello – the choice is yours. **Pages 86-7**

## 6 Palazzo Ducale

Gleaming on the waterfront like a frosted pink birthday cake with lacy white icing, the Doge's Palace is undoubtedly the city's most magnificent *palazzo*, a veritable masterpiece of Gothic architecture. Inside, the dazzling treasures of the Republic provide a fascinating insight into Venice's colourful history. **Page 89**

## 7 The Rialto

Don't just visit the famed Rialto Bridge, one of the classic picture-postcard sights of Venice. Take time also to visit the Rialto markets – ideally at the crack of dawn, before the crowds arrive – for a vivid insight into the hard-working life of everyday Venetians. **Pages 90-1**

## 8 San Marco

Piazza San Marco, celebrated by Napoleon as 'the most elegant drawing room in Europe', has been the heart of Venice for over a millennium. Fork out a fortune for a mid-morning coffee on the famous café terraces, then climb the Campanile for views (on a clear day) to the snow-capped Dolomites. **Pages 92-5**

## Tourist information

Venice's main tourist office (Azienda di Promozione Turistica) is just off **St Mark's Square**, at *Calle Larga dell'Ascensione 71; tel: 041 5298711, fax: 041 5230399, e-mail: aptve@provincia.venezia.it, www.provincia.venezia.it/aptve.*

# Accademia

*Campo della Carità 1050 (Dorsoduro). Tel: 041 5200345. Open: Mon 0900–1400, Tue–Fri 0900–2100, Sat 0900–2300, Sun 0900–2000 in summer; Mon 0900–1400, Tue–Sat 0900–1900, Sun 0900–2000 in winter. Guided tours: Wed and Thu 1000, 1100, 1200 (in English). £££.* Vaporetto: *Accademia.*

The Accademia holds the world's finest collection of **Venetian art**, including masterworks from the city's most famous sons. The works are housed in **La Carità**, a complex of church, convent, cloisters and *scuole* (colleges). The main entrance is in the former Scuola Grande di Santa Maria della Carità – the side entrance is reserved for students attending the adjoining art school.

The collection, displayed in **24 rooms**, is not always in chronological order – the first 11 rooms focus on the Renaissance, rooms 12 to 17 display 18th-century landscapes and genre paintings, while the remaining rooms revert to the Renaissance.

In **Room 1**, originally the meeting room of the Scuola, Veneziano's polyptych, *The Coronation of the Virgin*, bridges the gap between Byzantine art and the beginning of a truly Venetian school of painting. **Room 5** houses Giovanni Bellini's masterpiece *Pietà* (1505) and *The Tempest*, in which Giorgione laid the foundations for modern painting, abandoning any formal preparation and building the image instead through layers of paint. In **Room 10** you will find a celebrated *Pietà* by Titian and several Tintorettos. There are surprisingly few works by **Canaletto** in Venice, but you will find three in **Room 17**. Highlights in the last few rooms include Gentile Bellini's *Procession* (**Room 20**), showing St Mark's Square, and the nine brilliant canvases of Carpaccio's fabulous *The Legend of Saint Ursula* (**Room 21**).

> " *How does one recognise Venetian paint? By a brilliance of colour, some say ... by a greater luminosity, say others ... By the subject matter, many would confess, meaning the milky-breasted goddesses of Titian, Tintoretto and Veronese, or the views of Guardi and Canaletto. I would say it identifies itself ... by an enhanced reality, a reverence for the concrete world.* "
>
> **Mary McCarthy,**
> **Venice Observed** (1961)

# Ca' d'Oro

*Calle Ca' d'Oro (Canareggio). Tel: 041 5328790.*
*Open: daily 0900–1330. ££. Vaporetto: Ca' d'Oro.*

'The Ca' d'Oro is like the smile of a woman', remarked André Suarès. 'Its face breathes happiness and serenity, and the Grand Canal reflects it.'

Ca' d'Oro ('House of Gold') boasts the most beautiful façade of all Venetian palaces. The former home of the **Contarinis**, the powerful family that gave the city eight doges, it was originally completely gilded – hence its name. The gold has long since eroded, leaving a fanciful pink and white stone façade, carved into fragile, lacy Gothic patterns.

# Ca' Rezzonico

*Fondamenta Rezzonico 3136 (Dorsoduro). Tel: 041 2410100. Open: 1000–*
*1700 Apr–Sept; 1000–1600 Oct–Mar; closed Fri. ££. Vaporetto: Ca' Rezzonico.*

Not only is this one of the few *palazzi* on the Grand Canal to open its doors to the public, but it also happens to be an outstanding example of baroque architecture, designed by **Baldassare Longhena**. The **Rezzonico family** moved here in 1687. They were neither Venetian nor aristocrats, but they were rich and important enough to buy themselves noble rank from the Republic.

Today, the newly restored palace houses the **Museo del Settecento Veneziano** ('Museum of 18th-century Venice'). Within its sumptuous rooms you will find an enormous ballroom lavishly decorated with *trompe-l'œil* frescos, various **Guardi**, **Canaletto** and **Tiepolo** paintings, an unusual nuptial chamber with two dressing-rooms and an entire pharmacy reassembled from Campo San Stin. With so many original furnishings and paintings still in pristine condition, it is easy to conjure up a vivid picture of patrician life in 18th-century Venice.

> " *There are surely in Venice more paintings than in all the rest of Italy.* "
>
> **1561 guidebook to Venice**

# Churches

## Santi Giovanni e Paolo

*Campo Santi Giovanni e Paolo (Castello). Tel: 041 5235913. Open: Mon–Sat 1000–1700; Sun 1300–1700. Vaporetto: Fondamente Nuove or Ospedale Civile.*

Called **San Zanipolo** by Venetians, this is the largest church in Venice, on a par in importance with **St Mark's** and the **Frari**. Legend has it that, following a dream, **Doge Tiepolo** was inspired immediately to built an imposing Gothic church, striking in its architectural austerity.

The church is the unofficial pantheon of Venice, containing the tombs of many famous Venetians, including 15 doges. The most grandiose mausoleums were created by illustrious sculptors and adorned with works by the most noted Venetian painters. The luminous retable in the right aisle is by **Giovanni Bellini**; the ceiling frescos in the **Rosary chapel** are by **Veronese**. The **stained-glass window** in the right-hand transept was made by the glassmakers of Murano.

In the magnificent *campo* outside, the plain, red-brick façade of the church is beautifully offset by the white marble façade of the **Scuola Grande di San Marco**, now the city hospital, with its remarkable *trompe-l'œil* panels.

## Santa Maria Gloriosa dei Frari

*Campo dei Frari (San Polo). Open: Mon–Sat 0900–1800; Sun 1500–1800. £. Vaporetto: San Tomà.*

Santa Maria Gloriosa was built in 1250 by the Franciscans, hence its popular name, **I Frari** ('the friars'). Although the exterior is unprepossessing, the vast Gothic interior shelters some of Venice's most dazzling art treasures. The most famous is **Titian**'s *Assumption* (1518), over the main altar, one of the most influential paintings in 16th-century Venetian art.

The Frari was considered a most prestigious place of worship, and a number of important Venetians are buried here, including **Doge Pesaro** and **Doge Tron**. Composer **Monteverdi** is remembered by a simple white marble slab on the floor, while the pupils of sculptor **Canova** created a peculiar pyramidal tomb for him.

## Santa Maria dei Miracoli

*Campiello dei Miracoli (Canareggio). Tel: 041 2750462. Open: Mon–Sat 0900–1700; Sun 0900–1130 and 1300–1700. £.* Vaporetto: *Rialto.*

A masterpiece of the early Renaissance, this is one of the most charming churches in Venice. Built in the 1480s by **Pietro Lombardo**, to provide protection for the early 15th-century *Madonna and Child* portrait at the altar, it is distinguished by its architectural simplicity, its exquisite carvings and its revetment of coloured marble. It is squeezed on to a tiny island, which appears to be perfectly made for it. The interior has an almost magical quality about it, with a vaulted roof and starry dome.

81

## Santa Maria della Salute

*Campo della Salute (Dorsoduro). Tel: 041 5225558. Open: 0900–1200 and 1500–1730.* Vaporetto: *Salute.*

This magnificent and monumental **baroque church** is one of the great architectural sights of Venice – a shining white riot of domes and statues, supported by over a million timber piles and guarding the entrance to the Grand Canal. It was built to commemorate the end of the 1630 plague, which had wiped out over one-third of the population; *Salute* means health and salvation. Designer **Baldassare Longhena** worked on the church for half a century, creating an octagonal basilica encircled by chapels and surmounted by a great cupola.

The massive main entrance is opened only on 21 November, the **feast day** of Madonna della Salute. A bridge of boats is constructed across the Grand Canal, and people walk across the water to worship.

# Grand Canal: to the Rialto

*This extraordinary watery highway, known affectionately as the Canalazzo ('Little Canal'), has been described as 'the finest street in the world'. It winds proudly for nearly 4km (2 1/2 miles) in an inverted 'S' shape, splitting the city into two unequal parts. For many it is their first impression of Venice – a fascinating sight, lined by 200 palaces built between the 12th and 18th centuries, which seem to rise directly out of the water.*

Today the canal is crowded with *vaporetti*, launches, working barges and gondolas. The best way to appreciate this remarkable canal is to join them. Jump in a gondola, or *vaporetto* 1 or 82, grab a front seat, sit back and admire the works of art which line the banks.

*From Ferrovia Santa Lucia to San Stae landing stage.*
*Vaporetto: nos 1 or 82.*

The **railway station** at the western end of the canal as it passes through central Venice takes its name from the saint whose church used to stand here. This stretch of the canal boasts a variety of notable palaces, including several **Veneto-Byzantine** architectural gems, and **historic warehouses** dating back to the times of the Serene Republic. Although heavily restored, it is easy to visualise these as they once were, full of rice, spices, perfumes and dried fruits from the East.

After the **Ponte degli Scalzi**, one of only three bridges knotting the two halves of the city together, look for the impressive **Fondaco dei Turchi** ('Turk's Warehouse'), with its sumptuous marble arcaded façade. From 1621 to 1838 it was rented to Turkish merchants as the headquarters of the Ottoman trade delegation in Venice. At the same time it served as a mosque, a bath-house and a bazaar. Next door, the plain-brick **Deposito del Megio** ('Millet Deposit') served as the Republic's public granary. Opposite, the city's winter casino (*open: 1600–0230 Oct–Mar; smart dress*) is housed in the impressive early Renaissance **Palazzo Loredan-Vendramin-Calergi**, a model for many of the palaces built alongside the canal.

> *Venice is not an expensive residence ... I have my gondola and about fourteen servants ... and I reside in one of the Mocenigo palaces on the Grand Canal.*
>
> **Lord Byron in a letter to a friend, 1819**

### From San Stae to San Tomà landing stage

**Palazzo Barbarigo** (opposite San Stae pier) retains traces of its 16th-century exterior frescos, once a common feature of canal-front mansions. The yellow-fronted **Palazzo Grissoni-Grimani** next door but two was originally adorned by **Tintoretto** frescos. Just before Ca' d'Oro landing-stage, you can't miss the magnificent **Ca' d'Oro** (*see page 79*); further along, the 13th-century **Ca' da Mosto** (two along from Rio dei Santi Apostoli) is one of Venice's oldest Gothic palaces.

For centuries, the busy area around the **Rialto Bridge** (*see pages 90–1*) has been a centre of trade. Today, crowded quaysides, ancient administrative buildings and colourful food markets still border this stretch of the canal, while barges and fishing boats throng the water. Opposite and a little further on from the Ca' d'Oro pier, there has been a thriving fish market at **Campo di Pescheria** for six centuries; today, it takes place under the white arches of a mock-Gothic market hall. The pink and white market buildings of the **Fabbriche Vecchie** and the **Fabbriche Nuove** were built in the 16th century as offices of the judiciary for trade and commerce.

> *Obviously things have to smell of whatever they smell of, and obviously canals will reek in the summertime, but this really is too much.*
>
> **Burgundian president Charles de Brosses, 18th century**

83

# Grand Canal:
# from the Rialto

Just before the **Rialto Bridge**, which spans this commercial heart of the city, the elegant white 16th-century **Palazzo dei Camerlenghi** was originally the city treasury. Opposite, the austere white **Fondaco dei Tedeschi** was a major foreign merchants' headquarters during the Republic, and is now the main post office. On the other side of the bridge, visitors crowd the waterside tables on the **Riva del Vin** quayside, one of few places where you can sit so close to the canal – and correspondingly expensive! Facing across the canal, your view is of the fine 15th-century pink Gothic Palazzo Bembo, with its pointed windows and balconies.

Finally, just before San Tomà landing-stage, you'll see the faded yellow **Palazzo Marcello 'dei Leoni'**, named after the venerable stone lions guarding the doorway.

### From San Tomà to San Marco landing stage

**Dorsoduro**'s span of the Grand Canal has more than its fair share of patrician palaces, especially after La Volta ('the curve'), where the canal turns back on itself, and becomes wider and grander than ever.

The magnificent **Ca' Foscari** (beside Rio di Ca' Foscari), built for Doge Foscari in 1437, is now part of Venice University. Composer **Richard Wagner** lived next door, at **Palazzo Giustinian**, and wrote the second act of *Tristan und Isolde* here. **Ca' Rezzonico** (*see page 79*), with its imposing pillared façade, was once the home of English poets **Elizabeth Barrett** and **Robert Browning**.

After the wooden Accademia Bridge, **Palazzo Barbarigo** (on the corner beside Rio San Vio) is decorated with some mosaics of dubious taste, added in 1887. Alongside, the single-storey **Palazzo Venier dei Leoni** is more unusual – a truncated, white, unfinished palace housing **Peggy Guggenheim**'s collection of modern art (*see page 90*). Two palaces further on, and lavishly decorated with coloured marble, is **Palazzo Dario** (marked 'Darius' on the façade), said to bring bad luck to its owners, all of whom have died in a mysterious or violent way. Nearby, **Palazzo Salviati** (opposite Santa Maria del Giglio landing stage), richly decorated with modern glass mosaics, was built by one of Murano's glass barons.

> For this evening I have ordered the singing of the gondoliers ... the gondolier gives strength and energy to his song, so that it echoes in the distance and spreads over the surface of the water. Far away a companion replies with the next verse, then the first takes up the song again, as though the one were the echo of the other. The greater the distance between them, the more beautiful the song.
>
> **J W von Goethe,**
> *Italian Journey*
> **(1786–8)**

The Grand Canal ends with a flourish with the monumental **Santa Maria della Salute** (*see page 81*) and the **Dogana di Mare** (Maritime Customs). The view along the final stretch of the canal, towards **St Mark's Square** (*see pages 94–5*), is one of the grandest. It takes in several of the finest palaces of Venice; some now house celebrated hotels, some are museums and galleries, and many are famed for their celebrity links. **Palazzo Mocenigo** (formed by four palaces linked together just before La Volta, opposite San Tomà pier) served as lodgings to **Lord Byron**. At times, he would swim home from the Lido. The elegant, cream-coloured **Palazzo Grassi**, the last great palace to be constructed on the canal, is one of the most imposing *palazzi* on this stretch of water. It was bought by Fiat in 1984 and converted into a centre for art exhibitions.

The Grand Canal has always been an endless source of inspiration to artists and writers. Two palaces beyond Accademia Bridge, **Monet**, **Whistler** and **John Singer Sargent** all had studios in **Palazzo Barbaro**, **Robert Browning** gave recitations in the library and **Henry James** wrote *The Aspern Papers* here. Sculptor **Canova** had a studio in pretty **Casetta delle Rose**, one of the smallest houses on the canal, set back in tiny gardens next door to the huge **Ca' Grande**. Canova's jealous mistress bought the house opposite so that she could keep an eye on him.

The fairytale, pink-fronted **Palazzo Fasan** is known as the 'House of Desdemona' from Shakespeare's *Othello*. Just prior to the San Marco landing stage, guests at the Gothic **Palazzo Giustinian**, once a hotel, included **Verdi**, **Turner**, **Proust** and **George Eliot**, while **Ernest Hemingway** often propped up the bar at **Harry's** (at the landing stage).

# Islands of the Lagoon

*Visiting the islands of the lagoon puts Venice into perspective. La Serenissima is not simply a remarkable city born out of the sea, but part of an archipelago of over 40 islands scattered across a vast lagoon.*

## Burano

Colourful Burano, with its alarmingly tilted **bell tower**, is the most photogenic lagoon island. The brilliant reds, blues, pinks, lilacs, greens and yellows of its neat, gaily painted **cottages**, reflected in the narrow canals, make it a work of art.

The locals live chiefly on **fishing** (there are many fine fish restaurants here) and **lace-making**. Burano **lace** dates back to the 15th century, when a young girl reproduced the pattern of a beautiful piece of seaweed with a needle and thread to create a fine and fragile product. The lace rapidly became highly sought after by aristocratic Venetian ladies. To find out more, visit the **Scuola e Museo di Merletto** (*School and Museum of Lace-making, Piazza Galuppi; tel: 041 730034; open: Wed–Mon 1000–1700 Apr–Sept, Wed–Mon 1000–1600 Oct–Mar; ££*), on the main square.

> **"** *This [the Lido] was a holiday-place of all holiday-places … Too many people in the piazza, too many trunks of humanity on the beach, too many gondolas, too many motor-launches … too many ices, too many cocktails … too much sun … too many cargos of strawberries … too much enjoyment, altogether far too much enjoyment!* **"**
>
> **D H Lawrence, *Lady Chatterley's Lover* (1928)**

## The Lido

Venice's seaside resort, just 10 minutes from the city, developed as the world's first 'lido' from 1840 onwards. It now boasts glorious sandy beaches, wooden bathing huts, fabulous hotels, a swinging nightlife (during the summer season), a casino and Venice's only golf course. It also hosts the oldest international film festival in the world, staged annually in late August/early September since 1932.

# Murano

The famous glass-making centre of Murano resembles a miniature Venice, with handsome houses, canals, bridges and even a scaled-down Grand Canal.

In 1291, the **glassmakers** and their furnaces were moved to the island from Venice because of the high incidence of fires in a city predominantly built of wood. Murano thrived on glass production, and it remains the best place to buy Venetian glass. Many manufacturers offer demonstrations, and the **Museo Vetrario** (*Museum of Glass, Fondamenta Giustiniani 8; tel: 041 739586; open: Thu–Tue 1000–1700 Apr–Oct, Thu–Tue 1000–1600 Nov–Mar; ££;* vaporetto: *Museo*), housed in the grand **Palazzo Giustiniani**, tells the story of the industry.

There are grand mansions on Murano, as well as the magnificent **basilica of Santi Maria e Donato**, one of the oldest in the lagoon. The striking colonnaded apse faces the canal. Inside is an intricate mosaic pavement, with pieces of old Murano glass set into it.

# Torcello

> **"** *Mother and daughter, you behold them both in their widowhood – Torcello and Venice.* **"**
>
> **John Ruskin, Works (1904)**

The story of Venice began on tiny Torcello, which was settled as early as the 5th century AD, and had grown to become a thriving centre by the 10th century. Today, all that remains are silted-up canals, a handful of crumbling houses and a few ancient monuments. The Byzantine **basilica of Santa Maria Assunta** (*tel: 041 730084; open: 1030–1730 Apr–Oct, 1000–1700 Nov–Mar; ££*), has a dominant campanile and exquisite 12th-century mosaics; the adjoining **church of Santa Fosca** (*open: 1000–1230 and 1400–1700*) was first erected in 864 as a *martyrium*, and reconstructed in the 11th and 12th centuries. The **Estuary Museum** (*open: Tue–Sun 1000–1230 and 1400–1730 Apr–Sept, Tue–Sun 1030–1230 and 1400–1600 Oct–Mar*) displays the alleged 5th-century throne of **Attila the Hun**.

*Getting around: Motoscafo No 12 stops at one pier on Murano. Several lines go to the Lido: Nos 1 and 82, the night boats (marked 'N') and Nos 6, 14 and 51/52. For islands south of Venice, take the No 82 vaporetto.*

# Museo Storico Navale

*Campo San Biagio (Castello). Tel: 041 5200276. Open: Mon–Sat 0845–1330. ££. Vaporetto: Arsenale.*

The maritime museum is a must for all who are interested in the illustrious history of Venice as one of the world's greatest maritime powers. The extensive collection, housed in an old granary, ranges from models of the ships built in the neighbouring **Arsenale**, to human torpedoes used in the Second World War. Other highlights include a special section devoted to the history of the gondola – including **Peggy Guggenheim**'s private craft and the doge's gold-painted ship of state, the *Bucintoro*. Sadly, the original vessel was burned by **Napoleon**, but this is a magnificent copy.

# Museo Civico Correr

*Piazza San Marco (entrance in Ala Napoleonica) (San Marco). Tel: 041 5225625. Open: 0900–1900 in summer; 0900–1700 in winter. ££. Café and bookshop. Vaporetto: San Marco.*

An early visit to this, Venice's principal historical museum, will greatly enhance your walks around town. It is named after the wealthy abbot **Teodoro Correr**, whose paintings and documents, bequeathed to the city in 1830, form the core of the collection. The wide marble staircase was once the grand entrance to **Napoleon**'s prestigious palace. An entire floor is devoted to the history of the **Venetian Republic** and the **Risorgimento**, and several rooms are dedicated to the figure of the doge.

> *'Tis ridiculous to see how these ladys crawle in and out of their gondolas by reason of their zoccoli, and what dwarfs they appeare when taken down from their wooden scaffold.*
>
> **John Evelyn on ladies' footwear, *Diary* (1640)**

Upstairs, a further 20 rooms of art and sculpture provide a vivid insight into Venetian life and art from the 14th to 16th centuries. The **Bellini salon** houses works by three members of this great Venetian family, and **Carpaccio**'s infamous *Two Venetian Ladies*, in their saucy low-cut dresses. (Incidentally, also on display are the extraordinary *zoccoli*, foot-high platform shoes once worn by upper-class women and prostitutes.)

# Palazzo Ducale

*Piazzetta San Marco (San Marco). Tel: 041 5204287. Open: 0900–1900 Apr–Oct; 0900–1700 Nov–Mar (last admission 90 minutes before closing). £££ (audio-guide highly recommended).* Vaporetto: *San Zaccaria.*

The Doge's Palace is the grandest of all Venice's palaces and, until the fall of the Republic in 1797, its nerve centre. Strategically situated on the lagoon at the point where the city surveys the Adriatic, it was the seat of government and home to Venice's rulers.

The doge was the supreme magistrate of Venice, elected by an assembly of citizens, and remaining in office for life. The first doge, Paulo Anafesto, was appointed in 697. As Venice gradually achieved independence, influential families would try to dominate the increasingly important role. The doge's power had to be reduced, but his appearance became more and more magnificent: his fine scarlet robes were adorned with jewelled clasps and ermine, and his distinctive velvet head-dress (*zoia*) was studded with precious stones.

The first doge's 'palace' was built here in 814, and continually rebuilt, enlarged and embellished over the centuries. The end result is a gracious Gothic structure of gleaming pink marble and white stone arcades, dating mainly from the 14th and 15th centuries. The grand Renaissance courtyard within was a later addition.

The grandeur of the palace's interior is dazzling, with some fine paintings and frescoed ceilings by Veronese and Tintoretto. The grandiose Sala del Maggio Consiglio contains Tintoretto's *Paradise*, reputedly the largest oil painting in the world. Around the walls are portraits of the first 76 doges; that of Marin Falier, executed for treason in 1355, is concealed by a black curtain.

# Guggenheim Collection

*Palazzo Venier dei Leoni (Dorsoduro). Tel: 041 5206288. Open: Wed–Mon 1100–1800, with presentations in English at 1200 and 1600. ££. The museum is in the process of acquiring the Dogana di Mare as further exhibition space.* Vaporetto: *Accademia*.

The Guggenheim Collection is housed in the quirky **Palazzo Venier dei Leoni** (or 'Palazzo Nonfinito'), the unfinished single-storey white *palazzo* on the Grand Canal. The palace has seen its fair share of eccentrics: in the early 20th century, socialite Marchesa Casati of Milan sprayed the grounds lilac and filled them with apes and naked torch-bearing 'slaves' for a party. In 1949, the palace was purchased by American copper heiress **Peggy Guggenheim**, an ardent collector, dealer and patron of modern art. On her death, in 1979, the building and her remarkable collection were given to the Guggenheim Foundation, created by her uncle.

In the gardens, there are works by **Giacometti**, **Brancusi** and **Marini**. Inside, the collection is exceptional for its range, quality and comprehensiveness, representing all the major art movements of the 20th century, especially the Surrealists. The impressive list of artists includes **Bacon**, **Braque**, **Chagall**, **Kandinski**, **Klee**, **Magritte**, **Mondrian** and **Moore**. One entire room is dedicated to Peggy's own discovery, **Jackson Pollock**; the dining room contains major **Cubist works**, including **Picasso**'s *The Poet*; and there are several works by Peggy's second husband, **Max Ernst**.

Peggy is buried in the delightful gardens along with her 14 poodles, and a view of the Grand Canal.

# The Rialto

It is said that the very first inhabitants of Venice settled here on a cluster of small islands called **Rivus Altus** ('high bank') or Rialto. The height of the land afforded greater safety from flooding than the surrounding islands. By the 11th century, Rialto had become the commercial centre of an ever-expanding city.

# Rialto Bridge

*(San Polo/Santa Croce).* Vaporetto: *Rialto.*

The first Rialto Bridge, a simple wooden pontoon spanning the Grand Canal, appeared around 1172; the third version collapsed under a wedding procession in 1444. In the 16th century, it was decided to replace the wooden bridge with a sturdier structure. A competition was held and the daring design of the appropriately named **Da Ponte** was chosen. Begun in 1588, the single-arched bridge, lined with a double row of shops, took just three years to complete, although the foundations required over 12,000 piles. Until 1854, when the Accademia Bridge was constructed, the Rialto Bridge remained the only means of crossing the canal on foot.

> " *I will buy with you, sell with you, talk with you, walk with you, and so following: but I will not eat with you, drink with you, nor pray with you. What news on the Rialto?* "

**Shylock, in William Shakespeare's *The Merchant of Venice*, I.iii.30–4**

# Rialto markets

*(San Polo/Santa Croce) Erberia: open: Mon–Sat until noon; Pescheria: open: Tue–Sat until noon.* Vaporetto: *Rialto.*

The Rialto markets are an appealing blend of noisy, gesticulating locals, traders and tourists. For centuries this was the centre of business and trade, where you could buy everything from gold, silver and oriental silks and spices to fish, fruit and vegetables. Stroll through the streets and squares near the Rialto Bridge – along the **Erberia** quayside (fruit and vegetable market) and through the porticos of the **Pescheria** (fish market) – and absorb the 'ancient smell of mud, incense, fish, age, filth and velvet' (Jan Morris, *Venice*). It's still the most buzzing and picturesque place in Venice for shopping.

> " *If Saint Mark's Square is the royal throne room; the Quay the splendid balcony overlooking the lagoon; the Grand Canal the gallery of pictures and mirrors; Rialto is what might be called the city's larder …* "

**Diego Valeri, *Guida sentimentale di Venezia***

# San Marco

## Basilica di San Marco

*Piazza San Marco (San Marco). Tel: 041 5225697. Main part of church open:
daily 0945–1730; Museo Marciano (Loggia dei Cavalli) open: daily 0945–1600.
Admission free. Treasury open: daily 0945–1600. £. Golden Altar Screen open:
daily 0945–1600. £. Services eight or nine times a day. Guided tours in English
twice a week in summer months. Vaporetto: San Marco or San Zaccaria.*

The Basilica of St Mark is a 'church of gold'
with a captivating aura of mystery. The biggest
puzzle surrounds its construction: to this day, no
one knows who was responsible for its splendour,
although some say that a seated figure with
crutches, carved in the central arch of the central
doorway, represents the unnamed architect.

One fact is certain: the history of the basilica
dates back to 828 when two merchants returned
to Venice from Alexandria in Egypt, carrying
with them the relics of **St Mark**. The ruling
doge at the time, **Giustiniano Parteciaco**,
seems to have commissioned the theft to enhance
his prestige and that of Venice. He built a church
and shrine, basing it on the **Church of the
Apostles** in **Constantinople**, the richest city
in Christendom, and made St Mark the patron of the city.
Giustiniano's church served as the **Doge's Chapel**, being
continually embellished over the centuries by various
leaders, and became the city cathedral in 1807.

The original structure of the striking cross-shaped basilica is
largely 11th century. The process of adorning the plain brick
church with gold, mosaics and marble took a further two
centuries. Now, St Mark's is considered the most glorious
**Byzantine building** in the western world. Its striking main
**façade** is a masterful balance of columns, arches, marble
slabs and **mosaics**. One mosaic (on the left-hand side),

> " The church in Venice is something more than all things bright and
> beautiful. It is descended from Byzantium, by faith out of nationalism:
> and sometimes to its high ritual in the Basilica of St Mark there is a
> tremendous sense of an eastern past, marbled, hazed and silken. "

**Jan Morris, *Venice* (1960)**

reputedly smuggled out of Alexandria under slices of pork in a barrel, represents the earliest known depiction of St Mark, and shows the first basilica. The exquisite **carvings** on the arches of the central doorway provide an insight into 13th-century city life, showing seasonal labours such as fishing (lower right) and shipbuilding (lower left). The **loggia** is surmounted by replicas of the four famous horses of St Mark (the gilded bronze originals are now inside).

The glittering **interior** – dark and exotic, smothered in gold, marble and mosaics – will take your breath away. When illuminated, the entire church is radiantly bathed in golden light, described by W B Yeats as 'God's holy fire'. The most lavish mosaics grace the three main domes: the **Pentecost Dome** (nearest the door) portrays the *Descent of the Holy Spirit* in the form of a dove; the **Ascension Dome** in the centre shows *Christ in Majesty*; and the **Dome of Emmanuel** (in the sanctuary) shows *Christ with Prophets*. Swirling, multi-coloured patterns of glass, marble and porphyry make up the undulating pavement. In the 19th century, the authorities began a massive project to level the floor, until a British architect managed to persuade them that it had been a deliberate attempt to imitate the sea.

The basilica has been called 'the world's greatest stolen property office', filled over the centuries with booty from every corner of the city's once far-flung empire – capitals from Sicily, porphyry from Syria, columns from Alexandria and sculpture from Constantinople. Its most precious treasures include the Byzantine-style **Pala d'Or**, a jewel-spangled golden altarpiece, adorned with enamels and over 3 000 precious stones. St Mark's remains are said to lie beneath the high altar, although they were probably destroyed during a fire in 976.

The **Treasury** contains a priceless collection of Byzantine silver, gold and glasswork, and the **Museo Marciano** (reached by a tiny stairway from the atrium, marked 'Loggia dei Cavalli') houses the city's four highly valued huge **bronze horses**, the only *quadriga* (four-horse chariot team) to have survived from classical antiquity. The loggia offers memorable views of the piazza below, through the hooves of the replica horses outside.

# Campanile di San Marco

*Piazza San Marco (San Marco). Tel: 041 5224064. Open: daily 0900–1900; 0930–1545 in winter months. ££. Vaporetto: San Marco or San Zaccaria.*

St Mark's 100-m (325-ft) bell tower offers visitors the best panorama of Venice and, further afield, a view of the lagoon and, on a clear day, the Alps. Galileo first demonstrated his telescope from here in 1609. The roof of the first tower, built in 888, was covered with mirrored slabs that gleamed in the sun and could be seen from afar by sailors.

> *On Monday early, the Campanile was resplendent in the sunshine … Suddenly I saw it slowly sink directly downward behind a line of roofs, and a dense grey dust rose in clouds … I ordered my gondolier to the Piazzetta. On arrival the sight was pitiful. Of that splendid shaft all that remained was a mound of white dust …*
>
> **Report in *The Times* by an American architect, July 1902**

On 14 July 1902, the tower, constructed in 1511, suddenly fell down. Remarkably, the only casualty was the custodian's cat. The tower was immediately rebuilt according to the original design, and even the fragments of Sansovino's beautiful loggia were painstakingly pieced together. Today a lift takes visitors to the top – take ear-plugs if you're likely to be there when the five bells strike the hour!

# Piazza San Marco

*(San Marco). Vaporetto: San Marco or San Zaccaria.*

From sunrise to nightfall, St Mark's Square is *the* place to people-watch in Venice. Throughout its long history, the piazza has always been Venice's ceremonial gathering place; according to Napoleon, it was 'the most elegant drawing room in Europe'. It was originally conceived as a vista for the Doge's Palace, and later became the great showpiece of the Serenissima. Doge Agnello Parteciaco built the first palace here in 814, among orchards and vines. Now, the square boasts some of the city's finest buildings. Famously, it is one of the first places in the city to suffer at *acqua alta* (high tide), when everyone has to pick their way across duck-boards.

Under the square's arches are some of the city's most elegant shops and cafés. The first coffee shops opened here in the 17th century, when there were 27 in the square alone. Today, **Florian** and **Quadri** are perhaps the most famous, with their expansive terraces, orchestras and white-frocked waiter service, and, of course, exorbitant prices.

It is hard to resist the beautifully dressed shop windows in the busy, narrow streets close to St Mark's Square. The **Mercerie**, stretching from the Rialto to the square, has been Venice's main shopping street since the Middle Ages, while Via XXII Marzo, Calle dei Fabbri and the streets around the square boast glitzy big-name designer boutiques and smart speciality stores.

" *At night ... it seemed to me that the vast square of the winged lion was a single blaze of merry light and that the whole arcade was bustling with people, while other crowds enjoyed themselves in the splendid coffee houses looking onto the square ... When the bronze giants struck midnight, it seemed that all the life and animation of the city was gathered here ...* "

**Charles Dickens, *Pictures from Italy* (1846)**

VENICE

# Scuola Grande di San Rocco

*Campo San Rocco (San Polo). Tel: 041 5234864. Open: daily 1000–1600. £££*
*(includes 45-minute audio-guide).* Vaporetto: *San Tomà.*

The Scuola Grande di San Rocco is the most magnificent of the Venetian *scuole* (charitable lay confraternities) and one of the greatest city sights. Its remarkable collection of epic canvases by Tintoretto led John Ruskin to describe it as 'one of the three most precious buildings in Italy'.

*Scuole* began to flourish throughout Europe in the Middle Ages, supported by various guilds, and fulfilling a religious purpose as well as helping the sick and the needy (who would often make generous bequests or donations). The Scuola Grande di San Rocco was established in 1478 as a place for worship and to care for the sick following the 1477 plague. It was dedicated to **St Roc**, the protector of plague victims. The building we see today was constructed between 1489 and 1549, reflecting the transition from Renaissance to baroque.

Once the building was completed, the Scuola launched a competition to find someone to decorate the rooms. **Jacopo Tintoretto**, already famous, was the winner, and spent the next 25 years adorning the walls with 54 masterpieces. To view the works in chronological order, start in the Great Hall on the first floor, where you will find on the ceiling his **21 Old Testament scenes**, and on the walls **ten New Testament episodes**. The last canvases Tintoretto painted for the Scuola are on the ground floor. These focus on **key episodes in the life of Mary**, while his largest, and perhaps greatest, masterpiece, *The Crucifixion*, hangs upstairs in the Albergo Hall. It is particularly remarkable for its rapid brushwork.

> *We shall scarcely find four walls elsewhere that enclose within a like area an equal quantity of genius … It is not immortality that we breathe at the Scuola di San Rocco, but conscious, reluctant mortality.*

**Henry James (1843–1916)**

# Eating and drinking

## Cannaregio

### Caffè Costarica
Rio Terrà di S Leonardo 1563 (opposite Campo S Lunardo). Closed Sun. ££. One of Venice's oldest coffee houses, serving quick, stand-up espressos at the bar, and refreshing iced coffees (frappé).

### Osteria alla Frasca
Corte della Carità 5176. Tel: 041 5285433. Closed Thu. £. Country-style hostelry, where the pretty vine-covered terrace provides a delightful setting to enjoy a plate of pasta or tasty snacks.

### Palazzina
Rio Terrà di S Leonardo 1509 (beside Ponte delle Guglie). Tel: 041 717725. Closed Wed. ££. Highly regarded canalside restaurant with simple furnishings, a daily changing menu and excellent pizzas.

## Rialto

There are plenty of eateries to choose from around the Rialto markets.

### Cantina Do Spade
Calle Do Spade 860. Tel: 041 5210574. Closed Thu lunch and Sun. £. Hidden down a dark alley near the Rialto, this cosy osteria with its simple home cooking was a favourite haunt of Casanova.

### San Tomà
Campo San Tomà 2864a. Tel: 041 5238819. Closed Tue. ££. Popular trattoria serving delicious pizzas and pasta dishes outside in the pretty piazza or in a cool garden.

## Dorsoduro

### Al Profeta
Calle Lunga San Barnaba 2671. Tel: 041 5237466. Closed Mon. ££. This cheerful, popular restaurant serves delectable pizzas and a conventional trattoria menu in its pretty, sheltered garden.

### Cantina del Vino già Schiavi
Fondamenta Meravegie 992. Open: Mon–Sat 0900–1300 and 1515–2030. £. A friendly bar within a fine old wine shop, run by three generations of the same family. Standing room only. In summer, everyone spills out on to the picturesque canal quayside.

### Da Nico
Zattere ai Gesuati 922. Open: 0700–2200. The speciality of this ice-cream temple on the Zattere, reputedly the best in town, is giandiotto: praline ice cream with lashings of whipped cream.

## Picnic fare

The **Rialto** is the district to stock up for a picnic. Buy salad and fruit at the **market stalls** (Mon–Sat mornings); bruschetta and herb-flavoured grissini from the bakery **Mauro** (Ruga Rialto 603); regional cheeses (montasio, piave, asiao) from **Latteria Ronchi Francesco** (Ruga Rialto 1053a); and wine, cold cuts, olives and sun-dried tomatoes at **Aliani** (Ruga Rialto 654), the best delicatessen in town.

# Coffee

Coffee is an essential part of Venetian life. Indeed, the beverage was first introduced to Europe as a medicinal drink by traders of the Serenissima in the early 17th century. Venice's first coffee house opened in 1683 in St Mark's Square, starting a new Italian fashion. Italians rarely drink coffee with milk, favouring *espresso*, a tiny, extra-strong coffee prepared expressly for you (hence the name) and drunk piping hot early in the morning (to wake them up), after meals (helpful to digestion) and during the afternoon (as a break from work). For a less concentrated coffee, ask for a *caffè lungo*. For coffee with milk, choose *caffè con latte*, *caffè macchiato* (with just a dash of milk) or *cappuccino* (served in a large cup with hot frothy milk and a sprinkling of cocoa powder).

## San Marco

### Ai Do Ladroni
*Campo San Bartolomeo 5362. Tel: 041 715736. Open: Mon–Sat 0800–2400. £.* A simple, friendly *osteria* right by the Rialto Bridge, with delicious home-made pasta and a fun crowd. Late at night, it takes on a pub feel.

### Gelateria Paolin
*Campo San Stefano. ££.* One of the best ice-cream cafés in town.

### Harry's Bar
*Calle Vallaresso 1323. Open: 1030–2300. £££. The* original 'Harry's Bar', the most famous bar in Venice. Hemingway would stop off here regularly for a 'Bellini' (one-third peach juice, two-thirds *prosecco* ). The prices are a rip-off, but it's a once-in-a-lifetime experience.

### Vino Vino
*Ponte della Veste 2007a. Open: Wed–Mon 1030–2400. ££.* A typical, cosy *osteria* with wooden tables, paper place-mats and wholesome Venetian cooking. The adjoining bar has tasty *cicchetti* snacks and a large selection of wines.

## Islands of the Lagoon

### Bar Gelateria P Garbiso
*Viale Santa Maria Elisabetta 51c, Lido. ££.* A popular café, just inland from the beach, serving coffee, cakes, pastries and the Lido's best ice cream.

### Busa alla Torre
*Campo San Stefano 3, Murano. Tel: 041 739662. £££.* The reputation of this tiny fish restaurant in a delightful tree-shaded square is renowned well beyond the lagoon. Booking is recommended, especially in summer.

## Pizza

**Santa Croce** has more than its fair share of top pizzerias. **Al Nono Risorto** ( *Sottoportico de Siora Bettina; tel: 041 5241169; closed Wed; £* ) gets the student vote. **Da Crecola** ( *Campiello del Piovan; tel: 041 89481; ££* ) has the prettiest setting, with outdoor tables in a delightful canalside *campiello*. **Ae Oche** ( *Calle del Tintor; tel: 041 5241161; £* ) has the largest selection, while **Al Gallo** ( *Corte Amai; tel: 041 5205953; closed Sat; ££* ) has some of the most unusual toppings.

# Shopping

### Bevilacqua
*Fondamenta Canonica 337b.* A treasure trove of luxurious fabrics, tapestries, braiding and brocades, antique and modern, by the leading name in Venetian textiles.

### Boutique del Dolce – Gilda Vio
*Fondamenta Rio Marin 890.* Reputedly the best *pâtisserie* in Venice. The *tiramisù* is unforgettable.

### Bruscagrin Il Fornaio
*Strada Nova 3845.* This bakery offers an exceptional variety of bread and mouth-watering cakes. Try the *pan del Doge* (fruit bread).

### Codognato
*Calle Seconda de l'Ascensione 1295.* Venice's oldest jewellery shop.

### Domus Vetri d'Arte
*Fondamenta dei Vetrai 82, Murano.* More tasteful than many of the glass shops of Murano, selling vases, ornaments, dishes and other select pieces of island glass.

### Emilia
*Via San Mauro 296–303, Burano.* The largest lace shop on the island, selling the widest choice. Be prepared to pay a lot for the genuine article.

### Emilio Ceccato
*Sottoportici Rialto 16–17.* The place to buy a genuine gondolier shirt or stripy top.

### Guido Farinati
*Calle Larga 1658 (off Campo San Giacomo dell'Orio).* Farinati stained glass can be seen throughout Venice. Guido continues the age-old family tradition, producing fine pieces of mosaic-style glass giftware.

### Legatoria Polliero
*Campo dei Frari 2995.* The diaries, notebooks and photograph albums of this traditional bookbinder make exquisite gifts.

### Pastificio Artigiano
*Strada Nova 4292.* Home-made pasta, gondola-shaped packet pasta and unusually flavoured varieties (beetroot, curry, cocoa) that make fun presents.

# Nightlife

### Alla Rivetta
*Calle Sechera.* A tiny bar, popular for a glass of *prosecco* and some top-notch *cicchetti*.

### Old Well Pub
*Corte Canal 656.* Just off Piazzale Roma, a pub that serves an excellent pint and is always lively.

**Dorsoduro** is one of the liveliest *sestieri* for nightlife, with plenty of late-night bars and cafés. The most popular include **Il Caffè** and **Margaret DuChamp** in Campo Santa Margherita, and the student haunts **Café Blue Pub** and neighbouring **Café Black** (internet café by day and popular bar by night), both in Calle dei Preti Crosera and open until 0200.

# Carnival

*Close your eyes and imagine an enchanted evening during carnival: a tall man in a dark cloak and a tricorn hat sweeps past, whispering 'Benvenuto al carnevale', and disappears into the mist-wrapped streets; your gondola arrives and glides through the inky waters to a magnificent candlelit palace on the Grand Canal where you dance until dawn in a whirl of plumes, sequins and masqueraded revellers …*

As if Venice did not have enough visual attractions, the city is transformed every year (in the **days leading up to Lent**) into a spectacular **pageant** of wonderful costumes and elaborately decorated masks, of parties, parades, open-air concerts and, most lavish of all, the **Doge's Ball**.

Carnival celebrations began in Venice more than a thousand years ago when the period leading up to Lent became a time of excessive and wild partying. The **wearing of masks** began as a tradition to enable nobles to mix incognito with ordinary folk: men dressed up as women, masters as servants, servants as masters; a masked aristocratic lady could act out her fantasies, making love to a gondolier without him knowing her true identity. The whole city went berserk. By 1458, the revelry had become so licentious that an edict was issued preventing men from entering convents in women's clothing to commit *multas inhonestates*!

## Biscuits

The ancient *forni pubblici* (public bakeries) once stood in **Castello** (*at Riva Ca' di Dio 2179–2180*). It is here that the biscuit (from *bis-cotto*, meaning 'twice-cooked') was first conceived as a long-lasting staple for the mariners of the nearby Arsenale. Today's Venetian favourites include *busolai* (very sweet, and tasting of aniseed); yellow *zaletti*, made with cornmeal, raisins, lemon and vanilla; *buranelli*, not unlike shortbread; *pignoletti*, made from sugar, almonds and pine nuts; and crisp, dry *baicoli*, named after a lagoon fish whose shape it resembles. At carnival time, you will also see *frittelle* doughnuts filled with raisins, cream or *zabaglione*, and wafer-thin *crostoli*, thin flakes of deep-fried pastry dusted with icing sugar.

By 1790, carnival in Venice had grown so popular that it lasted from November until March. Many Venetians wore their masks throughout, and party-goers would travel across Europe to join in with the debauchery and thrill of the celebrations. However, **party-pooper Napoleon** put a stop to it all in 1797, outlawing the carnival. The tradition was not renewed again until as recently as 1979.

Today, Venice's world-famous carnival is a much tamer affair. Visitors are encouraged to take part and can buy a disguise from any number of street stalls and shops – anything from a traditional *Commedia dell' Arte* **character** to the most **extravagant and bizarre costumes**. The merry-making lasts for ten days, ending with the tolling of the bells of San Francesco della Vigna at midnight on Shrove Tuesday, but not before a **massive firework display** over the lagoon rounds off the celebrations in spectacular style.

# Emilia-
# Romagna

This extraordinarily varied region lies at the southernmost part of northern Italy between the River Po, the green Apennines bordering on Tuscany and the blue Adriatic Sea. One of Italy's most prosperous areas, it is also the country's gourmet capital, the site of Europe's oldest university, has a treasure trove of art riches and, for more sybaritic pleasures, boasts Europe's largest seaside resort.

# BEST OF
# Emilia-Romagna

*Getting there:* the area's main airports are at Rimini and Bologna and the rail network runs parallel to the main roads. By train, Bologna is 1 hour from Florence, and around 2 hours from Milan. Bologna is connected to Florence by the A1; the roads are generally good, helped by mostly flat terrain. Off the main roads, in the hills, the roads become twisting and narrow.

⑤

*River Po*

Castell'Arquato

④

Reggio

③

②

*River Po*

**ADRIATIC SEA**

Maranello

①

⑥

S Apollinaire in Classe

**North**

⑦

Riccione

0       50 km

0       25 miles

## (1) Bologna

The lovely capital of Emilia-Romagna has earned many nicknames, from *La Dotta* ('The Learned') to *La Rossa* ('The Red'), as much for the colour of its buildings as for its politics. It's also *La Grassa* ('The Fat') – a city that has not only given us *bolognese* sauce but has also elevated pasta to an art form with *tortellini*, said to be modelled on the shape of Venus's navel.
**Pages 106-7**

## (2) Ferrara

One of Italy's major cities of art, with beautifully preserved medieval buildings and magnificent Renaissance architecture, Ferrara is also the cycling capital of Italy. Get on your bike for the perfect way to get about on the flat terrain of the city. **Pages 108-9**

## (3) Modena

Birthplace of world-famous tenor Luciano Pavarotti, of fast Ferrari, Maserati and Bugatti cars and of balsamic vinegar, this is Emilia-Romagna's second city after Bologna. Its medieval centre is delightful and includes three World Heritage monuments. **Pages 110-11**

## (4) Parma

The sunny yellow palaces and the pink marble of the Baptistery make this a beautiful and elegant little city. It is rich in art treasures, as well as being the home of Parma ham and of the king of Italian cheeses, Parmesan.
**Pages 112-13**

## Tourist information

The main information centre for the Emilia-Romagna region is *Assessorato Regionale al Turismo, Viale Aldo Moro 30, Bologna; tel: 051 28 33 53, www.regione.emilia-romagna.it.*

## (5) Piacenza

Baroque sculptures and fine medieval and Renaissance buildings combine to make this a very pleasing, yet largely undiscovered city. Il Gotico is one of Italy's most beautiful medieval buildings and the massively powerful Farnese dynasty was born here along with Parma. **Pages 114-15**

## (6) Ravenna

Once the capital of the western Roman empire, Ravenna is the site of the world's largest and perhaps finest series of mosaics, the inheritance of superb late Roman and Byzantine art. Its central square, the Piazza del Popolo, is like an elegant drawing room, lined with bars, cafés and shops that become even more animated during the summer music festival.
**Pages 116-17**

## (7) Rimini

Immortalised by famous son Federico Fellini in his film *Amarcord*, Rimini is Italy's top party spot, with around 150 clubs and a huge sandy beach some 15km (9 miles) long. But it is also an old Roman city and home to one of Italy's finest Renaissance monuments, the Tempio Malatestiano.
**Pages 118-19**

> 66 *The sun shone 'on throngs of girls on bicycles on the roads of Emilia, on a filigree of trees against a white sky and on a big house where town gave way to country ...'* 99

**From Leonardo Sciascia's** *Il giorno della civetta* **(The Day of the Owl) (1961)**

# Bologna

*The ancient city of Bologna – La Dotta, La Rossa, La Grassa – has 40km (25 miles) of arcaded walkways and a skyline etched with towers, built by 12th-century families as emblems of status and wealth.*

Originally there were around one hundred towers, but only around 20 remain today, including the two main symbols of the city – the **Torre degli Asinelli** and the **Torre Garisenda** (*Piazza di Porta Ravegnana*). The Asinelli tower (*open: daily 0900–1800; £*) is 98m (321¹/₂ ft) high; its neighbour, the Garisenda tower, has a pronounced lean of around 3m (10ft). A stiff climb of 498 steps to the top of Asinelli is rewarded with fabulous views over the neighbouring hills and the Po plain, and the russet tiles and brick of Bologna *La Rossa* ('The Red').

The city meets in the adjoining **Piazza Maggiore** and **Piazza del Nettuno**, where a 16th-century bronze statue of Neptune towers over a fountain. The **Piazza Maggiore**'s magnificent **Basilica di San Petronio** (*tel: 051 22 21 12; open: daily; free*), dedicated to St Petronius, the 5th-century bishop and patron saint of Bologna, is the city's largest church and one

# Modest Neptune

*In baroque times the modesty of the scandalously proportioned sea god on the fountain of Bologna's Piazza del Nettuno was protected by a pair of bronze trousers.*

of the finest medieval brick buildings in Italy. The first stone was laid in 1390 as the beginning of a grand plan that would have rivalled St Peter's in Rome in size. Pope Pius VI curtailed the project and the funds and land were used instead for the university. The marble on the façade of the basilica only covers the bottom third, but the main portal is complete, with superb carvings, and a very beautiful *Madonna and Child* by the Sienese Jacopo della Quercia. Inside there is an ingenious chronometer – a long brass meridian line in the floor on to which a shaft of light falls from a pinhole in the roof, showing the time of day.

Bologna *La Dotta* ('The Learned') is the site of Europe's oldest university, founded in 1088. Just south of the basilica is the university's first official building, the **Archiginnasio** ( *Via Clavature* ), started in 1562. The palace of Archiginnasio was built to gather together the schools of *Legisti* (civil and canon law) and *Artisti* (philosophy, maths, physics and medicine), and it was here that instruction in the dissection of human bodies was first introduced in the **Teatro Anatomico** ( *tel: 051 23 64 88; open: 0900–1300; free* ). Although Bologna was badly bombed during the Second World War, the wood-panelled theatre, with its tiers of seats, was rebuilt using all the existing material. The canopy that hangs over the anatomy professor's rostrum is supported by two skeletal figures known as *gli spellati*, or 'the skinned ones'.

Don't pass up the chance to eat out in Bologna *La Grassa* ('The Fat'), which prides itself on its fine, family-run restaurants, and its wonderful food shops. This is, after all, the city that gave the world *bolognese* sauce, and has elevated pasta to an art form; its *tortellini* is said to be modelled on Venus's navel.

*Tourist information: Piazza Maggiore 6. Tel: 051 23 96 60. Open: Mon–Sat 0830–1900; Sun 0900–1400.*

" *In Bologna … the porticoes, the arcades, the domes, everything reminds one of curvaceous flesh. Even the dialect, the accent, is exuberant and has a special roundness.* "

**Guido Piovene, *Viaggio in Italia* (1958)**

# Ferrara

*A sign here welcomes you to the 'city of cyclists'. As well as being the cycling capital of Italy, Ferrara is one of the major cities of Italian art, with beautifully preserved medieval buildings, lovely Renaissance architecture and 9km (6 miles) of city walls.*

The greatest symbol of the powerful Este family, who ruled from the 13th to the 16th centuries, and focal point of Ferrara is the vast, moated fortress, the **Castello Estense** (*Largo Castello; tel: 0532 29 92 33; open: Tue–Sun 0930–1700; £–££*). Commissioned in 1385 by Nicolò II, it was both an impressive defence rampart and a magnificent palace hosting famous writers such as Petrarch and Ariosto and painters of the calibre of Bellini, Titian and Mantegna. As a grim fortress, it had its own *sala di decapitazione* (beheading room); later, it was converted into a habitable palace, and Lucrezia Borgia lived here as Duchess of Ferrara. The atmospheric medieval interior includes the fabulously frescoed Salone dei Giochi (games room), and the gruesome dungeon. On the wall outside the castle, in Corso Matiri della Libertà, is a reminder of man's inhumanity; memorial plaques remember the 11 Ferrarese citizens shot by Fascists on 15 November 1943.

## Unfair reputation

*The myth of Lucrezia Borgia as a serial adulteress and wicked poisoner is partly the result of the deeds of her over-protective brother and father, partly a later male fantasy; in fact, she was a good source of both patronage and inspiration.*

Ferrara's original substantial Jewish community was welcomed by the Este family and tolerated under papal rule. The **Ghetto** in the old quarter centred on the Via Vignatagliata and Via Mazzini. Ercole I's *addizione ercolea* was an extension of

## Thriving community

*The Jewish community of Ferrara is still, after five centuries, one of the most important in Italy and one of the major players in the social, cultural and business life of the city.*

the old city, dating from 1493 to 1503. This quarter was increasingly vulnerable to attack and overcrowding, so, in a very early example of modern town planning, the Viale Cavour, Corso Giovecca and Corso Ercole I d'Este were created. The result was described by historian Jacob Burckhardt as 'the first modern city of Europe'.

At the end of the Corso is the elegant **Palazzo dei Diamanti** (*Corso Ercole I d'Este 21; tel: 0532 20 99 88; open: Tue–Sat 0900–1400, Sun 0900–1300; £–££*), the home of the **Pinacoteca Nazionale**. The national art gallery houses leading Renaissance works of art and a series of prints by Andrea Mantegna, and also hosts important visiting art exhibitions. The exterior of the 'Palace of Diamonds' is covered with more than 12,000 stones sculpted in the shape of a diamond – legend has it that inside just one of the stones there is a real jewel!

Southwest of here, the **Palazzo Schifanoia** (*Via Scandiana 23; tel: 0532 641 78; open: daily 0900–1900; £*) is one of the wonders of Ferrara. The palace was the summer retreat of the Este family, where the locals 'avoided boredom', as the Italian name suggests. The Salone dei Mesi ('Room of the Months') displays the best example of 15th-century frescos in Ferrara.

*Tourist information: Castello Estense. Tel: 0532 20 93 70; www.provincia.fe.it. Open: Mon–Sat 0900–1300 and 1400–1800; Sun am. Rent a bike: Palazzina via Kennedy 2; tel: 0532 76 51 23/20 20 03.*

# Modena

*Modena is the capital of the province of the same name and the second-largest city, after Bologna, of Emilia-Romagna. The region as a whole has the second-highest per capita income in Italy; Modena has the country's highest. This is the home of luxury sports cars – Ferrari, Bugatti, Maserati and de Tomaso – and also of the tenor Luciano Pavarotti. It also has some of the country's finest Romanesque architecture and famous collections of art, and is a gourmet's paradise.*

Modena's central square, the **Piazza Grande**, has been designated a Unesco World Heritage Site. It is dominated by the 11th-century **Duomo** (*Corso Duomo; tel: 059 21 60 78; open: Tue–Sun 0630–1200 and 1530–1900, closed during religious services; donation*), one of Italy's most beautiful Romanesque cathedrals. The west façade is richly decorated by Wiligelmo, a 12th-century Lombard sculptor. Inside, the attractive *tribuna* (rood screen) is topped by a 12th-century crucifix, supported by Lombardic lions.

Outside, the city's distinctive landmark is a leaning 87-m (285-ft) campanile, the **Torre Ghirandina** ( *open: Sun and holidays 1000–1300 and 1500–1900; £* ), started in 1169, but not completed until 200 years later. A five-minute walk west through a maze of old streets brings you to the city's other famous sight, the **Palazzo dei Musei** ( *Via Emilia; tel: 059 22 21 45* ). The *palazzo* houses the city museums and art galleries, of which the **Galleria Estense** ( *open: Tue–Sun 0900–1900, closed Wed, Thu and Sun pm; £–££* ) is the highlight, with works of early Emilian and Tuscan art, and paintings by Titian, Correggio, Tintoretto, Veronese and many others. The pieces were collected by the Este family, who moved here from Ferrara in 1598 and held Modena under the House of Este until 1859, when the Duchy became part of the Kingdom of Italy.

*Tourist information: Piazza Grande 17. Tel: 059 20 66 60. Open: Mon–Sat 0830–1300 and 1500–1900; closed Thu pm.*

# Galleria Ferrari, Maranello

The Este family did much to boost the cultural level of Modena, and this is still reflected today in every corner of the city, where quality is a byword. The luxury car factories surrounding the city are worth an out-of-town trip. Founded by Enzo Ferrari, who died in 1989, the Ferrari factory today produces some 2 500 cars a year. The factory is not open to visitors, but next door is the museum (**Galleria Ferrari**), where you will find one of the world's largest collections of Ferraris, classic engines, vintage cars, trophies won by the Ferrari team and a reconstruction of Enzo's study.

*Getting there: 17km (11 miles) south of Modena; regular buses run from the bus station. Via Dino Ferrari 43, Maranello. Tel 0536 94 32 04. Open: Tue–Sun 0930–1230 and 1500–1800. ££.*

## Spring flowers

*The pretty medieval village of Vignola ( 22km (13 1/2 miles) south of Modena ) is ablaze with cherry blossom in spring; its fruits are among the most delicious in Italy.*

# Parma

*Small is beautiful in this pleasingly proportioned and prosperous city. A stroll around the little streets and squares, admiring the elegant shops and the mouth-watering food displays, instantly conveys the impression of a community devoted to life's finer things. Whether it's retail therapy, music, history, art or literature that you seek, this city should not disappoint you.*

A good starting point is the former Benedictine convent, Il Monasterio di San Paolo (*Via Melloni; tel: 0521 28 22 17; open: daily 0900–1345; £*). In 1519, the socialite Abbess Giovanna instructed Antonio Allegri from Correggio (better known simply as 'Correggio') to decorate her private dining room, the Camera di Correggio (Corregio Room). He painted sensuous nudes, cherubs (*putti*) and images heavily influenced by antique symbols instead of pious religious figures, and the result is a feast for the senses. The ribbed, vaulted ceiling, which looks as though it is made of bamboo, is surrounded by a frieze interspersed with smiling rams' heads. Above the fireplace the Abbess is depicted as Diana the Huntress; the inscription, *Ignem Gladio Ne Fodias* ('Do not stir the fire with your sword'), was directed at the bishop, requesting him not to interfere in her unconventional convent. After Giovanna's death, the cloistered way of life was reinstated by the relieved bishop.

Correggio's fame and fortune continued to grow. The centrepiece of Parma's Piazza Duomo is the beautiful 11th-century Lombard-Romanesque Duomo (*open: daily 0900–1230 and 1500–1900; £*), whose cupola houses Correggio's complex fresco masterpiece, the *Assunzione della Vergine* (the Assumption), created between 1526 and 1530. The figure of Christ descends to lift Mary amid a throng of apostles and angels, watched over by playful *putti*; it is a remarkable work, full of light and movement. Also worth seeing within the Duomo is Benedetto Antelami's

*Deposition* (Descent from the Cross), created in 1178 from a single piece of marble. The carving, Antelami's earliest-known work, is deeply moving.

Antelami's mastery is also evident in the other great building on the piazza, the beautiful pink marble octagonal **Battistero** (baptistery) (*Piazza Duomo; open: daily 0900–1230 and 1500–1800; £*). Antelami not only designed this exquisite structure, said to be one of the country's best and most harmonious examples of medieval art, but he also created the friezes on the door arches. Inside, his 14 superb stone tablets carved in relief show the months of the year and allegories of winter and spring.

Parma's largest monument is the **Palazzo della Pilotta** (*Piazzale della Pilotta 15; tel: 0521 23 33 09*), named after the Basque ball game of *pelota*, which used to be played in the courtyards. The huge brick building dates back to 1583 and now houses the city's main art gallery, **Galleria Nazionale**, the **Museo Archeologico Nazionale** (archaeological museum) and the **Teatro Farnese** (*theatre tel: 0521 23 33 09; open: Tue–Sun 0900–1930; £*), built in 1618 entirely of wood, with Italy's first revolving stage.

*Tourist information: Via Melloni 1b. Tel: 0521 21 88 89. Open: Mon–Sat 0900–1900; Sun 0900–1300. Market days: Wed and Sat.*

## An afternoon in Parma

*Although Stendhal attributed his great work* La Chartreuse de Parme *to Parma's Charterhouse, there is no evidence to suggest that he spent any longer than an afternoon in Parma, although he did spend a lot of time in Bologna.*

# Piacenza

*At the most northerly part of Emilia-Romagna, Piacenza stands between the Ligurian Apennines and the River Po. At first sight, the red-brick city can seem somewhat austere, but closer inspection reveals a lovely medieval historic centre.*

The centrepiece of the town is the **Palazzo del Comune**, also known as 'Il Gotico' (now the town hall), in the **Piazza dei Cavalli**. This beautiful red brick and marble 13th-century palace, crowned with battlements, in the Lombard-Gothic style, is flanked by two splendid bronze equestrian statues, from which the square takes its name. Dating from 1625, these baroque masterpieces depict the Farnese Duke Ranuccio I and his father, Alessandro Farnese, crafted by the Tuscan sculptor Francesco Mocchi.

The **Palazzo Farnese** is a few minutes' walk northwest of here; started in 1558, it was never completed. Today, it contains three small museums, including the **Civico Museo** (*Piazza Cittadella; tel: 0523 32 82 70/32 69 81; open: Tue– Sun 0830–1300, Sat–Sun 1430–1730; £* ), where two cycles of frescos, richly framed in stucco, depict the stories of Pope Paul III and Alessandro Farnese, and paintings on display include the *Madonna and Child with John the Baptist* by Botticelli. In the archaeology and armoury section, the main point of curiosity is the **Fegato di Piacenza**, a bronzed Etruscan sheep's liver, inscribed with deities. The Etruscans commonly used animals' entrails to tell the future.

*Tourist information: Piazzetta Mercanti 7. Tel: 0523 32 93 24; www.piacenzaturismi.net. Open: Tue–Sat 0930–1230 and 1530–1830.*

## The Pilgrims' Way

*In the Middle Ages Piacenza was a pilgrimage centre, with several* hospitalia *(hostels) catering for travellers on their way to Rome, on the* Via Francigena *or Pilgrims' Way. Piacenza was the thirty-eighth stop, the main point between northern and central-southern Italy. According to medieval sources, pilgrims followed the itinerary in order to pray for salvation for themselves and their loved ones, but they were also driven by a desire to escape their everyday life and by the eternal urge to explore the world inherent in everyone.*

## Castell'Arquato

The hill region around Piacenza is very picturesque, with many castles and medieval villages. One of the most impressive medieval complexes is **Castell'Arquato**, beautifully situated on the hillside overlooking the Arda valley. It has a lovely medieval piazza, where the cafés and restaurants are always very busy at weekends. The castle, which dates back to 1293, is being partly restored, but the two inner courtyards can be visited. Nearby is the **Ponte Gobbo** ('Hunchback Bridge'), supposedly the work of the devil and his demons. St Columba promised that the first to cross the bridge would lose his soul to the devil. The devil expected the saint to be his victim, but he was outwitted by the holy man, who sent over an old bear in his stead.

*Getting there: 32km (20 miles) south of Piacenza; take the A1, leaving at the exit for Fiorenzuola, or the more scenic Strada Statale (major road 9, also known as the 'Via Emilia') to Fiorenzuola and follow signs from there for 10km (6 miles). Open: Sat–Sun 1500–1830; Sun 1000–1230. £.*

# Ravenna

*Ravenna was already important in the 1st century AD, when the emperor Augustus built a naval base and port at Classe, 5km (3 miles) away. However, by AD 402, it had achieved the status of the capital of the western Roman empire.*

## Tip

*The only surviving building of Classe, the ancient port of Ravenna, is the Basilica di S Apollinare ( 5km (3 miles) south ), richly embellished with 6th- and 7th-century mosaics. A massive excavation project is under way, due for completion in 2003. Already, a number of mosaics similar to those of Ravenna have been discovered, and the expectation is that the site will yield more extraordinary finds, and eventually rank alongside the largest archaeological sites in Italy.*

The city soon fell to the Goths, in 476, but retained its importance throughout the highly significant Byzantine rule of the 5th and 6th centuries – a golden age whose legacy is the world's largest and finest series of mosaics of superb late Roman and Byzantine art, matched only by Istanbul (Constantinople, capital of the eastern Roman empire).

Today, Ravenna's glories slumber within its churches. The most spectacular treasures are the 6th-century mosaics in the octagonal, rather plain **Basilica di San Vitale** ( *Via Fiandrini; tel: 0544 342 66; open: daily 0900–1900, closes 1630 Oct–Mar; £* ), whose sober exterior belies a gorgeously ornate interior. The floor mosaics are of marble, while those on the walls of the apse are of gold, enamel, mother of pearl and glass; the colours change endlessly in the transforming

# Byron in Ravenna

*In the 19th century, Lord Byron lived here, at Palazzo Guiccioli, Via Cavour 54, while conducting an affair with Countess Teresa Guiccioli. He wrote productively, including three cantos of Don Juan. However, in October 1821, when the affair was over, he left Ravenna writing,* 'It is awful work, this love, and prevents all a man's projects of good or glory'.

light. On the side walls are the two famous processional panels of the 6th-century emperor Justinian and his wife, Theodora. Theodora had a colourful past as a child prostitute, courtesan and sex-show performer, before making herself known to the emperor; as empress, she was a dangerous woman to cross. On the panel, she stands bejewelled and controlling, in the rigid pose so characteristic of Byzantine art.

Outside the church is the little chapel, **Mausoleo di Galla Placidia** (*same opening as San Vitale; admission included*). Dedicated to Placidia, the wife of a 5th-century Barbarian emperor, it is home to Italy's most beautiful 5th-century mosaics, more naturalistic and less stylised than the work of the Byzantines. The glorious gold and ethereal blue mosaics that fill the vaulted ceiling apparently inspired Cole Porter to write his classic song *Night and Day*.

A short walk south, the central square, the **Piazza del Popolo**, is like an elegant drawing room, lined with shops, bars and cafés spilling out on to the piazza. The scene becomes even more animated during the summer music festival. Two minutes away is the **Sepolcro di Dante** (Dante's tomb) (*Via Dante Alighieri; open: daily 0900–1900 in summer, 0900–1200 and 1400–1700 in winter; £*). After his exile from Florence, Dante was taken under the protection of the Da Polenta family here until his death in 1321. His tomb was erected in 1780, and remains a site of pilgrimage for many, including a group of Florentines who come every year to donate the oil for the lamp that stands sentinel at his tomb.

*Tourist information: Via Salara 8/12, off Via Cavour. Tel: 0544 35755/ 35404. Open: Mon–Sat 0830–1800; Sun 1000–1600.*

# Rimini

*Rimini, the provincial capital of the most southern part of the Romagna coast, was known to the Romans as* Ariminum, *a colony for its citizens and the port where the Roman road ended.*

Today, Rimini is the end of the line for holidaymakers drawn by a 15-km (9-mile) sandy beach and a buzzing nightlife, which has made it Italy's clubland capital. This is now Europe's largest seaside resort, yet beyond the seafront strip lies a charming old city with a famous – and infamous – past.

At the southern edge of the historic centre stands the Roman arch, the **Arco d'Augusto** (*junction of Via Aemilia and Via Flaminia*). Erected in 27 BC in honour of Augustus, it is made of Istrian stone, now rather crumbly, but remains the oldest surviving Roman archway. Carrying along the Corso d'Augusto you come to Tiberius' bridge, **Ponte di Tiberio**, which was begun by Augustus but finished by Tiberius (AD 14–21). The other significant Roman remains are of the 2nd-century AD **Anfiteatro** (Roman amphitheatre) (*Via Roma; for access contact the City Museum, which organises tours, tel: 0541 214 82; £*). At present work is being undertaken to open the amphitheatre to the public for open-air performances.

West of here are the two charming main squares of the old town, **Piazza Tre Martiri** and **Piazza Cavour**, which are very popular with buskers and the ubiquitous Vespa-riding teenagers. Just off here is one of Italy's finest Renaissance monuments, the **Tempio Malatestiano** (*Via IV Novembre 35; tel: 0541 242 44; open: daily 0800–1230 and 1530–1830; free*). Built initially as a Gothic Franciscan church, in 1450 it was transformed by Florentine architect Leon Battista Alberti into a personal temple for **Sigismondo Malatesta**, a ruthless and debauched man whose crimes included murder, rape, incest and perjury. The interior reflects his life in scenes of pagan and bacchanalian excess, and angels and *putti* (cherubs) hover over the tombs of the tyrant and his beloved third wife, Isotta degli Atti. Isotta's chapel houses the 14th-century crucifix, attributed to Giotto, and a splendid fresco by Piero

# Birthplace of Fellini

*The film director Federico Fellini (1920–93) was born and raised in Rimini, and immortalised the region in the 1970s with his Oscar-winning film* Amarcord. *Much of the atmosphere still exists in the small houses and narrow streets of the Borgo San Giuliano and the famous old lady of Adriatic hotels, the Grand, in the park named after him. There is a fascinating archive collection at the* Fellini Association *(* Via Angherà, 22; tel: 0541 50085 *).*

della Francesca decorates the Reliquary Chapel, but Pope Pius II was not hoodwinked by these religious symbols. He condemned the site as 'a temple of devil-worshippers', and had an effigy of Malatesta burned on the streets.

Some say that Rimini is still a place of too much excess. Indeed, its 150 clubs have made it into Italy's top party scene, with a well-known reputation for transsexual and heterosexual prostitution. However, it is also very popular with Italian families. One good family day out is provided by the famous water park of **Aquafàn** (*bus no 11 from Rimini to Riccione Gardini or by car on A14, exit Riccione; Via Pistoia, Riccione; tel: 0541 60 30 50; open: 1000–1830, then disco all night; £££*).

*Tourist information: Piazzale F Fellini 3. Tel: 0541 56902. Open: Mon–Sat 0800–1900; Sun 0930–1230.*

# Eating and drinking

## Bologna

### Birreria Meddix
*Via Mascarella 26. £.* One of only two genuine *birrerie* (bars specialising in beers) in Bologna. Sandwiches and snacks also available.

### Pappagallo
*Piazza della Mercanzia 3c. Tel: 051 23 12 00/ 23 28 07. Closed Sun. £££.* A firm favourite, not only for its location, near the two towers, but also for its Bolognese specialities.

### Trattoria Fontoni
*Via del Pratello 11a. Tel: 051 23 63 58. Closed Sun and Mon pm. ££.* Popular *trattoria* whose specialities include ricotta-filled cannelloni and good *tiramisù*.

## Ferrara

### Centro Stórico Bar
*Corso Martiri della Libertà 16/18.* This 'American Bar', ice-cream parlour and cake shop is right opposite the Duomo and serves delicious snacks and drinks on the terrace right in the heart of the historic centre.

### Testamento del Porco
*Via Mulinetto 109–111. Tel: 0532 76 04 60. Closed Tue and Sat lunch. ££.* Cheerful, good restaurant where big appetites are well catered for and *speck, prosciutto* and other pork variations feature strongly.

## Parma

### Gelateria K2
*Strada Carioli. Open: 1100–2400, closed Wed.* Glorious *gelato* – try the *bacio* – a 'kiss' of the most delicious ice cream of chocolate and amaretto.

### Gran Caffè Cavour
*Via Cavour 30b (off Pza Garibaldi).* Tables spill out on to the cobblestones here in this very popular bar with the drop-dead gorgeous crowd; the interior is pretty gorgeous too, with its sparkling chandelier and frescoed ceiling.

## Ravenna

### Ca'de Ven
*Via Ricci 24. Tel: 0544 30 163. Open: Tue–Sun 1100–1400 and 1730–2215. ££.* The name is local dialect for 'wine bar' and few are more atmospheric than this set in a 'medieval inn' in the old centre.

### Tazza d'Oro
*Piazza del Popolo 11. £–££.* Enjoy a cooling drink and snack at an outside table on the central piazza.

## Rimini

### La Cantinetta
*Via Pescheria 10.* In the old town, this is where the Riminese congregate.

### Saraghina's
*Via Poletti 32. Tel: 0541 78 37 94. Open: Tue–Sun eves. ££–£££.* Good fish restaurant in the centre of town. Specialities include *fritto misto* and the house white wine is Soave.

# Shopping

## Bologna

*Monari*
*Via Scandellera 7a. Closed Sun, Mon am and Thu pm*. Wine from the award-winning Poderi delle Rocche vineyards, *grappa*, olive oil and honey.

Designer clothes can be found in **Galleria Cavour, Via Farini** and **Via d'Azeglio**; **COIN** department store in **Via Barberia** sells cheaper clothes and has an old Roman theatre under a glass pavement.

## Modena

**Modena** produces most of the country's supply of **balsamic vinegar** and free visits to the vinegar distilleries are available (*Consorzio Produttori di Aceto Balsamico Tradizionale di Modena, Via Ganaceto 134; tel: 059 23 69 81*).

**Lambrusco** is the sparkling red wine of the region around Modena. Details of guided visits to vineyards and tastings are available from Consorzio Tutela del Lambrusco di Modena (*Via Schedoni 4; tel: 059 23 50 05*).

## Parma

**Parma ham**: information from the Consorzio del Prosciutto di Parma (*Via dell'Arpa, Parma; tel: 0521 24 39 87*). **Parmesan cheese**: information

from the Consorzio del Formaggio Parmigiano Reggiano (*Via Gramisci 26, Parma; tel: 0521 29 27 00*).

## Ravenna

There is a good **mosaic** factory and souvenir shop at Galleria San Vitale (*Via Manfreddo Fanti 8, Ravenna; tel: 0544 36070; ££*).

For details of **mosaic courses** in June, July and August, contact the CISIM (Centro Internazionale di Studi per l'Insegnamento del Mosaico) (*Via Corrado Ricci 29; tel: 0544 48 23 78*).

# Nightlife

**Bologna's Teatro Comunale** (*Piazza Verdi; tel: 059 52 99 99*) is the major year-round venue for theatre, opera and concerts. The summer arts festival, **Bo Est**, has concerts at night in the courtyards of civic buildings.

**Modena's Teatro Comunale** (*Corso Canal Grande 85; tel: 059 22 51 83*) has opera during the winter season.

**Parma's** Piazza Pilotta is the venue for open-air concerts in summer. The town's **Teatro Regio** (*Via Garibaldi 16a; tel: 0521 21 86 89*) has excellent opera. The **Teatro Due** (*Viale Basetti 12a; tel: 0521 23 02 42*) is home to one of Europe's top theatre companies, the Colletivo di Parma.

The **International Ravenna Festival** takes place annually in June and July. It attracts celebrities in every field, from opera to dance, theatre to classical and contemporary music (*ticket office, Via Mariani 2; tel: 0544 32577; www.ravennafestival.org*).

# Food

*The Emilia-Romagna region is the gourmet capital of Italy; the regional capital city, Bologna – La Grassa ('The Fat') – offers an exquisite and plentiful supply of delicious food.*

This city gave us its famous *bolognese* sauce, the rich tomato and meat sauce that has been plagiarised worldwide. *Ragù alla'bolognese* is at its authentic best in Bologna, and is never served with spaghetti, as it is elsewhere in the world – the locals will tell you that fresh *tagliatelle* is the proper accompaniment.

*Fresh* is the key word in the making of **pasta**, which is lovingly sculpted with exquisite craftsmanship, elevated into an art form: *tortellini* was reputedly modelled on Venus's navel; the larger version, *tortelloni*, are parcels that are often filled with cheese, butter and herbs; in addition, there are any number of *sfoglia*, the generic name for hand-made pasta, often served with a *ragù* (sauce) of wild mushrooms, also a local speciality. The region is also famous for **parma ham**, *prosciutto di Parma*, which is said to owe its delicious flavour to the whey, the by-product of cheese, which is fed to the specially reared pigs. Even more prestigious is the sweet and long-matured *culatello* (hind cut of pork) from Zibello, near Parma. Try also the delicious *mortadella* where for once small is not beautiful – in fact, the bigger the better!

The local king of all **cheeses**, *Parmigiano-Reggiano* or Parmesan, was known even to the ancient Romans. Today, around 600 dairies hand-produce the great wheels of cheese 365 days a year.

Maturation takes anything from 12 to 24 months, resulting in the delicious nutty flavour, which is even more delicious served with a few drops of **balsamic vinegar**. Most of the country's balsamic vinegar is from Modena where it is aged for up to 14 years in oak barrels. It comes from an ancient tradition in which grape must (the product left over from the making of wine) is cooked and left to ferment, resulting in a bittersweet strong taste. Used for flavouring meats (and delicious on strawberries), it is also called balm vinegar, as it was thought to have medicinal properties, and was reputedly used by Lucretia Borgia during childbirth.

There are excellent **vineyards** in the hills of Emilia-Romagna, which produce delicious wines, including Val Trebbia, Malvasia and Sangiovese – a particularly fine full-bodied red that goes well with meat, particularly wild boar, which still roam in these hills.

**EMILIA-ROMAGNA**

Florence

Florentines discovered three-dimensional perspective, football, opera and ice cream – not bad for a community of money-lenders and cloth-makers. The architecture of their city has been repeated the world over in private and public buildings, and virtually every Italian Renaissance artist of any rank made his mark here. Despite tourist invasions and summer heat, Florence can still offer sanctuary to the art-loving visitor – many of its galleries, churches and museums are far from the madding crowd.

# BEST OF
## Florence

*Getting there:* although Florence's small Peretola airport is used mostly by business people, it is handy for Florence, Tuscany and northern Umbria, too (car hire available). Florence is well served by trains and long-distance buses from all parts of Italy. Anyone arriving by car is well advised to park it in a secure long-stay car park, such as the one to be found beneath Santa Maria Novella railway station, or on Piazza delle Libertà.

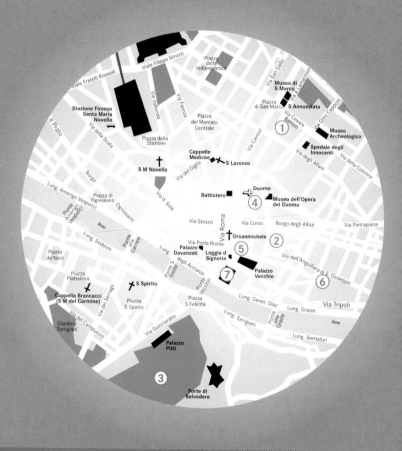

## ① Accademia

Come here to see Michelangelo's original *David*, controversially moved indoors in 1873 to a room that does little justice to its brave monumentality, but at least protects the precious carving from the effects of weather and pigeon droppings. **Page 128**

## ② The Bargello

Stuffed with important Renaissance works, from Michelangelo's drunken *Bacchus* to Giambologna's comical turkey, this grim former prison building is now a showcase for some of the most famous and influential sculptures produced in Florence during the Renaissance era. **Page 129**

## ③ Giardino di Boboli

Take a break from art by wandering the pathways of this green city oasis, once the private garden of the Medici Dukes, now a place of quiet occasionally enlivened by fountains, statues and enrapturing views along the cypress-lined alleyways. **Page 130**

## ④ Piazza del Duomo

Visit the cathedral square for the Baptistery, with its gilded doors and medieval mosaics, the cathedral itself, crowned by Brunelleschi's famous dome, the marble-clad tower built by Giotto and the Museo dell'Opera del Duomo, the Cathedral Works Museum, with its great carvings by Michelangelo and Donatello. **Page 132**

## ⑤ Piazza della Signoria

The main square in Florence has witnessed many turning points in history, and is dotted with statues and fountains commemorating people and events from the turbulent past – not to mention pavement cafés where you can sit and take in the historic surroundings, including the Palazzo della Signoria, the city's medieval town hall. **Page 138**

## ⑥ Santa Croce

One of the most imposing of the medieval churches in Florence, Santa Croce is covered in frescos by Giotto and his followers, and lined with tombs and memorials to artists, poets, philosophers and humanists from the great age of the Renaissance. **Page 140**

## ⑦ Uffizi

Once the private art collection of the Medici Dukes, the paintings and sculptures in the Uffizi amount to a living history of the Renaissance, with key works from every artist who ever worked in the city – not least the crowd-pulling works of Botticelli – his *Primavera* and the *Birth of Venus*. **Pages 142–3**

127

*Tourist information*

*APT Firenze, Via Cavour 1. Tel: 055 2908323; fax: 055 2760383.*

# Accademia

*Galleria dell'Accademia, Via Ricasoli 60. Tel: 055 238609; www.sbas.firenze.it/.*
*Open: Tue–Sun 0830–2200; Fri–Sat 0830–2330; hols 0830–2000. ££.*

The **Accademia di Belle Arte** in Florence was the first teaching establishment set up in Europe to train artists in the basic techniques of drawing, painting and sculpture. With such distinguished patrons as Michelangelo, it was founded in 1563 and still functions as an art school.

The Gallery alongside was set up in 1784 to provide examples of distinguished art for the students to copy. Of these, the works of **Michelangelo** are by far the most important works in the Gallery. Here you can see the original *David* (1504), moved here in 1873 and replaced in Piazza della Signoria by a copy, and his *Quattro Prigioni (Four Slaves)* (1521–3).

The twisting, writhing figures of the Four Slaves are a famous example of Michelangelo's lifelong habit of leaving works unfinished. Art historians (and visitors to this gallery) love to debate whether Michelangelo deliberately left them in this raw state, with the figures appearing to wrestle with the very rock that binds them, powerfully expressing the psychological and physical effects of slavery. In their unfinished state, they have an elemental power that might have been lost if Michelangelo had worked on them further.

Few other works in the museum can compare with Michelangelo's heroic figures, but the **Salone della Toscana** is well worth a visit: it is full of neo-classical sculptures by 19th-century academicians, including busts of such renowned Romantic poets and musicians as Byron and Liszt.

# The Bargello

*Museo Nazionale del Bargello, Via del Proconsolo 4. Tel: 055 2388606. Open: Tue–Sun 0830–1350 (same hours for hols). ££.*

The Bargello is strangely neglected in favour of the Uffizi even though its collection of sculpture rivals that of any museum in the world. The 13th-century palace, built for sessions of the city council, symbolised the triumph of elected government in Florence. Three centuries later, it stood for the opposite, after Medici tyrants turned it into a prison.

The Bargello's repertoire of nude bodies in stone – twisting, raging, lusting and musing atop their pedestals – represents a revolution in taste (the Renaissance) and an obsession with the human body.

The ground floor displays the only bust **Michelangelo** ever carved, *Brutus*, with its distinct Republican overtones – it could be seen as a reference to the assassination of the Medici tyrant, Alessandro I. His *Drunken Bacchus* carries a somewhat different message. The same room contains his *David-Apollo* as well as **Benvenuto Cellini**'s bust of *Cosimo I* and **Giambologna**'s *Flying Mercury*. Upstairs is **Donatello**'s

homoerotic, under-age *David* – the first nude statue of the Renaissance, and one of the most remarkable works of art in Florence. Other high points include Ammannati's *Leda and the Swan* and Ghiberti's powerful *The Sacrifice of Isaac*. On the wall of the first floor are two panels submitted by Brunelleschi and Ghiberti in a competition for the commission to create Florence's **Baptistery doors**. If you have any attention span left, there are still 30,000 odd coins and medallions to look at.

# Giardino di Boboli (Boboli Gardens)

*Instead of a theme park or virtual reality, the 16th-century Medici rulers had this vast fantasy-filled garden in which to kill time. The Florentine public didn't get its first peek until 200 years later. Avenues lined with cypresses intersect ensembles of Roman and Renaissance statues and stately cedars of Lebanon shade strange grottoes. Performances of Europe's first operas took place in its amphitheatre. **Fountains** are ubiquitous, from the fabulous Mannerist Oceanus to secluded, leering fauns that spit water into Roman sarcophagi.*

The originals of Michelangelo's *Slaves* once decorated the Grotta del Buontalenti (left of the entrance) until the early 1900s. Copies have replaced them. Deeper inside, beneath the stalactites, is **Giambologna**'s alarmingly endowed *Venus*. The steep climb up from the Pitti Palace to the top of the Boboli Gardens is rewarded with a cinematic view of Florence and the surrounding Tuscan countryside.

*Palazzo Pitti. Tel: 055 218741. Open: daily 0900–1830 Apr, May, Sept and Oct; 0900–1930 June–Aug; shorter hours in winter. Closed first/last Mon of month. £.*

# Cappella Brancacci

*Alongside the church of Santa Maria del Carmine, Piazza del Carmine. Tel: 055 2382195. Open: Tue–Sun 1000–1700; hols 1300–1700. ££*

Tucked away at the rear of an ugly 18th-century church (rebuilt after a fire in 1771) is this astonishing chapel, covered in freshly restored frescos that mark some of the earliest (and most successful) experiments in **perspective** and **realism** that became commonplace as the Renaissance blossomed. Begun by **Masolino** and continued by **Masaccio** (both of whom died while the work was still in progress), the frescos date from 1425–8, and were completed by **Filippino Lippi** in 1480. They tell the story of St Peter in a deliberately stripped-down style that enhances the spirituality of the central figure – whose very shadow was said to have the power to heal the sick and dying.

The paintings are remarkable, too, for their setting of the saint's story against a background of contemporary architecture, dress and street scenes – including recognisable Florentine buildings. Like performing Shakespeare in modern dress, this has the effect of making the story more immediate and telling, and increasing its relevance.

Many great artists, including Leonardo da Vinci and Michelangelo, came to this chapel to study the pioneering work – for them, the artistic achievement lay in the mastery of **three-dimensional perspective**. To a modern eye, it is perhaps the psychological realism that is most compelling – especially in the two side scenes depicting **Adam and Eve** being expelled from Paradise, their faces wracked by anguish and sorrow, and the realisation of all that they have lost through one thoughtless act of ingratitude and disobedience.

# Piazza del Duomo

The Piazza del Duomo is the ancient, clotted heart of Florence. It brings together the conventional ecclesiastical Renaissance combination of baptistery, cathedral and bell tower. Climb the steps to the top of the cathedral dome for views of red-tiled rooftops and a plunging look into the church interior. An even more dizzying view is possible over the edge of the Campanile.

The current building of the **Battisterio** (baptistery) (*Piazza del Duomo/San Giovanni; open: Mon–Sat 1200–1830, Sun 0830–1330; £*) – described by art historians as 'proto-Renaissance' – dates from 1059 to 1128. It stands at the intersection of the town's two former main Roman roads. Lorenzo Ghiberti worked for almost half a century on the **north door** (1403–24), which has 28 scenes from the lives of Jesus and the four evangelists, and the **east door**, his crowning achievement. (The originals are in the **Museo del Duomo**.)

Giotto was appointed architect of the cathedral in 1334 but never got beyond building only one-third of the **Campanile** (bell tower) (*open: daily 0900–1900 Apr–Oct, 0900–1630 Nov–Mar; ££*). His colour scheme – white marble (from Carrara), green marble (Prato) and red marble (Maremma) – was later applied to the cathedral. The reliefs, portraying the history of humanity, were added over the next century by Andrea Pisano, Luca della Robbia and Donatello.

When it was built, the **Duomo Santa Maria del Fiore** (*open: Mon–Sat 1000–1700, Sun 1300–1700; £*) was the largest church in the world – 53m (174ft) long and 38m (125ft) wide. Brunelleschi's world-famous **dome** (1420–34) was the first of its size since the Pantheon in Rome.

# Spedale degli Innocenti

*Piazza della Santissima Annunziata 12. Tel: 055 2491708. Open: Thu–Tue 0830–1400; hols 0800–1300. ££.*

**Spedale degli Innocenti**, or the Hospital of the Innocents, was founded as an orphanage in 1444, the first such institution in Europe. No less an architect than **Brunelleschi** was chosen to undertake the construction of such an important building. His design for the façade and the two inner cloisters is deceptive in its simplicity – hemispherical arches rest on slender columns – but it was daring in its deliberate rejection of ecclesiastical Gothic, and its deliberate return to the old 'pagan' ways of the Romans. With this one building, Brunelleschi set in train the **revival of classical architectural values**, and provided a template for the many graceful Renaissance buildings that are to be found in the city.

In the spandrils of the arches are **Andrea della Robbia**'s lovely glazed terracotta roundels, showing babies in swaddling clothes looking like little angels holding out their hands in supplication. The reality was that many of the children who ended up here were the result of unwanted pregnancies, rather than true orphans. At the left-hand end of the portico you can see the *rota*, a revolving stone cylinder, into which

mothers could place their unwanted infants without being seen. They rang the bell alongside and the child would be taken in by turning the stone.

The **Gallery** inside the building displays artistic treasures donated to the orphanage, including an outstanding work by **Ghirlandaio**: the *Adoration of the Magi* (1488) shows the three kings in all their glory worshipping the new-born Messiah, while Herod's soldiers go about their grim slaughter of Bethlehem's new-born innocents in the background.

# Museo Archeologico

*Via della Colonna 36. Open: Tue–Sat 0900–1400; Sun 0900–1300; guided visit 1030. ££.*

The Archaeological Museum is as surprising for what it doesn't contain as for what it does. There are few Etruscan and Roman objects on display, though the museum has a rich collection. On the other hand, there is a stunning collection of ancient Egyptian material, well worth seeing in its own right.

Of indigenous material, the museum's greatest treasure is the Etruscan bronze Chimera (5th century BC). This beast, part lion, part goat and part snake, was ploughed up near Arezzo in 1554, and was greatly admired by the artists of the day – to them it was proof that they and their ancestors were of one blood. Today, we might say that the genetic heritage of the ancients – their skills as artists and bronze casters – had been passed down to the artists of Renaissance Florence. Benvenuto Cellini, one of the greatest metal workers of his age, was entrusted with the task of repairing the damage inflicted by the plough as the statue was turned up from the soil.

The Egyptian material in the museum resulted from a joint French and Italian expedition of 1889, which recovered a rich assortment of organic materials, preserved by the dry desert conditions. Amongst the material on display is a complete chariot from the 14th century BC, plus well-preserved clothing, ropes, baskets and wooden furniture.

# Museo dell'Opera del Duomo

*Piazza del Duomo. Tel: 055 2302885. Open: Mon–Sat 0900–1900 Apr–Oct; also Sun 0900–1400 in summer; Mon–Sat 0900–1730 Nov–Mar. ££. To see the workshop that is now used to repair the Duomo, walk around the corner to Via dello Studio 23.*

Without seeing this museum, you haven't really seen the monuments of Florence – many of the most impressive pieces of the **Battisterio**, **Duomo** and **Campanile** are kept here to preserve them from pollution and vandalism. The 13th-century building behind the cathedral served as its **workshop** for centuries. This is where Michelangelo sculpted *David* during the years 1501–4.

Sculptures from the unfinished cathedral façade that was torn down in 1587 line the walls of the ground floor. The 80-year-old **Michelangelo** sculpted the *Pietà* (1548–55) for his own tomb in Rome, portraying himself in the figure of St Nicodemus – the old man in a cowl. Dissatisfied, late one night, he fell into a rage and tried to smash it, leaving Christ scarred by the hammer blows and missing his left leg. **Donatello** is represented by early, powerful sculptures of the prophets Jeremiah and Habakuk (1420) and a late Maria Magddalena in wood (1455). There are also pulpits by him and **Luca della Robbia**, the latter's famous for its rows of dancing children. The panels of the recently restored baptistery doors 'of Paradise' are on the ground floor.

# Orsanmichele

*Via Calzaiuoli. Open: daily 0900–1200 and 1600–1800. £.*

The name of Orsanmichele is a contraction of *Orto di San Michele* (St Michael's garden), the monastic garden on whose site the present church was built. Remarkably it was not built as a church, but as a grain store, to be used to hold grain to be distributed to the poor in times of hardship. This accounts for the odd shape of the church, which was converted from the granary in the 1340s and given two parallel naves.

Most of the interest in the church lies outside, in the 14 niches set into the exterior walls. The various **trade guilds** operating in Florence were invited to supply statues of their patron saints to fill these niches, and the Florentines, competitive as ever, sought to outdo each other in the artistry and quality of the statues they commissioned.

Many of the statues are remarkable, but the one that garners most attention is the figure of **St George** (now replaced by a copy – the original is in the Bargello – *see page 129*). This is the work of **Donatello**, and the artist succeeds in conveying something of the fear and uncertainty, along with the courage and determination, with which the warrior saint prepared to encounter the dragon that it was his destiny to fight and slay.

# Palazzo Davanzati

*Via Porto Rossa 13. Tel: 055 23885. Open: Tue–Sat 0900–1200; Sun 0900–1300 (temporarily closed at time of writing). ££.*

By contrast with the vast palaces of the Medici, the Palazzo Davanzati is a palace built on a more homely and domestic scale, with a beautiful courtyard at its core, emphasising just how much the inner courtyards of Florentine houses functioned as another room, a place of cool shady retreat in the heat of the summer. Touring the palace gives you an insight into family life for wealthier merchants in 16th-century Florence.

One indicator of wealth is the **well** to the right of the entrance, with its buckets on a pulley system allowing water to be drawn up to the higher floors of the palace (including the top-floor kitchens). Having your own **private water supply**, when most other people had to fetch all their water from public fountains, was a considerable luxury.

The living rooms on the first floor are gorgeously frescoed; the **Sala dei Pappagalli** ('Room of the Parrots') is named after the exotic birds depicted in the borders. The furnishings in the rooms are all contemporary, and include beds, chests, stools and even – luxury of luxuries – **flushing toilets** complete with terracotta waste pipes.

The top floor has the kitchens – located here so that cooking smells and smoke would leave through the roof and not permeate the living rooms. The equipment on display includes **pasta-making equipment**, indicating that the typical diet of Florentine households has not much changed over the centuries.

# Palazzo Pitti

*Piazza Pitti. Tel: 055 2388615.*

The vast Pitti Palace was built on the edge of Florence by Luca Pitti and greatly expanded by Medici tyrant Cosimo I in his determination to put a little space between himself and liberty-loving Florentines who might try to get up close and personal.

Cosimo ordered his court architect, Giorgio **Vasari**, to join the palace to the Uffizi by way of a **corridor** over the Arno so he could sneak in and out of the Palazzo Vecchio (his former residence) and escape quickly across the river. His paranoid son, Ferdinand I, went a step further and built the Forte di Belvedere above the gardens of the palace – its cannons were aimed at Florence.

The palace contains no less than **eight museums** (mercifully, two are closed indefinitely), devoted to fashion, silver, coaches, and so on. The **Galleria Palatina** ( *tel: 055 2388614; open: May–Oct, Tue–Sat 0830–2100, Sat until 2400 Jul–Aug, Sun 0900–1400, Nov–Apr, Tue–Sat 0830–1900, Sun 0830–1400; ££* ) is one of Europe's great art museums. It has a brace of Caravaggios, 11 paintings by Raphael, 13 Titians, works by Rubens, Tintoretto and Giorgione, to say nothing of the gifted and possibly mad Rosso Fiorentino. Two signature works alone would more than justify a visit: Rubens' *The Consequences of War* and Raphael's *Portrait of a Lady*.

# Piazza della Signoria

*The imposing Piazza della Signoria was the scene of the Bonfire of the Vanities, when Savonarola convinced Florentines to burn their carnival costumes and licentious paintings only a few short months before*

*they subjected him to the same treatment (after he was declared a heretic).*

Beneath the three graceful arches of the **Loggia dei Lanzi** is a most remarkable open-air ensemble – Roman, Renaissance, Mannerist and 19th-century sculpture. Most of the figures are engaged in fighting, rape or decapitation. The name 'dei Lanzi' refers to the Swiss mercenaries of Cosimo I, who stood on guard here.

## Palazzo Vecchio

*Piazza della Signoria. Tel: 055 2768465. Open: Mon–Wed and Fri 0900–1900; Sun 0800–1300. ££.*

The palace on the Piazza della Signoria is still the **city hall** of Florence. It was the work of **Arnolfo di Cambio** (1299–1314) but **Michelozzo** created the early Renaissance courtyard in 1453. Two centuries after its completion, **Vasari** decorated the walls with frescos, now badly faded, of Austrian cities to celebrate a wedding between the house of Medici and an Austrian princess. The clock, added in 1667, still ticks.

## War damage

*The Germans dynamited all of Florence's bridges in 1944 except the Ponte Vecchio – they blew up houses at each end instead.*

## Ponte Vecchio

One of Europe's most photographed structures, the 'Old Bridge' occupies a place used in Roman times as a **crossing** over the Arno for the *Via Cassia*. Today's bridge was built in 1345. Originally, there were butcher shops and tanners (who dumped their bloody scraps in the river). Ferdinand I wanted the bridge to be more upmarket, reserving its shops for **jewellers** and **goldsmiths**, and so it has remained.

## San Lorenzo and Cappelle Medicee

**San Lorenzo** (*Piazza di San Lorenzo; tel: 055 216634; open: daily 0700–1200 and 1530–1830; ££*) is just a stone's throw away down the Via de'Pucci. The unfinished façade hides one of the most perfectly proportioned buildings of the Renaissance: Filippo **Brunelleschi** rationalised every inch of the space divided between nave and chapels. The bronze reliefs on the pulpit are late masterpieces by **Donatello**, who also decorated the Sagrestia Vecchia. The altar has an annunciation by **Filippo Lippi**.

The entrance to the **Cappelle Medicee** (Medici chapels) is behind the church (*Piazza di Madonna; tel: 055 2388602; open: Tue–Sat 0830–1700; hols 0830–1350; ££*). Michelangelo designed the **Sagrestia Nuova** as a monumental tomb for the Medici family, achieving a sense of harmony between sculpture and architecture unknown in western art since classical Greece.

# Santa Croce

*Piazza di Santa Croce. Tel: 055 244619. Open: daily 0800–1830 Apr–Oct; 0800–1230 and 1500–1830 Nov–Mar. Admission charge to museum, cloister and Capella de'Pazzi.*

The narrow street of Borgo dei Greci leads into Piazza Santa Croce, gateway to a neighbourhood where residents actually outnumber tourists and there is a feeling of community.

The largest Franciscan church in Italy, **Santa Croce** was the work of Arnolfo di Cambio (but the façade is 19th century). It has been called the Westminster Abbey of Florence. Inside are masterpieces by artists from Giotto to Donatello, and tomb-spotters will quickly alight on Michelangelo, Machiavelli, Galileo and Rossini. Dante's exile finally ended after 500 years when a pompous memorial was built for him in 1863. Few people pay the price of admission to see the **Cappella de'Pazzi** ('Pazzi Chapel') (1430–46) next door, which is now part of a museum – the **Museo dell'Opera di Santa Croce** (*tel: 055 244619; open: Thu–Tue 1000–1200 and 1430–1900 in summer, 1000–1230 and 1500–1700 in winter; £*). It is arguably the most perfect of all the designs created by Filippo Brunelleschi, built according to the **golden mean** (the principle behind the Acropolis in Athens). Brunelleschi was also responsible for the **cloister**.

# San Marco

*Piazza di San Marco. Tel: 055 287628. Open: Thu–Tue 0830–1400. ££.*

This graceful group of monastic buildings resulted from the patronage of **Cosimo de'Medici**, who, in order to emphasise his own piety (which was probably genuine), paid for the convent to be rebuilt using the services of his favourite architect, **Michelozzi**, in 1437. Michelozzi eschewed all frills and created a building whose simplicity is exactly right for monastic contemplation. That simplicity is enhanced by the stark and mystical **frescos of Fra Angelico** (painted 1435–8). The frescos are painted on the walls of the **monks' cells**, and are intended to be a focus for prayer and contemplation: an *aide-mémoire*, if you like, of the various torments suffered by Christ on his way to Calvary.

Along from the cells where the monks spent much time in private prayer is a **library** full of precious books, including early translations of the Greek philosophers whose work did so much to inspire the Renaissance. The Dominican preacher **Savonarola**, who briefly ruled Florence before being burned at the stake for heresy, was prior of San Marco in 1491, and there are various momentoes of his time here – as there are of Cosimo de'Medici, who had a private cell, to which he would come on retreat from time to time.

# Santa Maria Novella

*Piazza di Santa Maria Novella. Open: daily 0700–1130 and 1530–1800. £.*

Santa Maria Novella is a beautiful church, with a façade of grey, green and white stone. Prominent among the patterning is the symbol of the **Rucellai family** – a billowing **ship's sail**, representing trade. This wealthy family paid for the building of the façade in 1470. Inside are some renowned frescos: on the left is **Masaccio**'s *Trinity, Mary and St John* (1427), an early Renaissance work and a landmark in the development of three-dimensional perspective. Behind the altar is the heart-warming series of frescos on the *Life of the Virgin* (1485–90) by **Ghirlandaio**, full of colour and details of domestic life in 15th-century Florence.

141

The **cloisters** alongside the church are home to **Uccello**'s powerful dramatic frescos depicting the story of *Noah and the Flood* (1450), but these were themselves badly damaged by the flood that devastated Florence in 1966 and are now not as compelling as they once were.

# Uffizi

*Giorgio **Vasari** designed the **Uffizi** ('offices') for Medici ruler Cosimo I and his **bureaucracy** in the 16th century. Today, it is Italy's most popular museum (around 1.5 million visitors a year and growing), with 1 000 works of art from the 13th to the 17th centuries displayed in 45 rooms. Its most famous icon, Botticelli's **Birth of Venus** (or 'Venus on the half shell') challenges the Mona Lisa for the status of world's most recognised painting.*

Of all Italy's museums, the embarrassment of riches here is the most embarrassing. It inspired Mark Twain's stoical boast that he had wandered 'weary miles of picture galleries' in Florence. If your focus is the Renaissance, plan to spend the day in the first 15 rooms. Don't forget, however, that the Uffizi is also one of Europe's great international collections, with major works by northern Europeans such as Dürer, Cranach, Brueghel and Rembrandt.

Everyone who visits the Uffizi finds at least one work that they like, even those who don't particularly enjoy religious art. Renaissance artists shared an enthusiasm for rich colours with their Gothic predecessors (whose works are displayed in the first room in the gallery), with the difference that Renaissance colours are more natural – skies are blue instead of gold.

Renaissance artists extended the range of subjects well beyond that of purely religious art, so that the Uffizi has examples of early **portraiture** ( *The Duke and Duchess of Urbino* (1460) by Piero della Francesca), **battle scenes** ( *The Battle of San Romano* (1456) by Paolo Uccello) and **nudes** (Lorenzo di Credi's *Venus* ), not to mention subjects derived from Greek and Roman mythology and philosophy (Botticelli's celebrated works).

Despite a backlash against profane art led by Savonarola in the 1490s (during his reign of terror, countless works of art were burned on great 'Bonfires of Vanity'), the trend was established whereby artists had the freedom to depict whatever subjects and stories they or their patrons required. In the later galleries there are many portraits, including exquisite pictures by **Bronzino** of various members of the Medici family. There is also **Titian**'s celebrated *Venus of Urbino* (1538), an enigmatic work that evokes strong responses: Mark Twain called it 'the obscenest picture the world possesses', and there is no doubt that the sexual flush on the goddess's cheeks and the 'come hither' look in her eyes makes it a powerfully erotic picture.

143

Elsewhere in the gallery we find experimental pictures in which the artists develop new techniques for expressing their vision and temperament: **Michelangelo**'s *The Holy Family* (1506–8) is a remarkable example of the style that became known as **Mannerist** because of its exaggerated poses, while the works of **Caravaggio** and **Rembrandt** are full of unusual lighting effects and colours.

*Loggiato degli Uffizi, 6. Tel: 055 294883; fax: 055 264406. Open: Tue–Sun 0830–2230; Fri and Sat until 2330; hols 0830–2000; reservations Mon–Fri 0830–1830. £££. Booking a ticket avoids the queues, but costs a little more. The present, extended, opening hours are experimental and subject to change.*

# Eating and drinking

Florentine cuisine is simplicity itself. *Crostini* is toasted Tuscan bread with chicken-liver pâté, tomatoes or mushrooms, or simply dipped in unspeakably good olive oil. Soup often takes preference over pasta, *ribollita* in winter and *pappa di pomodori* in summer. Florentines also like to eat hare, wild boar and pheasant. The *bistecca alla fiorentina* is a steak of local Tuscan beef, from the Valdichiana, marinated in herbs, garlic and the finest olive oil, and cooked to perfection over wood coals. *Tortino di carciofi*, an artichoke omelette, and *funghi alla griglia* ('grilled mushrooms') are among the few dishes for a vegetarian. The more expensive restaurants sometimes have bargain lunch menus. In Florence, restaurants are likely to charge for *pane e coperto* ('bread and cover charge') and sometimes for *servizio* (10 per cent), but this will always be stated clearly on the menu.

## Cantinetta del Verrazzano
*Via dei Tavolini 18r. Tel: 055 268590. Closed Sun. £.* Very near the Duomo and an ideal place for a break. Excellent for a small meal – a *focaccia* or a sandwich made from *prosciutto di cinghiale* ('wild boar') or roasted *porcini* mushrooms washed down with a glass of wine or an espresso. Raspberry and honey *tortini* are luscious.

## Il Cibreo
*Piazza Ghiberti 35. Tel: 055 2341100 (no reservations). Closed Sun and Mon, and last week of Jul and Aug. ££.* This *trattoria* is an annexe to a more expensive restaurant next door. The food is truly outstanding at modest prices. However, it doesn't accept reservations and is always packed. The best tactic is to arrive early, say at 7.30 pm. *Anatra ripiena al forno* ('stuffed roast duck') is a speciality. One oddity – they don't do pasta.

### Enoteca Pinchiorri
*Via Ghibellina 51r. Tel: 055 242777.*
*£££*. Tuscan cuisine with a heavy
French accent (and two Michelin
stars). The wine cellar ranks with any
in Europe and inspires near-religious
awe among connoisseurs.

### Mario
*Via Rosina 2r. Tel: 055 218550. £*.
Lunch-only no-nonsense *trattoria*
with generous quality and quantity
price ratio, also near the Mercato
Centrale. Come early, before it fills
up with students.

### La Pentola dell'Oro
*Via di Mezzo 24r. Tel: 055 241808.*
*£*. Chef Giuseppe Alessi goes tradition
one better by serving Renaissance-
style dishes – *Piatti Rinascimentale*
– and vegetarian meals.

### Da Sergio
*Piazza San Lorenzo 8r. Tel: 055
281941. Closed Sun and Aug. £*. Right
off the Mercato Centrale. The menu is
limited but impeccable. In addition to
*bollito misto* ('stewed meats') there are
lots of things *in umido* ('in broth'),
such as cod, tripe and rabbit.

145

# Shopping

Florence's **Mercato Centrale** (central market) ( *Via dell'Ariento; Mon–Sat 0730–
1300, Sat also 1600–2000* ) was inspired by the market at Les Halles in Paris, which
no longer exists. It is the town's main market and one of the best places in Italy to
buy food or eat lunch – try **Da Nerbone** in the market or **ZaZa** on the piazza. Both
will serve a roast suckling pig sandwich and a glass of Chianti. *Coniglio* or *verdure
fritte* (fried rabbit or vegetables) are also classics; braver stomachs will want to try
*trippa alla fiorentina* (tripe in tomato sauce) and the tender, almost eggy *lampredotto*
(stewed cow's stomach), served in broth ( *umido* ) or as a sandwich ( *panino* ).

# Florence – 'Cradle of the Renaissance'?

**1050** Power struggle between the Holy Roman Emperor and the Pope contributes to the growth of autonomous city states, including Florence.
**1125** Florence destroys Fiesole and begins to expand its territory. The Florentines fight wars with the Ghibelline cities of Pisa and Siena.
**1269** Florence defeats Siena near Colle Val d'Elsa.
**1284** Building boom of town halls: Florence (1299).
**1342** Economic crisis in Florence.
**1378** A wealthy Florentine family – the Medici – becomes banker to the Pope.
**1406** Florence conquers Pisa and wages war with Naples, Milan and Lucca. During a period of unrest in Florence, Cosimo de'Medici sides with the people's party and is driven into exile.
**1434** Cosimo Il Vecchio returns to Florence in triumph and remains in power until his death (1464). The beginning of the Medici dynasty.
**1478** War between Florence and the Pope.
**1501** Michelangelo's *David* graces the square before the town hall in Florence.
**1530** The end of Florence as a Republic. The Medici rule as tyrants with the help of Spanish troops.
**1555** Florence besieges Siena, and puts an end to the last Republic in Italy.
**1569** Cosimo I, proclaimed Duke of Tuscany, controls the entire region except for Lucca, Massa-Carrara and the islands.

## Romanesque and Gothic

These five hundred years of fluctuating fortunes, and some times of enormous wealth, have left a fascinating architectural legacy in Florence. The city is celebrated as the cradle of the Renaissance, but there is evidence here (as elsewhere in Tuscany) of the earlier styles of Romanesque and Gothic. Romanesque (10th–12th centuries) unites geometric shapes with unprecedented ambition to build upwards. The **Florentine Romanesque** style – seen in the Baptistery (1059–1128) – was also influenced by Byzantine and Islamic architecture.

The **Gothic** style here, unlike further north, retained the dome, used less vertical thrust and gave frescos centre stage. Florence's most important example is the **Duomo** (1294).

# Renaissance

The 15th century was a revolutionary period that profoundly changed many aspects of European life – housing, language, warfare, diet, cities, technology and education. The Florentines saw this as an age of the rebirth of classical learning and artistic ideals and called it a *Rinascità* ('Rebirth'). However, the idea of the Renaissance as a sudden Florentine watershed between the medieval and the modern is an over-simplistic 19th-century theory. More modern theories see the late medieval period as 'proto-Renaissance'.

Its dominant artistic figure was Giotto (1266–1337), the first artist since antiquity to create realistic representations of people, space and objects.

Art historians have picked 1420 – the year when Brunelleschi won the contract to put a dome on top of Florence's cathedral – as the moment when the early Renaissance began. He had already rediscovered linear perspective (familiar to the ancients) and his approach to architecture was radically new. It can be seen in Florence in the Spedale degli Innocenti (1419–24); Sagrestia Vecchia in San Lorenzo (1419); Cappella dei Pazzi in Santa Croce (1442); and San Lorenzo (begun in 1425).

The most important figures of the High Renaissance were Michelangelo, Leonardo da Vinci and Raphael. This period spanned little more than a generation, roughly 1490–1520. Raphael's work possesses the grace and harmony to which Renaissance artists aspired. Michelangelo carried on until 1564, and the incredible age of 89, counting among his achievements in Florence the San Lorenzo Sagrestia Nuova (1520).

## Mannerism

The term 'Mannerism' was originally a put-down by Tuscan artist Giorgio Vasari, referring to artists who came after Michelangelo and who worked *alla maniera di Michelangelo*. Ironically, the Tuscan Renaissance bang ended in a whimper, with a self-conscious, angst-ridden style alien to the classical spirit but with some striking parallels to modern art.

# Tuscany, Umbria and the Marches

*Tuscany is paradise on earth in the minds of many: a region of hill towns bristling with medieval towers, of lush vineyards and olive groves, rolling hills, Renaissance art and a Mediterranean coastline. In spring, the land is covered with entire fields of sunflowers, and poppies, Spanish broom, cornflowers and marigolds. Umbria, the green heart of Italy, is distinctly different, with a deeply rural atmosphere, stretches of solitary wildernesses and deep mystic roots.*

TUSCANY, UMBRIA AND THE MARCHES

# Tuscany, Umbria and the Marches

***Getting there:*** *the main airports in the region are at Pisa and Rome, although the former is more convenient for reaching Tuscany. Both cities are about two hours' drive on the Autostrada from Perugia, Umbria's capital. British Airways (tel: 0345 222 111; www.british-airways.com) and Alitalia (tel: 020 7602 7111; www.alitalia.it) have flights several times a day to Rome, Milan and Pisa. There are also cheap charter flights to these cities as well as to Bologna and Rimini.*

## ① Assisi

Follow in the footsteps of the patron saint of Greenpeace International, St Francis, and make your pilgrimage to see the miraculous frescos of Assisi's basilicas. Despite recent earthquake damage, they are still worth at least a day of anyone's time. **Pages 154–5**

## ② Lucca

Do as the local *Lucchesi* do and take your evening *passeggiata* around the perfectly intact ramparts of this beautiful city. Roman remains lie alongside art-nouveau façades, and there's an architectural surprise round every narrow medieval street corner. **Pages 157–8**

## ③ Perugia

A monumental Etruscan arch, the Virgin's wedding ring, Umbria's most fabulous art gallery and the 'most beautiful public building in Italy', this lively university town has it all. And you surely won't leave without buying some 'kisses' – local speciality chocolates. **Pages 160–1**

## ④ Pisa

Will the tower still be standing by the time you get there? It may be a world-famous icon, but many people don't realise that it's just one element of a miraculous ensemble – the Field of Miracles – alongside an equally spectacular baptistery and cathedral. Go before it's too late! **Pages 162–3**

## ⑤ San Gimignano

The remarkable sight of a forest of towers greets the visitor to this lovely medieval hill-top town. Once upon a time there were 72 of them – today, there are just over a dozen; climb to the top of the Torre Grossa for views of the surrounding Tuscan countryside. **Page 165**

## ⑥ Siena

Fiercely independent and more than happy to be different from arch-rival Florence, Siena has an unforgettable shell-shaped main square, a baptistery full of fabulous works of art and a rich heritage of customs and traditions. If you want to visit to experience the intensity of the *Palio* horse races, plan ahead! **Pages 168–71**

## Travel information

If you want to travel outside the major cities, **hiring a car** will give you maximum flexibility: all the major rental companies have offices in Rome and Pisa for pick up and delivery. If you just want to travel between the major cities, Italy's **state railway** (FS) runs an efficient network of trains: Florence and Pisa are the main arrival points for trains from Europe and the rest of Italy.

# Arezzo

*Italians recently voted Arezzo as one of Italy's best places to live. The Etruscans thought so too – it was part of their League of 12 Cities. It became Roman* Arretium *in 294 BC and still has a well-preserved amphitheatre. The poet Petrarch (1304–37) would recognise parts of the* Centro Storico *today; native son and Renaissance man Giorgio Vasari (1511–74) would find it even more familiar, since he designed much of it.*

## Tip

*There is a vast antique fair in Arezzo's* Centro Storico, *around the Piazza San Francesco, on the first weekend of each month (*information, tel: 0575 377678*).*

The nexus of the old, hilly part of town is the Piazza Grande, framed by Vasari's Palazzo delle Logge, the Palazzo della Fraternità dei Laici and the splendid Romanesque church of **Pieve di Santa Maria**, a massive collection of porticoes, columns, blind arcades and loggias, crowned by a bell tower (1330) known as 'the tower of a hundred holes'.

The jewel in Arezzo's art-history crown is in the main choir chapel of the **church of San Francesco**. This fresco cycle – the **Legend of the True Cross** (1452–66) (*Piazza San Francesco; viewing only in guided groups – ask at the tourist office or call 0575 355668; ££*) by Piero della Francesca – is one of the most important works of art created in the Renaissance. The frescos may have been commissioned to boost interest in the increasingly unpopular Crusades.

The **Casa di Giorgio Vasari** (*Via XX Settembre 55; open: daily 0900–1900; £*) was the home of this artist, who was also consultant to the Medici Duke Cosimo I. Vasari decorated the rooms himself, with frescos and paintings in Mannerist style. The Camera della Fama ('Hall of Fame') has Vasari assuming a heroic pose in a group of famous artists whose lives he described as a biographer.

Arezzo's cathedral, the **Duomo San Donato** (*Piazza del Duomo; open: daily*), occupies the highest point in the city. Begun in 1277, it was not finished for several hundred years – the 'Gothic' campanile and façade were actually completed in the 19th and 20th centuries. Guillaume de Marcillat, a Dominican monk from Chartres, created the rare 16th-century stained-glass windows. In the left aisle is the tomb of Bishop Guido Tarlati, with its marble reliefs of miracles and battles; just to the right is a fresco of Maria Maddalena by Piero della Francesca.

*Tourist information: APT, Piazza della Repubblica 28, by the train station. Tel: 0575 377678; fax: 0575 20839. Open: Mon–Sat 0900–1300 and 1500–1830; Sun 0900–1200.*

## Giostra del Saracino

*The 'Joust of the Saracen' takes place on the third Sunday in June and the first Sunday in September. Two hundred and fifty participants – soldiers, musicians, valets, flag jugglers and knights – parade to the Piazza Grande. Eight knights in heavy armour, two from each of Arezzo's four quarters, take turns charging a huge effigy of a Saracen. They score by striking his shield with their lances and avoiding the effigy's counter-attack when it rotates and strikes back with a whip. The winner receives a golden lance.*

# Assisi

*Assisi, the birthplace of St Francis, is one of the world's most important pilgrimage destinations. Its two-storeyed basilica attracts millions of tourists, eager to gaze on frescos by Giotto, Cimabue, Simone Martini and Pietro Lorenzetti. The city – largely medieval – is of a pinkish travertine that changes colour at sunset, glowing several shades redder.*

## Basilica di San Francesco

*Upper and lower churches open: daily 0630–1930; sometimes closed 1200–1400 Nov–Mar; depending on services, the upper basilica might be closed part of Sun. £.*

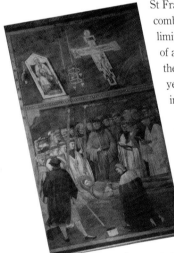

St Francis is buried in a two-storeyed edifice, combining earthy Romanesque features with limitless engineering ambition, resting on a series of arcaded buttresses. The first stone was laid the day after Francis's canonisation, only two years after his death in 1226. His remains are interred in the crypt.

The ceilings and walls of the lower basilica are covered in some of the most important medieval frescos in Europe. **Simone Martini** worked on the Cappella di San Martino chapel from 1322 to 1326 and was responsible for all the decorations, including the stained-glass windows and the marble decoration of the floor. Despite the earthquake damage in 1997, the luminous upper basilica is still the highlight. Its simple plan has remained untouched since its completion in 1253. The apse and transepts are covered in frescos by **Cimabue** and his assistants; **Giotto**'s fresco cycle illustrating the *Life of St Francis* transformed the emphasis of western art.

*Tourist information: Piazza del Comune 12. Tel: 075 812534; fax: 075 812450.*

# Earthquake damage

*Following the earthquake of September 1997, modern technology has played a key role in the restoration of the damaged frescos in the upper basilica. The 120,000 fragments of a Cimabue fresco were recorded by restorers in a database and then reassembled with the help of a virtual model.*

*To see the basilica's frescos clearly, bring a powerful hand torch or a pocket full of change to feed the coin-operated spotlights.*

# Other sites

Still a town hall after all these centuries, the Palazzo dei Priori is made up of four linked buildings, pierced by tunnels, one of which is painted with colourful grotesque ornament. The 14th-century façades are decorated with massive wrought-iron lamps. Unadorned San Damiano could be mistaken for a farmhouse were it not for the simple arcade in front of the church and the cloisters, added in the 16th century. Inside the church are 14th-century frescos, and a remarkable crucifix that was left unfinished overnight, and found to be miraculously completed the next day.

San Rufino has an outstanding Romanesque façade, and a massive and stately Romanesque campanile. It is divided into three parts, both vertically and horizontally. Three caryatids support the central rose window. (San Rufino suffered serious earthquake damage, and is currently undergoing restoration.)

Huge flying buttresses were added to the church of Santa Chiara in the late 14th century to prevent the whole structure from collapsing. Begun in 1257, the Romanesque-style west front has decorative bands of alternating rose and white limestone. The remains of St Clare are displayed in the crypt beneath a rather ugly neo-classical high altar.

Below the former temple of Santa Maria Sopra Minerva, via the Museo Civico ( *open: daily 1000–1300 and 1500–1900 mid-Mar–mid-Oct, 1000–1300 and 1400–1700 mid-Oct–mid-Mar; £* ), you can visit the subterranean remains of what was once the city's *Foro Romano* (Roman forum), and walk down the lane of the Roman town of *Assisium* beneath the medieval piazza of Assisi.

**155**

# St Francis (1181–1226)

*The son of an Assisi cloth merchant, St Francis began by kissing lepers and wearing hair shirts – but he went a step further and declared his love to the sun, the moon, the elements and all God's creatures. He referred to his body as an 'ass', poverty as his 'bride' and death as his 'sister'. Francis has been seen as a medieval animal rights activist, social worker and Christianity's first environmentalist (Greenpeace International made him their patron saint).*

# Gubbio

*Tourist information: APT, Piazza Oderisi 6. Tel: 075 9220693; fax: 075 9273409.*

Gubbio claims to have been one of the first five towns founded after the biblical Flood. In many respects, it is the perfect medieval hill town, its tall austere buildings seemingly as ancient as time, representing a patchwork of centuries.

The Roman part of the town is mostly in the plain, with a well-preserved 1st-century **Roman theatre** (*off the Viale dei Teatro Romano*). Later, the Gubbians shifted higher up the Monte Ingino, constructing two narrow terraces shored up by walls over 20m (65 ½ ft) high. The layout is best appreciated from the Pensili garden in front of the Palazzo Ducale.

The town's focal point is the **Piazza dei Consoli** with its magnificent town hall, the **Palazzo dei Consoli**. In the **Museo Civico and Pinacoteca Comunale** (museum and art gallery), an extraordinary loggia overlooks the rooftops.

The **Duomo** is just a few streets uphill from the Piazza dei Consoli. The interior has fine stained-glass windows and an unusual vaulted ceiling. The 15th-century **Palazzo Ducale** just opposite is interesting for its period Renaissance interiors. From here, it is a steep 2-km (1-mile) walk to the **Basilica Sant'Ubaldo** (827), the church dedicated to the city's patron saint – 300m (985ft) above the city. Alternatively, take the old **funicular** (*Porta Romana; open: daily 0830–1930 July–Aug, 1000–1315 and 1430–1700 Sept–June, closed Wed Oct–May; £*) from the Porta Romana. On the saint's feast day, *ceri*, or candles, are carried in an annual, uphill race from the cathedral. The view from the top is superb.

## The madmen of Gubbio

The *Fontana dei Matti* ('Fountain of the Mad'), in front of Gubbio's Palazzo del Bargello, is so named because it was once believed that anyone who waded round the basin three times would go crazy. Today, on holidays, young men wade around the fountain, hoping to qualify as 'honorary madmen of Gubbio'.

# Lucca

*Tourist information: APT, Piazza Guidiccioni 2. Tel: 0583 491205; fax: 0583 490766. Or Piazzale Verdi, Porta San Donato. Tel: 0583 419689; fax: 0583 442505.*

Lucca rivals any city in Italy for fascination and beauty. One century flows into the next – and right up to the present – as you walk past shops with medieval and art-nouveau façades, cross a Roman amphitheatre-turned-piazza and stroll along the magnificent 16th-century ramparts that are now a pleasure garden.

The façade of the **Duomo San Martino** (*Piazza San Martino; tel: 0583 957068; open: daily 0700–1830 in summer, 1730 in winter*) is a series of loggias resting on pillars. Inside, the cathedral houses the much-worshipped **Volto Santo** ('Holy Face'), an ancient wooden statue of a bearded Christ on the Cross, fully dressed, with a feminine face. Once a year, on 13 September, it is paraded by candlelight through Lucca's *centro storico* by local people in medieval dress. The marble figure of **Ilaria del Carretto** (*Apr–Oct Mon–Sat 1000–1800, shorter hours in winter; £*), by sculptor Jacopo della Quercia, immortalises the 19-year-old wife of a nobleman, who died in childbirth at the beginning of the 15th century.

Lucca is one of the few towns in Italy with a set of perfectly intact defensive walls (**Le Mure**). The intimidating 4-km (2½-miles), 12-m (39-ft) high circuit was started in 1554 and took nearly a century to complete. It consists of 11 curtain walls, 10 bastions and one platform, and its base is 30m (98ft) thick. No one ever dared to besiege the city. Maria Luisa Bourbon transformed the ramparts into a public garden and, today, the people of Lucca still take a ritual evening walk beneath ancient trees.

The **Piazza San Michele** stands on the site of the former Roman forum. The brilliant white façade of the church of

## Il buccellato

*Taddeuci in Piazza San Michele is the best place to buy the local speciality,* il buccellato, *a raisin and aniseed cake. The shop has an untouched 19th-century interior of wood panels and mosaic tiles.*

San Michele in Foro (*open: daily*) is a dreamy fusion of Gothic and Romanesque styles. The adjoining bell tower is the highest in Lucca. Behind it are perfectly preserved 14th-century houses.

San Frediano (*Piazza San Frediano; open: daily*), the oldest church in Lucca, faces east – the wrong direction – because it was built next to a city wall. Inside, it is a monumental basilica with some capitals recycled from the nearby Roman amphitheatre. The unmissable right-hand chapel is one of the most popular places to pray – in the presence of the mummified St Zita. A servant born in 1218, she stole bread to give to the poor and lied about it, but the lie became truth when the scraps of bread turned into roses.

The narrow Via Fillungo is lined with medieval palaces and towers, and shops with *fin de siècle* or art-nouveau façades. There is also a small art-nouveau passage (*No 102*).

# Montepulciano

*Tourist information: Via Ricci 9. Tel: 0578 757450.*

At 605m (1 985ft), Montepulciano is one of the highest situated cities in Tuscany. Architecturally, it is a fascinating mix of Sienese Gothic and Florentine Renaissance architecture. The ring of fortifications was erected in 1511 at the behest of Cosimo I.

The Corso winds its way from the main square up to the Piazza Grande, the highest point in the city. The Palazzo Comunale (*Piazza Grande 1; tel: 0578 757034; closed Sun*) dates from 1243, and was given a facelift by the Florentines in 1393. The impressive Palazzo Nibili-Tarugi, on the northern side of the square, was built entirely with travertine.

Perhaps the most remarkable building in Montepulciano is the Renaissance basilica of Madonna di San Biagio (1518–45) (*Via di San Biagio 14; open: daily*) in a solitary setting just outside the city gates. It is entirely built of travertine on a Greek-cross plan and surmounted by a central dome.

# Orvieto

*Tourist information: Piazza Duomo 24. Tel: 0763 341772; fax: 0763 344433. The* Carta Orvieto Unica *pass covers admission to several museums and monuments, use of the town's mini-buses and parking for 5 hours in the funicular car park.*

Orvieto is thrust up into the Umbrian sky by a plateau of extinct volcanoes; at the foot of its sheer cliffs, vineyards have been grown for centuries. The volcanic soil gives the city's white wine its distinct crispness.

Orvieto's **Duomo** is a fine example of this city's unique cultural heritage. It is the finest of its period in Italy, a refined Sienese-style building of horizontal bands of white travertine and dove-grey tufa. The rare, sumptuous mosaic on the façade contrasts with an uncluttered interior, with a floor of ox-blood coloured marble.

The fabulous, world-famous frescos (1499–1504) by Signorelli in the **Cappella di San Brizio** ( *open: daily 1000–1245 (except Sun) and 1430–1715, until 1915 in summer; £; tickets from the tourist office or gift shops on Piazza Duomo* ) depict the Apocalypse, the torments of hell and the Resurrection.

The **Palazzo Faina** ( *Museo Civico e Claudio Faina; open: daily 1000–1300 and 1400–1800 Apr–Sept, Tue–Sun 1000–1300 and 1430–1700 Oct–Mar; ££* ) houses one of the most important archaeological collections in Umbria, including Etruscan sculpture and pottery.

Alongside the public gardens that surround the remains of the 14th-century Fortezza is a 63-m (207-ft) well, the **Pozzo di San Patrizio** ( *Viale Sangallo; tel: 0763 343768, fax: 0763 344664; open: daily 0930–1845 Apr–Sept, 1000–1745 Oct–Mar; £* ), dug in 1527 on the orders of Pope Clement VII, preparing for a siege that never came. A double helix staircase was constructed to allow packhorses to descend to collect water and ascend via a separate set of steps.

159

## Wine tradition

*Winemaking in Orvieto dates back to the Etruscans. Pope Gregory XVI commanded in his will that his body be washed in Orvieto Abbocato, a traditionally made, naturally sweet wine.*

# Perugia

*Time travel is easy in Perugia. The city sits on a mountaintop that has been inhabited for at least 3000 years. Its art gallery has masterpieces by Fra Angelico, Piero della Francesca and Perugino, its palace, square and fountain rival any in Italy, and it retains a monumental Etruscan arch. And the cathedral claims to have the Virgin's wedding ring. Today, Perugia is known for* baci *– 'kisses' (chocolates with nougat cream) – its university and one of Europe's best jazz festivals.*

The **Arco Etrusco** is Perugia's best surviving city gate, originally part of an encircling wall of almost 3km (1³/₄ miles). It is indeed 'Etruscan' in its lower reaches; the upper level of the gate was added to by the Romans and crowning the whole structure is a delicate 16th-century loggia.

In 1496, the Exchange Guild commissioned the local artist Pietro Vannucci – known to posterity as Umbria's greatest painter, **Perugino** – to paint the walls at its **Collegio del Cambio** (*Corso Vannucci 25; open: Mon–Sat 0900–1230 and 1430–1730, Sun 0900–1230, Mar–Oct, Tue–Sat 0900–1400, Sun 0900–1230, Nov–Feb; £*). The resulting frescos, uniting pagan and Christian imagery, are masterpieces of the Italian Renaissance. Perugino painted himself between the allegorical figures of *Strength* and *Temperance* as a fat man with a double chin.

The **Galleria Nazionale dell'Umbria** (*Palazzo dei Priori, Corso Vannucci; open: Mon–Sat 0900–1900, Sun 0900–1300, closed first Mon of each month, some extended hours, including late evenings; ££*) houses the richest artistic collection in the region. Unsurprisingly, Umbrians are well represented. There are a dozen works by Perugino, including his early masterpiece *The Adoration of the Magi* (1475–7). There are many masterpieces from beyond Umbria's borders, too, including Fra Angelico's luminous *Madonna and Child with Angels and Saints* and a legendary polyptych by Piero della Francesca painted at about the same time as the cycle of frescos in Arezzo (*see page 153*).

From the 15th to the 18th centuries many important artists contributed their works of art to the **Duomo San Lorenzo** (*Piazza Dante; £*), among them Agostino di Duccio, Perugino, Luca Signorelli and Federico Barocci. The **Cappella del Sant'Anello** contains what is said to be the Virgin's wedding ring.

The **Fontana Maggiore**, created by medieval sculptors Nicola Pisano and son Giovanni, has remarkable realism and balance. The themes are an eclectic mixture of Christian and pagan, secular and religious, fabulous and mythical subjects. The fountain was an engineering as well as artistic achievement, completed in 1277 with the help of Friar Bevignate, a hydraulic genius who pumped water into Perugia from Monte Pacciano nearly 3km (1¾ miles) away.

Perugians call their **Palazzo dei Priori**, polished by 600 years of sunshine and rain, the most beautiful public building in Italy. Since the Middle Ages, the palace has been the heart of political life in town. It was built in pink and white stone intermittently between the 13th and 15th centuries but a sense of unity somehow prevails.

161

*Tourist information: APT, Via Mazzini 21. Tel: 075 5725341; fax: 075 5725341. Or Ufficio Informazioni Piazza IV Novembre (Palazzo dei Priori). Tel: 075 5736458; fax: 075 5723327.*

# Pisa

*In the 11th century, the Pisans defeated the Saracens and launched a new era in trade and commerce, and architecture and sculpture. The Renaissance might have taken place in Pisa rather than Florence had it not been for the city's disastrous naval defeat of 1284 and the silting up of its port. Pisa's Field of Miracles is one of the most remarkable sights in the world, the setting for one of the symbols of Italy – the Leaning Tower.*

## Campo dei Miracoli (Field of Miracles)

*Combined tickets available (££) for two, four or five attractions, out of Museo dell'Opera del Duomo, Museo delle Sinopie, Battistero, Camposanto and the Cattedrale. All are open: daily 0800–1940; 0900–sunset in winter.*

The **Battistero** (baptistery), separate from the cathedral, was essentially the work of father and son Nicola and Giovanni Pisano. The hexagonal pulpit by Nicola (1260) launched a new style of sculpture in Italy. The building has remarkable acoustics.

Surely the most bizarre fact about the **Campanile** (Leaning Tower) is that most of it was built *after* it had started to lean. The Pisans who began this tower in 1173 had only completed 10m (33ft) before things went awry. The 13th-century architects made the best of it by lengthening the south-side columns by 70mm (2in), giving it a slight banana shape.

The **cathedral of Santa Maria Assunta** was begun in 1063, and represents the high point in Pisan-Romanesque architecture. It was the first church in Italy to use a Latin-cross floor plan with a dome over its intersection. The architect used as his models the Byzantine basilica and the Islamic mosque. The bronze doors were cast in 1180 by Bonanno Pisano, the huge mosaic of Christ in the apse is by Cimabue, and the pulpit, which abbreviates the New Testament in stone, is by Giovanni Pisano (1302–11).

During the Crusades, the Pisans imported 50 ships filled with earth from Golgotha for their cemetery, the **Camposanto**.

## Leaning Tower of Pisa

*How much longer will this symbol of Italy remain standing? Instruments reveal that the 55m- (180 1/2 ft-) high campanile is inclining further out of plumb each year (already over 5m, or 16ft); furthermore, it is actually rotating in the soft subsoil. Massive cables are now in place, connected to concrete bunkers embedded in the ground, in case it does fall. In the meantime, engineers are removing soil from beneath the tower's foundations in order to bring it back closer to the vertical.*

The city's most prominent citizens were laid to rest in the holy earth until the 18th century. Alarming frescos depicted *Il Trionfo della Morte* ('Triumph of Death'), the *Last Judgement* and *Inferno*, inspired by the plague epidemics that swept across Italy from 1348, and the sadistic visions of Hell that became a trademark of the Dominican order.

The **Museo dell'Opera del Duomo** offers a striking view of the Leaning Tower from its courtyard and upper floors. Formerly a Dominican cloister, it forms a good setting for sculpture by both the Pisanos, and Islamic objects brought back by Crusaders. The **Museo delle Sinopie** displays the preliminary drawings for the frescos of the Camposanto. They were made using a special kind of red chalk manufactured in the town of Sinope on the Black Sea.

The Roman forum was probably located on the **Piazza dei Cavalieri**, and it was the commercial nexus of medieval Pisa. The Pisans' Medici rulers built the massive **Palazzo dei Cavalieri** in 1560 and decorated it with coats of arms and busts of Florentine dukes. Napoleon later turned it into a school (and it remains as such).

*Tourist information: Piazza del Erbe 1. Tel: 0583 65169. Open: daily 0900–1300 and 1530–1830 Apr–Sept; until 1930 June–Sept; shorter hours in winter.*

# Pienza

*Tourist information: Palazzo Communale. Tel: 0578 749071. Open: daily 0930–1300 and 1500–1830.*

When scholar and humanist Aeneas Silvio Piccolomini became Pope Pius II, in 1458, he resolved to turn his birthplace, Corsignano, into a **Città Ideale**, an 'ideal city' of perfect architectural forms. The result, although never finished, was Pienza – one of the most beautiful cities built during the Renaissance, a harmonious ensemble of buildings constructed of honey-coloured travertine that glows at dusk and dawn.

**Piazza Pio II** at the city's core is a trapezoidal square based on the ideas of humanistic Renaissance culture. The cathedral of **Santa Maria Assunta** is built over the spot where the ancient Pieve di Santa Maria church was situated; the papal coat of arms adorns its façade. Inside, you can pace its Latin cross of travertine columns, a common feature of the *Hallenkirche* ('hall church') of central Europe. Under the apse there is a crypt, where you can see fragments of the Romanesque sculptures that decorated the original church.

On the left of the cathedral, the **Palazzo Piccolomini** (1459–62) served as the Pope's rural retreat. Each of the three floors has mullioned windows set between pilasters that give panoramic views over valley and mountain – nature and architecture were meant to co-exist harmoniously in the *Città Ideale*. The court is surrounded by an elegant arcade with arches over columns with Corinthian capitals. The *palazzo* is now a museum (*Museo Piccolomini; open: Tue–Sun 1000–1230, and 1600–1900 in summer, 1500–1700 in winter; £*), housing the library of Pope Pius II and a collection of papal paraphernalia.

## Local cheeses

*Pienza is in the capital of Tuscany's cheese zone. Many of its shops sell delicious local pecorino, made from sheep's milk. The Fiera del Cacio – an annual cheese fair and festival – takes place on the first Sunday in September.*

# San Gimignano

*Tourist information: Piazza Duomo 1. Tel: 0577 940008; fax: 0577 940903. Open: 0900–1300 and 1500–1900 Mar–Nov. A* Bilietto Cumulativo *offers admission to all museums for a single price.*

San Gimignano is invaded by eight million visitors a year. During the Middle Ages, the town was an important stop on the *Via Francigena* pilgrimage route, and also made a killing in saffron. In medieval times, Tuscan towns bristled with towers from every *palazzo* – there were 72 in San Gimignano, just over a dozen of which remain today.

San Gimignano's heritage was created by imported leading artists from Florence and Siena. The **Palazzo del Popolo** (town hall) houses the **Musei Civico e Pinacoteca** (*Piazza del Duomo; open: daily 0930–1930 Mar–Oct, Tue–Sun 0930–1330 and 1430–1630 Nov–Feb; ££*), with 13th- to 16th-century works from Florentine and Sienese schools, and offers access to the **Torre Grossa** (*Piazza del Duomo; open: daily 0930–1930 Mar–Oct, shorter hours in winter; ££*), the only one of San Gimignano's towers that you can climb.

The 12th-century **Duomo** now houses the **Museo della Collegiata**. Plain on the outside, the majestic interior is a revelation of fresco painting. Some of the frescos are rather alarming, particularly in the **Cappella di Santa Fina** (*Museo della Collegiata and Cappella di Santa Fina, Piazza del Duomo; open: Mon–Fri 0930–1930 Apr–Oct, Sat until 1700, shorter hours in winter; ££*).

## Vernaccia di San Gimignano

*Vernaccia is a type of grape, not a brand of wine. The word translates roughly as 'belonging here' and it has been cultivated around San Gimignano since the 13th century. The English began drinking it in the 16th century. There are two contrasting types of wine made from the same grape: a mass-marketed, crisp and colourless drink, almost neutral in flavour that seems ubiquitous at summer parties, and the straw-coloured vintage with a rich flavour that was one of Michelangelo's favourite wines.*

Behind the equally plain Romanesque-Gothic façade of the **church of Sant'Agostino**, at the north end of town, is a magnificent collection of art, particularly the vivid fresco cycle about the life of St Augustine by Benozzo Gozzoli (in the apse).

165

# San Marino

*'Welcome to the Country of Freedom' proclaims the sign to Europe's oldest republic. With a population of just over 25,000 and an area of 61 sq km (23½ square miles), it's also one of the smallest states in the world, attracting a constant stream of tourists and day-trippers from nearby resorts during the season.*

This tiny country, with its own 1 000-strong army, football team and coinage, and a dramatic hill-top site, is best viewed from a distance. A closer inspection reveals a tangle of tourist shops selling 'duty-free' goods. However, it is worth a visit for its curiosity and photogenic value – and perhaps even to get another stamp in your passport (for a small fee).

San Marino is popular with **philatelists**. Its **Museo Filatelico e Numismatico** (Stamp Museum) ( *Piazza Belzotti, Borgomaggiore; open: Tue, Wed and Fri 0815–1415, Mon and Thu 0815–1800; free* ) has a huge range of stamps issued by the Republic since the mid-19th century, in every design and shape apart from square, as well as a vast coin collection.

Above **Borgomaggiore** is the old **medieval-style town** of San Marino ( *accessible by cable car; ££* ). Its main square is **Piazza della Libertà**, dominated by the neo-Gothic

Government House, **Palazzo Pubblico**. Government has changed little here over the last 900 years; the two main figures are the Captains Regent, selected from the 60 members of the Grand Council. The colourful public ceremony of their installation takes place (in medieval costume) on 1 April, 1 October and 3 September, San Marino's National Day. Just north of here is the **Basilica di San Marino** (*Piazzale Domus Plebis; open: daily; free*), which contains the remains of St Marinus, a monk and stonemason who fled here from religious persecution and, allegedly, founded San Marino in AD 301.

On the right of the basilica is the chapel of **San Pietro**, where two holes hewn into the stone are reputedly where St Marinus and his friend St Leo slept. Southeast of here are three watch-towers, on the highest ridges, and, on the highest peak, **Cesta o Fratta**, standing at 745m (2 444ft). From here there are magnificent views over Rimini to the Adriatic and Dalmatian coast and of the Apennines.

For a great view of San Marino itself, drive 16km (10 miles) southwest on a steep, winding road to another hill-top fortress. **San Leo** (*open: daily 0900–1200 and 1400–1830, closes earlier in winter; ££; information: Piazza Dante 14; tel: 0541 916306; open: daily 0900–1900*) is one of the country's most impressive sights, a 15th-century fortress in a glorious setting on top of a limestone rock. Dante was so impressed by the rock that he was inspired to use it in the landscapes of his *Divine Comedy (Purgatorio)*.

*Getting there: cars must be left in one of the many car parks, within walking distance of the town. Parking charges are expensive, with a minimum hourly fee. Tourist information: Palazzo del Turismo, Contrada Omagnano 20. Tel: 0594 882 400. Open: daily 0815–1415 and Mon and Thu pm.*

# Siena: Piazza del Campo

*Siena and Florence, two cities that fought bitterly in the Middle Ages to control Tuscany, remain worlds apart. The major monuments of hill-top Siena were built in a mere six decades between the 13th and 14th centuries, until the Black Death came to town in 1348 and swept away two-thirds of the population. Its lifeblood ebbed further with the decline of the* Via Francigena *trade and pilgrimage route, and Florence conquered Siena in 1555 after a terrible siege.*

## Piazza del Campo

The Piazza del Campo is the historic centre of Siena and perhaps the most beautiful square in Italy, encircled by the red brick and stone façades of medieval houses. It was formerly a market place that sloped downhill – a document from 1196 shows today's piazza – and is now paved with nine bands of travertine fanning out from the centre.

The Gothic **Palazzo Pubblico**, 'Siena's Declaration of Independence', forms part of the piazza's harmony, rather than dominating it. The 'Sienese arch' used on the town hall (and other buildings in the city) looks Gothic but was probably an import from the Orient. The black and white coat of arms of the town of Siena – the *Balzana* – is above the tympana of the doors and windows. Its other symbol – a she-wolf and the twins Romulus and Remus – appears on a granite column. The striking Torre del Mangia (tower) ( *Piazza del Campo; open: daily 0930–1830, Sun 0930–1330; ££* ) rises from the lowest point of the piazza alongside the Palazzo Pubblico to a height of 102m (335ft). It was built between 1325 and 1348 (additions in 1680).

The façade of the Palazzo Sansedoni curves around the piazza. It is a complex of several medieval houses joined into one palace in 1339, and its windows are of the same type as those of the Palazzo Pubblico, in accordance with the city's 13th-century building code.

In July and mid-August, the legendary Palio horse races take place around the Piazza del Campo. Every *contrada* ('neighbourhood') of Siena enters a horse in the race (after having it blessed in church). The colourful festival dates back to the Middle Ages.

# Cathedrals and around

Siena's Duomo Santa Maria ( *Piazza del Duomo; open: daily 0730–1900 mid-Mar–Oct, 1000–1300 and 1430–1700 Nov–Dec, 0730–1330 and 1430–1700 Jan–mid-Mar; free admission* ) is at the highest point in the city (346m, or 1 135ft). A tale of two styles, it was begun in 1200 in Romanesque fashion, then, in 1258, Cistercian monks took over, and built the transept, dome and choir in a revolutionary new Gothic style. Giovanni Pisano worked on the marble façade between 1284 and 1297. The campanile was finished in 1313.

169

The interior is in the form of a Latin cross, with a nave and two aisles divided by Romanesque pillars and arches. A cornice of the nave and presbytery is overpopulated with 172 busts of popes above and 32 busts of emperors below. The floor is divided into 52 panels of inlaid, etched and coloured marble representing various tales ( *not all on show every day* ). In the left (north) transept is the cathedral's greatest work of art, the pulpit (1266–8) by Nicola Pisano ( *take coins for the lighting* ).

# Siena: cathedrals and around

The **Libreria Piccolomini** (*Piazza del Duomo; open: daily 1030–1330 and 1500–1730 mid-Mar–Oct, 1000–1300 and 1430–1700 Nov–mid-Mar; £*) has a lavish Renaissance interior and is covered in Pinturicchio frescos (1502–9) that tell the life story of Aneas Silvio Piccolomini, the poet who became Pope (*see page 164*).

The **Battistero di San Giovanni** (*Piazza San Giovanni; open: daily 0900–1930 mid-Mar–Sept, 0900–1800 Oct, 0900–1330 in winter; £*), built in 1316, sits behind the Duomo where the crypt should be. The white marble façade of the baptistery and its three large doorways were added later (1382). The magnificent baptismal font is attributed to Jacopo della Quercia, and there are also works by Donatello and Lorenzo Ghiberti, bronze figures by Giovanni di Turino and Goro di Neroccio, as well as frescos by Vecchietta (*c* 1450), Michele di Matteo Lambertini and Benvenuto di Giovanni. The sumptuous cross-vaulted ceiling is reflected in wood-framed mirrors that might save you a stiff neck.

The Santa Maria cathedral is only a small part of the **Duomo Nuovo** ('new cathedral') planned by the city fathers in 1316, which might have been completed had not the plague intervened. Their ambition – to use the existing cathedral as the transept of a gargantuan new edifice that would surpass anything in Pisa or Florence – bordered on lunacy. The cathedral choir was moved to the east and the baptistery constructed, while work commenced on the enormous façade and three naves.

The **Museo dell'Opera del Duomo** (*Piazza del Duomo; open: daily 0900–1930 mid-Mar–Sept, 0900–1800 Oct, 0900–1330 in winter; £*) houses sculptures, paintings, gold objects, illuminated manuscripts and hangings mostly from the Duomo: works by Giovanni Pisano, Jacopo della Quercia and, its crowning glory, Duccio's glorious *Maestà*, the supreme masterpiece of the Sienese school, painted between 1308 and 1311.

Climb to the very top of one of the walls of the Duomo Nuovo for a dizzying view over the roofs of Siena and a chance

to visualise what might have been the strangest cathedral in Italy.

The **Pinacoteca Nazionale** (*Via San Pietro 29; open: Mon 0830–1330, Tue–Sat 0900–1900, Sun 0900–1330; ££*) is Siena's famous art gallery, partly housed in the Palazzo Buonsignori, and partly in the adjacent Palazzo Brigidi. It has a huge number of Madonnas, from the *Madonna of the Franciscans* by Duccio di Buoninsegna (1255–1319) to the *Madonna and Child* by Simone Martini. The *Città sul Mare*, by Ambrogio Lorenzetti, is regarded as one of the first landscape paintings in modern history.

The frescos by Domenico di Bartolo in the great hall – Sala del Pellegrinaio – of the **Ospedale di Santa Maria della Scala** (*Piazza del Duomo; open: daily 1000–1800 in summer, shorter hours in winter; £*) are one of the artistic glories of Siena. The hospital of Santa Maria was founded in the 9th century and remained in operation until the 1980s. The frescos offer fascinating insights into the blood and guts reality of 15th-century hospitalisation. Underground is the Oratorio di Santa Caterina della Notte chapel, where Siena's patron saint had visions and ecstasies.

*Tourist information: Centro Servizi e Informazioni Siena, Piazza del Campo 56. Tel: 0577 280551; fax: 0577 270676. Open: Mon–Fri 0830–1300 and 1500–1900; Sat 0830–1300.*

# Spoleto

*Tourist information: APT, Piazza della Libertà. Tel: 0743 49890; fax: 0743 46241.*

The Umbrians, Romans and Lombards who built Spoleto appreciated its prime location on a hill guarding a fertile valley. By the 9th century, it was one of the most important cities in central Italy. Today, there is no better place than Spoleto to contemplate Romanesque art.

From the **Piazza della Libertà**, you can see a Roman theatre (*access through the Archaeological Museum*) to the south. The **Palazzo Municipio** houses the city's **Pinacoteca** (*art gallery open: Tue–Sun 1000–1300 and 1500–1800; £; at some time in the future the collection will be moved to the Rocca*) and, in its vaults, the well-preserved remains of a 1st-century AD Roman house.

The **Piazza del Duomo** is striking; its cathedral has a graceful façade, exquisite rose windows dating from 1190, and a free-standing campanile built on regular blocks of Roman masonry. Inside, there are floors of inlaid marble and vibrantly coloured frescos by Filippo Lippi.

The **Rocca** is a monumental fortress that towers above the town. Built with stone looted from the Roman amphitheatre, it has served as a luxurious palace for Lucrezia and Cesare Borgia, as a maximum-security prison and, now, as an art museum. The **Ponte delle Torri**, an extraordinary aqueduct built in 1345, spans the gorge between Monte Sant'Elia, on which the Rocca is built, and Monteluco, opposite. Water no longer flows along its channel (though it can be turned on if necessary) and it is possible to walk across the top of the structure, 230m (755ft) long and 80m (262ft) high.

## Two Worlds Festival

*Since the 1950s, Spoleto has become internationally famous for its Festival dei Due Mondi ('Two Worlds Festival'), founded by the Italian-American composer Giancarlo Menotti and held at the end of June and beginning of July.*

# Todi

*Tourist information: APT, Piazza Umberto I, 6. Tel: 075 8942686; fax: 075 8942406. Informazione: Piazza del Popolo 38. Tel: 075 8942626; fax: 075 9652763.*

A town of great beauty, with views over unspoiled countryside, in a strategic position on a hill between the valleys of the Tiber and the Naia, Todi was settled early by the Umbrians.

The town's people were nicknamed *Marzia* after the Roman god of war, because of their reputation for defending their liberty with great ferocity. Three set of walls – Etruscan, Roman and medieval – still encircle the city. Inside, many of the medieval houses have been restored as weekend and holiday homes.

San Fortunato church is at the highest point in the town. Its magnificent Gothic portal is set into a half-finished façade that is bursting with biblical figures. The interior feels buoyant, thanks to slender composite columns rising up to massive Corinthian capitals from which the roof vaults spring.

To the left of the church, a path leads down to the Porta Marzia, the town's one surviving Etruscan gate. The Corso Cavour, the main street, leads to the broad Piazza del Popolo, which has hardly changed since the end of the 14th century. Four gates at the corners of the piazza allowed the whole square to be sealed off and defended in the event of an attack. The Duomo, built on the site of an Etruscan temple, incorporates Romanesque, Gothic and Renaissance features. Upstairs, the entire west wall is painted with a 17th-century copy of Michelangelo's *Last Judgement* in the Sistine Chapel.

173

## Coat of arms

*Todi's coat of arms shows an eagle with a napkin in its talons. A legend says that the town was founded on the spot where the eagle let the napkin drop, after seizing it from an Etruscan banqueting table.*

# Urbino

*Tourist information: Piazza Duca Federico 35. Tel: 0722 2788/2613;
www.comune.urbino.ps.it. Open: Mon–Sat 0900–1800 in summer;
closed pm in winter.*

Like the 'Chiantishire' of Tuscany and Umbria, the lesser
known Marche (The Marches), are also studded with a
Milky Way of medieval hill towns, of which Urbino is the
shining star. In Urbino, all streets lead to a breathtaking
view, the pace is gentle, and the atmosphere relaxed and
uncontrived. It remains one of Le Marche's best-kept secrets.

Urbino's rose-coloured buildings, standing high amid the slopes
of the Apennines, gleam in the golden light, little changed
since the 15th century, when the town was the prestigious
model for courtly life in Europe. The magnificent **Palazzo
Ducale** ( *Piazza Duca Federico 35; tel: 0722 2613/2788; open:
Sun 0900–2100, Tue–Sat 0900–1900 and Mon am* ), an
elegant blend of serene, harmonious architecture, was
commissioned by wise leader Duke Federico da Montefeltro
in 1444. It has been called Italy's most beautiful Renaissance
palace. On the first floor is the Marches' National Gallery,
**Galleria Nazionale delle Marche**, home to three of Italy's
great masterpieces, Raphael's *La Muta* and Piero della
Francesca's *Madonna di Senigallia* and his enigmatic,
profoundly disturbing *Flagellation of Christ*.

" *Where Castiglione's protagonist, Count
Ludovico de Canossa, defines for the
court of Urbino the virtue of* sprezzatura
[nonchalance], *which became an
influential concept throughout Europe:
'I have discovered a universal rule …
namely, to steer away from affectation
at all costs, as if it were a rough and
dangerous reef … and to practise in all
things a certain nonchalance which
conceals all artistry and makes whatever
one says or does seem  uncontrived and
effortless'.* "

**Baldassare Castiglione, *The Book
of the Courtier* (1528)**

Federico's court painter was
Raphael's father, Giovanni
Santi. The house where
Raphael was born, in 1483,
the **Casa Natale di Raffaello**
( *Via Raffaello 57; open: Mon–
Sat 0900–1300 and 1500–
1900, Sun 1000–1300; £* ),
lies just down the road from
the palace. One of his earliest
works, *The Madonna and
Child*, is on display and
in the courtyard outside
is the stone on which
father and son ground
their artists' pigments.

# Volterra

*Tourist information: Via Giusto Turraza 2. Tel/fax: 0588 87257.*
*Open: Mon–Sat 1000–1300 and 1400–1800; Sun 1000–1300.*

Volterra is isolated and forbidding but not without charm. Etruscan walls and tombs slide into the abyss at one edge of town while the exquisite medieval town hall remains open for business in the centre. Volterra's role as one of the major Etruscan *lucumoni*, or city states, has been proven by many archaeological finds, and an impressive Roman theatre was unearthed in 1951.

The **Museo Etrusco Guarnacci** (*Via Don Minzoni 11; open: daily 0900–1900 mid-Mar–mid-Oct, 0900–1400 mid-Oct–mid-Mar; £*) houses one of the most important Etruscan collections in Italy, with 600 funerary urns of carved sandstone, alabaster and terracotta, dating as far back as the Hellenistic era. The top floor has many of the best pieces, as well as a view of the rooftops of Volterra.

In the Middle Ages, Volterra was a major stop on the pilgrimage route from Compostela to Jerusalem. The attendant prosperity created many superb artistic and architectural treasures. The **Palazzo dei Priori** (1208) is the oldest municipal palace still in use in Tuscany. The lower part of the well-preserved façade is decorated with enamelled, marble and stone coats of arms. The **Museo Civico e Pinacoteca** (*Via dei Sarti 3; open: daily 0900–1900 mid-Mar–Oct, in winter 0900–1400; £*) exhibits notable works by Sienese painters and Florentine artists, including Ghirlandaio. The **Duomo** is a Romanesque-Pisan style basilica with unsubtle Renaissance additions such as a gaudy coffered ceiling and *trompe-l'oeil* marble pillars.

175

# Eating and drinking

## Arezzo

### Buca di San Francesco
*Piazza San Francesco 1, Arezzo. Tel:
0575 23271. ££.* One of Arezzo's best.
The dining room is a sumptuously
decorated cellar of a medieval palace.

### La Torre di Gnicche
*Piaggia San Martino 8, Arezzo. Tel:
0575 352035. Closed Wed, and for
two weeks in Jan, one in Aug. £.* In a
13th-century palace with a view of
Piazza Vasari. Excellent soup, pasta
and traditional dishes such as *grifi
all'aretina* served with local wine.

## Assisi

### La Piazzetta dell'Erba Via
*San Gabriele dell'Addolorata 15b, Assisi.
Closed Mon and two weeks in Jan. £.*
Small *trattoria* where the choices are
few but all good. Start with Umbrian
soup or a sandwich made with a
traditional bread called *torta al testo*.

## Lucca

### Da Giulio in Pelleria
*Piazza S. Donato, Lucca. Tel: 0583
55948. Closed Sun and Mon. ££.* A
crowded *trattoria* serving home-made
pasta and local standards such as
*bollito misto* ('stewed beef') with herb
sauce, chicken roasted in a brick oven,
and the non-PC horsemeat tartar.

### Osteria Baralla
*Via Anfiteatro 5–9, Lucca. Closed Sun.
£.* An atmospheric bar/inn, where you
can eat anything from *bruschetta*
(toasted bread with liver pâté or
tomatoes) to a full traditional meal.

## Orvieto

### Bar-Pasticceria Montanucci
*Corso Cavour 21–23, Orvieto. ££.*
The oldest café in the city and the
perfect place for some home-made
*baci* – chocolate 'kisses'. You are
not supposed to lunch on kisses,
so have a *panino* ('sandwich') first.

## Perugia

### Aladino
*Via della Prome 11, Perugia. Tel: 075
5720938. ££.* Regional Umbrian
cuisine with creative variations and
the occasional seafood dish. There are
two *degustazione* menus accompanied
by local wines.

### Cesarino
*Piazza IV Novembre 5, Perugia. Tel:
075 5728974. Closed Wed. £.* Excellent
*trattoria*-pizzeria in a 13th-century
palace, serving delicious pizza and home-
made *tagliatelle*. Often very crowded.

## Pisa

### Osteria dei Cavalieri
*Via San Frediano 16, Pisa. Tel: 050
580858. Closed Sat lunch, and Sun
and in Aug. ££.* Extremely popular
for simple, creative food, with a short
menu and wine by the glass.

### Trattoria La Mescita
*Via Cavalca 2 at the corner of Piazza
delle Vettovoglie, Pisa. Tel: 050 544294.
Closed Mon. £.* Near the market, family
restaurant serving savoury dishes such
as *spaghettoni con lardo di Colonnata*
(thick spaghetti with herbed lard) and
*baccalà bollito* ('stewed cod').

# Siena

Typical Sienese dishes are *ribollita* (a 'twice-cooked' vegetable and bread soup), minestrone, grilled meats, tripe and fried zucchini flowers. The classic dessert is *cantucci* ('almond biscuits') accompanied by Vin Santo dessert wine. *Panforte* is a dense, chewy cake of candied fruit, almonds, honey, and orange peel. *Ricciarelli* are biscuits made of almonds, egg white, sugar and vanilla.

### La Taverna del Capitano
*Via del Capitano 8, Siena. Tel: 0577 288094. ££.* Traditional restaurant near the cathedral serving dishes such as *panzanella di farro* (dried spelt bread, herbs and vegetables) *pappardelle* ('broad noodles') with meat sauce, and an outstanding veal cutlet.

# Spoleto

### Pecchiarda
*Vicolo San Giovanni 1, Spoleto. Closed Thu except in summer. £.* Spoleto's best culinary bargain. The gnocchi filled with ricotta are perfect, and so is the house speciality, *pollo alla Pecchiarda*, a chicken de-boned and stuffed with ground meat and artichokes. The owner serves his own wine.

# Urbino

### Vecchia Urbino
*Via dei Vasari 3/5, Urbino. Tel: 0722 44 47. Closed Tue. ££–£££.* Set in the historic centre, this attractive restaurant specialises in the 'fruits of the woods' – exotic truffles and wild mushrooms, in season.

# Shopping

### Casa del Parmigiano
*Via Sant'Ercolano 36, Perugia.* Cheese and salami from all over Umbria. *Pecorino di botte* (sheeps' cheese) is packed in a bottle in such a way that it continues to age; the rare *il roccaccio* is a cheese made near Todi, aged for 10 to 18 months.

### Drogheria Manganelli
*Via di Citta 71, Siena. Tel: 0577 280002.* Gourmet delicatessen with regional specialities at elevated prices – olive oil, honey, wine, truffles, marmalade, vinegar.

### Medio Evo
*Zona Ind le Ponte d'Assi, 06024 Gubbio. Tel/fax: 075 9272596; e-mail: medioevo@medioevo.com.* 'Middle Ages' specialises in the reproduction of ancient weapons, from crossbows, pikes or mallets to iron chastity belts for both sexes. The delivery of a suit of armour or full-size guillotine takes two months.

### La Panetteria Ceccarini
*Piazza Matteoti 16, Perugia.* The best baker in Perugia – 30 kinds of bread, festive and seasonal sweets and pastries such as *torciglioni* and *torte al formaggio* e *biscotti*.

# Festivals

*The calendar of Tuscany and Umbria is full of festivals. Most are purely local events that celebrate a region's food (mushrooms, pecorino, chestnuts, truffles, wild boar, grilled thrush); they offer the perfect chance to eat, drink and make merry with Tuscans and Umbrians.*

The more famous 'medieval' pageants are a mysterious mix of tourist hype and authentic local tradition. One of the most hyped (and insanely crowded) of all festivals is the *Palio di Contrade* in **Siena**, which nevertheless has deep roots in the city's history and psyche. Some of the seasonal festivals in the region, though adapted to Christianity, have their origins in pagan ritual. One event that stands out in this respect is the *Corsa dei Ceri* in **Gubbio**. Music, theatre and art festivals fall into a third category. The one with the most cachet is the *Festival of Two Worlds* in **Spoleto** but there are many others.

The local tourist office is always a good source of information about festivals. Here is a brief overview:

### APRIL/MAY
*Maggio Musicale* in Florence (Apr–June). Musical performances all over the city, in various venues.
*Calcio Storico* in Florence. Anything-goes football in medieval costume, with dozens on each side (also in June).
*Coloriamo i cieli* ('Let's paint the skies') in Castiglione del Lago. Kite festival (even-numbered years) on the banks of Lake Trasimeno (second Sun in May).
*Calendimaggio* in Assisi. Three-day celebration in commemoration of St Francis with singing, theatre performances, dance, processions, archery, banner-waving, not to mention knights and maidens in full regalia (early May).

*Corsa dei Ceri* ('Candle Race') in Gubbio. Young runners carry three gigantic wooden 'candles', each weighing about 50kg (110lb) and mounted with statues of saints, up to the Basilica di Sant'Ubaldo, on top of Monte Ingino.

## JUNE
*Festival dei Due Mondi* in Spoleto. International prose, theatre, dance and musical performances by leading artists from Europe and the Americas – one of the high points of the Italian social and artistic calendar. Book well in advance for tickets, and for a hotel room in the city (June and July).
*Palio della Balestra* in Gubbio. Contests with medieval bows and arrows between Gubbio and Sansepolcro.
*Gioco del Ponte* in Pisa.
*Rockin' Umbria* in Perugia. This rock festival has taken place each year since 1986 not just in Perugia, but also in Umbèrtide and Città di Castello. No big rock stars, but plenty of up-and-coming performers (last ten days in June–first ten days in July).

## JULY
*Palio di Contrade* in Siena. Traditional horse races around the Piazza del Campo (also in August).
*Umbria Jazz* in Perugia and other Umbrian cities. One of the most important jazz festivals in Europe (last two weeks in July–first week in Aug).

## AUGUST
*Bravio delle Botti* in Montepulciano.
*Giostra del Saracino* in Arezzo. Medieval jousting tournaments, with costumed locals attacking a figure of a Saracen (also in September).
*Palio di Contrade* in Siena.

## SEPTEMBER
*Todi Festival* in Todi. A wide variety of works in the fields of music, ballet and film produced by young, up-and-coming artists hailing from Italy and abroad.
*Sagra Musicale Umbra* in Perugia. A highly regarded event in the European music world at which 20th-century religious music is performed.

## NOVEMBER
*Rassegna Antiquaria* in Perugia. An exhibition of antiques.

## DECEMBER
*Celebrazioni di Santo Natale* in Assisi. Christmas concerts held in many churches and the Nativity scene portrayed by live animals and actors.

## JANUARY/FEBRUARY/MARCH
*Holy Week* in Assisi.
*Carnevale* in Viareggio. A growing event, with hundreds of costumed participants, its own 'village' of tents and big-tops, and its own website.

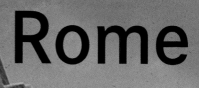

# Rome

Rome has been variously called 'Mother of Civilisation', Roma dea ('Goddess Rome'), Caput Mundi ('Head of the World') and the 'Eternal City'. As everyone knows, this unique city wasn't built in a day – indeed, it has over 2 750 years of history – and it now has enough monuments to last the average sightseer a lifetime. Everyone will find their own Dolce Vita here, whether it's in the cool and tranquillity of an ancient church, or in the lively atmosphere of a sun-baked piazza.

# BEST OF
## Rome

*Getting there/getting around: city **buses** and **trams**, run by **ATAC** (based at Piazza dei Cinquecento; freephone 167 431784), are orange. Buy the Roma Metro-Bus map, and check numbers and destinations at individual bus stops (fermate). The two-line **Metro system** is safe and easy to master. **Tickets** are single (biglietto a tempo), valid for one trip of up to 75 minutes, or valid for one day (biglietto giornaliero) or seven days (carta settimanale). Buy a ticket or pass before boarding (from ATAC counters, tobacconists, news-stands or automatic machines in stations), then validate it in the right machine before travelling. Licensed taxis are white or yellow, available from taxi ranks around the city.*

## ① Musei Capitolini

The Capitoline Museums, with their outstanding collection of Greek and Roman sculptures, provide an excellent overview of ancient art and history for first-time visitors to the city. **Pages 184–5**

## ② Colosseum

Once inside this 'must-see' monument that has so remarkably endured the test of time, it is easy to imagine the ecstatic crowds cheering the wild animals and the hapless gladiators fighting to the bitter, bloody end.
**Page 186**

## ③ Foro Romano

Walk the streets where Caesar once trod, the epicentre of an empire which embraced most of the known world, and the very heart of ancient Rome.
**Pages 189–91**

## ④ Pantheon

The Pantheon remains long in one's memory. Of all the city sights, its extraordinary near-perfect condition helps to bridge the two millennia in a way the many ruined buildings of ancient Rome cannot. **Page 193**

## ⑤ Piazza Navona

More of a giant stage set of famous fountains and terracotta façades than a square, this is where Rome's heart beats the loudest, where the theatre of daily Roman life is re-enacted daily in one of Italy's greatest piazzas. **Page 196**

## ⑥ The Spanish Steps

Sit awhile on the Scalinata di Trinità dei Monti (the 'Spanish Steps') at the heart of Rome's liveliest shopping district and watch the world go by. And on a blisteringly hot summer day, join tired shoppers cooling their feet in the well-placed fountain at the base!
**Pages 194–5**

## ⑦ Trevi Fountain

Discovering the Trevi Fountain for the first time is one of Rome's most pleasant surprises – a monumental extravaganza of sea gods, horses and rock pools, squeezed into a tiny piazza amidst a maze of twisting lanes and alleyways. Before you leave, toss in a coin – to ensure your return one day.
**Page 197**

## ⑧ Vatican City – San Pietro in Vaticano

Not only is St Peter's the largest church in Christendom and one of the world's most visited sights, but at sunset its massive dome is one of the most memorable silhouettes of the Roman skyline. **Page 199**

## ⑨ Vatican City – Museums and the Sistine Chapel

The Vatican Museums count among the finest in the world, 7km (4 miles) of galleries and passageways culminating in Michelangelo's remarkably frescoed Sistine Chapel – probably the greatest work of art of all time. **Pages 200–3**

183

## Tourist information

The main **EPT** (Ente Provinciale per il Turismo di Roma) is at *Via Parigi 5; tel: 06 48899253; open: Mon–Sat 0815–1915*. Other offices are at **Fiumicino** airport (*tel: 06 65956074*) and Stazione **Termini** in front of platform 3 (*tel: 06 4871270*). **Enjoy Rome** is a private agency offering information and accommodation at Via Varese 39 (*tel: 06 4451843*). A handful of **Info-tourism kiosks** (*open: daily 0900–1800*) are dotted around the city near large tourist attractions.

# Musei Capitolini (Capitoline Museums)

*The Capitoline Museums contain some of the finest and rarest treasures of ancient Rome, together with some major 16th- and 17th-century European paintings. These gorgeous collections are displayed inside two palazzi flanking Piazza del Campidoglio, designed by Michelangelo and lavishly decorated with gilt and coffered ceilings and frescoed walls.*

On the north side, **Palazzo Nuovo** is devoted mainly to sculpture. Most of the finest pieces are Roman copies of Greek masterpieces, showing the fondness for Hellenistic art in ancient Rome – the poignant statue of the *Dying Gaul*, the athletic *Discobolus,* portraying the twisted torso of a Greek discus thrower, a red porphyry marble *Drunken Faun* taken from Hadrian's Villa at Tivoli, and the voluptuous *Capitoline Venus*, walled up for centuries to avoid destruction by early Christians.

## Founding of Rome

*According to legend, Romulus and Remus were the founders of Rome. They were thrown into the Tiber by their uncle Amulus, the evil king of Alba, who had already ousted their father from the throne and saw them as potential claimants to his crown. However, they were washed ashore and suckled by a she-wolf until a kindly shepherd took them home. Subsequently, they founded a city on the site where they had been saved and called it 'Roma'.*

For those keen to put faces to the city's early rulers, or to the poets and thinkers of ancient Greece, the 'Hall of the Emperors' and the 'Hall of the Philosophers' contain characterful collections of busts. Look out also for the *Infant Hercules* wrestling with a snake, believed to be a portrait of Caracalla – the poor thing was already ugly at the age of five; the marble *Portrait of a Flavian Lady*, with her mass of elaborate and fanciful curls, a hairstyle that was all the rage among female aristocracy in the 1st year AD; and the bronze equestrian statue of a debonair Marcus Aurelius, the most recent addition to the palace.

On the opposite side of the square, the **Palazzo dei Conservatori** houses the rest of the Capitoline Museum. The courtyard is dominated by an amusing giant head, foot and pointing hand of the emperor Constantine – the remains of a colossal 10m- (33ft-) high seated statue from the forum (*see pages 189–91*).

Inside, on the second floor, is a treasure trove of famous paintings, including important canvases by Veronese, Tintoretto, Rubens, Titian, Caravaggio and others, while noteworthy sculptures on the ground floor include *Spinario*, a beautifully poised bronze of a boy removing a thorn from his foot, and *Esquiline Venus*, dating from the 1st century BC. The most celebrated piece is undoubtedly the *Capitoline She-Wolf*, an Etruscan bronze from the 5th century BC, which has become the symbol of Rome. The infants she is suckling were Renaissance additions, to illustrate one of the city's best-known legends – the story of Romulus and Remus.

*Piazza del Campidoglio. Tel: 06 67102071. Open: Tue–Sat 0900–1900; Sun 0900–1330. Closed Mon. £££; free on the last Sun of the month. (One ticket gains entrance to both palazzi.)*

# Colosseum

*Piazza del Colosseo. Tel: 06 7004261.*
*Open: daily 0900–dusk. £££.*

The Colosseum has to be seen to be believed. This four-tiered elliptical arena, built by the emperor Vespasian in AD 72, is the world's most famous amphitheatre. The most impressive of all the buildings of ancient Rome, it is 57m (187ft) high, with 80 arched entrances allowing easy access for over 55,000 spectators. The emperor Titus opened it in AD 80 with one hundred days of games in which 9 000 animals – including a rhinoceros – were killed.

In its heyday, the entire building was encrusted with marble and ornamented by columns of Egyptian granite, fountains spurting perfumed water and stairways painted purple and gold. On hot days, a giant **sailcloth** awning sheltered spectators from the elements. The marble front-row seats were reserved for emperors, senators and civil servants, the second concrete tier was for the bourgeoisie, the third was for commoners. Women were confined to the uppermost reaches, except Vestal Virgins, who sat near the emperor.

The bloodthirsty **games** were part of daily life in Rome. From the higher tiers, you can still see the underground passages, where wild animals were kept in cages before being winched to arena level to devour condemned criminals. If a cowardly gladiator ever tried to retreat underground, he was 'encouraged' back to the arena with whips and red-hot irons.

> " *I really did not gain a suggestion of the astonishing size of [the Colosseum] until I entered through one of the many arches … It was impossible not to be impressed by the thought of the emperors sitting on their especial balcony; the thousands upon thousands of Romans intent upon some gladiatorial feat.* "
>
> **Theodore Dreiser, *A Traveller at Forty* (1914)**

With the fall of the Roman empire, the Colosseum fell into disuse. During the Renaissance, the ruins were stripped of their precious materials, which reappeared in palaces and churches. In 1744, Pope Benedict XIV consecrated the arena in memory of the Christian martyrs who died there.

# Churches

## Santa Maria Maggiore

*Piazza di Santa Maria Maggiore. Tel: 06 483195. Open: daily 0700–1900. £.*

The largest of Rome's 80 churches dedicated to the Virgin, and arguably the most beautiful, Santa Maria Maggiore is especially famed for its blend of architectural styles – from 5th-century to baroque, via medieval and Renaissance – its shimmering mosaics and its sumptuous papal chapels, extravagant even by baroque standards.

Pope Liberius planned the **original basilica**, following a dream in which the Virgin instructed him to build a church on the spot where snow would fall the next morning, 5 August, AD 352. This miracle is commemorated annually at the feast of the *Madonna della Neve* (**Our Lady of the Snow**), when thousands of white petals are released from the roof of the church. Santa Maria Maggiore is also the only church where Mass has been celebrated every day since the 5th century.

The most fabulous treasures of the church's interior are its gleaming mosaics: the 36 scenes from the Old Testament in the nave date from the 5th century. There are gold-tinged Byzantine-style scenes in the altar's triumphal arch, but most spectacular of all are the 13th-century mosaics in the apse – considered by many to be the height of Rome's mosaic tradition.

The basilica most prizes its relic of five pieces of wood bound with iron, said to be pieces of Christ's crib from Bethlehem, putting it on view only on the 25th of every month.

## Bohemian Rome

*Don't miss the atmospheric neighbourhood of Trastevere, long known as Rome's 'bohemian' district. By day, children kick footballs around church squares, locals sit gossiping in doorways and laundry hangs over the medieval flower-splashed façades of ochre-coloured houses. Its patchwork of tiny streets, its tumbledown houses and its sun-bleached piazzette, with their galleries and craft shops, might appear sleepy but, by night, this is where Rome's heart beats the loudest, as Romans come flocking to Trastevere's popular pizzerias and trendy bars.*

# Santa Maria in Trastevere

*Piazza Santa Maria in Trastevere. Open: 0700–1300 and 1530–1900. £.*

Of the many historic churches in the ancient – and now fashionable – district of Trastevere ('Across the Tiber'), Santa Maria is the greatest treasure. Its shimmering golden mosaics, adorning both the inside and the outside, count among Rome's finest.

This beautiful basilica was the first to be dedicated to the Virgin. It was founded in AD 222 on the site of a miraculous fountain of oil which, according to legend, sprang from nowhere the day Christ was born.

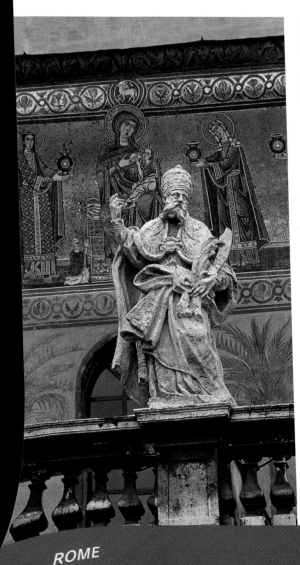

Its present appearance dates from the 12th century, the work of *Trasteverino* Pope Innocent II; the arched portico with its papal statues was added 500 years later. The choir contains six mosaics – bold, innovative works by Cavallini depicting episodes from the *Life of St Mary*. Cavallini's delicate 12th-century mosaic on the façade shows Mary feeding baby Jesus, flanked by ten maidens with lamps. This golden mosaic provides a stunning backdrop for **Piazza Santa Maria in Trastevere**, a popular meeting-place both day and night, and an ideal spot to while away the hours.

ROME

# Forums

## *Foro Romano* (Roman forum)

*Via dei Fori Imperiali (to the north) and Via San Gregorio (to the east). Tel: 06 6780782. Open: Mon–Sat 0900–1800 (1500 in winter); Sun 0900–1300. Closed 1 Jan, 1 May, 25 Dec. £. Portable sound-guides (££) available at the Via dei Fori Imperiali entrance (bring ID as a deposit).*

The expression 'All roads lead to Rome' dates back to ancient times, when all roads led to the forum – a magnificent cluster of temples, arches, memorials and halls of dazzling white marble with gleaming golden roofs that formed the heart of the ancient city. This is where Republican Rome began; where Cicero stirred the masses with his rousing orations; where Mark Antony came 'to bury Caesar, not to praise him'; where the sacred fire of the Eternal City was maintained; and where victorious emperors showed off their spoils from the battles that made Rome *caput mundi*, capital of the world.

> " *'Veni, vidi, vinci.' ('I came, I saw, I conquered.')* "
>
> **Julius Caesar, 1st century BC**

The forum was the centre of political, commercial and judicial life, as well as a community centre where people strolled under the porticoes and attended sports events. Over the centuries it was embellished with splendid temples and basilicas built by successive emperors, each seeking to immortalise themselves in stone. Since the fall of Rome, the forum has survived fire and earthquakes, barbarian invasions, grazing cows and Renaissance marble diggers. Serious excavation of the site began in 1898, and continues today.

Enough remains of the forum to take you right back to ancient Rome. Enter the complex on Via dei Fori Imperiali and start in the right-hand corner near the main road. The **Curia (Senate House)** was the very first assembly hall of the Roman elders, begun by Caesar in 44 BC. This was the political heart of the Republic, where white-toga-ed senators conducted meetings behind *open* doors – allowing the public to be kept informed. The current building (a replica of Diocletian's version, with the original red and green marble floor) dates from 1937.

# Forums continued

In front of the Curia, the **Lapis Niger (Black Stone)** is one of the most sacred objects of the forum, supposedly marking the tomb of Romulus. Behind stands the grandiose **Arch of Septimus Severus**. Beside the arch, a piece of stone, once part of a 3rd-century circular temple called the *Umbilicus Urbis*, marked the symbolic centre of Rome. Nearby stood the **Milarium Aureum (Golden Milestone)**, where a marble column recorded in gilded bronze letters the distances to all the major cities of the new empire.

To the left lie the semi-circular steps of the **Rostra** public platform, named after the bronze prows ( *rostra* ) of defeated enemy ships that once adorned it. In the surrounding area, the three plants considered essential for Mediterranean prosperity – vines, olives and figs – have been planted. The eight tall columns beyond the Rostra once formed the entrance to the **Temple of Saturn**. Built in 497 BC, it was the scene every December of the merry pagan *Saturnalia* festivities, when masters and slaves were briefly equal. The temple marks the start of the *Via Sacra* **(Sacred Way)**, along which victorious generals rode in triumphal procession to the Capitoline Hill to give thanks to Jupiter.

The next monument on the right is the **Temple of Castor and Pollux**, with three Corinthian columns topped with a frieze from the time of Augustus. It was dedicated to the two mysterious horsemen who led the Romans to victory over the Etruscans in 499 BC. Little is left of the **Temple of Caesar**, the building that began the cult of Emperor worship. Following his death, in 44 BC, Caesar's body was cremated here. The people kept his funeral pyre burning for days, buried his ashes and built a temple on the site.

The **Temple of Antoninus and Faustina**, built in AD 2, really indicates the monumental size of Rome's ancient temples. The original six columns and porch, decorated with a beautiful frieze, were saved from destruction by the temple's re-consecration as the Renaissance **church of San Lorenzo in Miranda**. Opposite, the circular, white-marble **Temple of Vesta** contained the sacred fire that symbolised Rome's eternity. It was kept alight by Vestal Virgins, the only female priesthood in Rome, who lived in the neighbouring **Atrium Vestae (House of the Vestal Virgins)**.

Continuing along the *Via Sacra*, you will pass the tiny round **Temple of Romulus**, incorporated into the 6th-century Franciscan church of SS Cosmas and Damian, known for its early mosaics and frescos. Beyond it lie the scattered remains of the **Basilica of Constantine and Maxentius**, one of the last great constructions of Imperial Rome.

Next door, the 10th-century church of **Santa Francesca Romana** incorporates part of the **Temple of Venus and Roma**. Once the largest temple in Rome, it was partly bulldozed by Mussolini to make way for his grand military boulevard. Marking the eastern end of the forum, the **Arch of Titus** is the oldest triumphal arch in Rome, with beautifully preserved reliefs.

## *Fori Imperiali* (Imperial forums)

*Via dei Fori Imperiali*

The Imperial forums were built as an extension to the Roman forum, as Rome's empire grew, and named after five rulers of the day: Augustus, Caesar, Vespasian, Nerva and Trajan. Some of the remains lie unexcavated beneath Via dei Fori Imperiali, paved over by Mussolini.

**Trajan's Forum** covers an area greater than four football pitches. The pristine, white-marble **Trajan's Column**, 40m (131ft) high, was once topped with a bronze statue of Trajan, since replaced by one of St Peter. Some 26,000 carved figures spiral up the column, chronicling Trajan's military victories. The figures would originally have been painted in bright colours.

Nearby, a six-storey, semicircular shopping mall – the **Mercati di Traiano (Trajan's Markets)** – once boasted over 150 shops, selling fruit and flowers on the ground floor, oil and wine on the next, pepper, spices and other exotic goods on the third and fourth floors, with offices on the fifth and fishponds on the sixth *(entrance on Via IV Novembre 94; tel: 06 6790048; open: Tue–Sat 0900–1800, Sun 0900–1300, closed Mon; ££).*

# Palatine

*Via dei Fori Imperiali (on the north) and Via San Gregorio (on the east). Tel:*
*06 6780782. Open: Mon–Sat 0900–1800 (1500 in winter); Sun 0900–1300.*
*Closed 1 Jan, 1 May, 25 Dec. £££.*

One of Rome's seven hills, the Palatine is the
city's legendary birthplace. With its romantic
garden, it's a peaceful, shady retreat away
from the noisy, frenetic city centre. The first
of Rome's seven hills to be inhabited, this is
where Romulus allegedly founded the city;
you can still see traces of huts from as early
as 800 BC.

For centuries, *Palatino* was a highly sought after address.
The emperor Augustus had a series of fine houses built on
the hill, for himself and his wife Livia. The small rooms of
the **Casa di Livia (Livia's House)** still contain remnants
of mosaic floors, wall paintings and engraved lead piping.

All the emperors after Augustus added their own new
palaces. The entire Palatine hill was soon covered with
grand residences, and the words 'palatial' and 'palace' were
coined. The last emperor to build on the Palatine, Septimius
Severus positioned his seven-storey **Domus Severiana**
on the south-east tip of the hill. Today, only the massive
arcaded foundations remain, overlooking the **Circus
Maximus**, the biggest horse-and-chariot racecourse
in the Roman empire.

Later, two wealthy Renaissance families, the Barbarini and
the Farnese, sealed the hill's illustrious reputation by building
summer houses here. The Farnese also filled in the Domus
Tiberiana and planted the **Orti Farnesiani (Farnese
Gardens)**, the world's first botanical garden. From its
terraces, the views are unsurpassed.

> **❝** *Cypress and ivy, weed and wallflower grown*
> *Matted and mass'd together, hillocks heap'd*
> *On what were chambers, arch crush'd, column strown*
> *In fragments, choked up vaults, and frescos steep'd*
> *In subterranean damps …* **❞**

**Lord Byron (1788–1824)**

# Pantheon

*Piazza della Rotonda. Open: Mon–Sat 0900–1830 (1600 in winter); Sun 0900–1300. £.*

Created in 17 BC, the Pantheon is indisputably the best-preserved major monument of Imperial Rome and a marvel of ancient architecture. If possible, visit it during a storm, when the rain splashes straight on to the colourful original marble flooring!

The Pantheon is one of the great symbols of Rome. Even in imperial times, when this district was packed with grand gardens, the Circus of Domitian, the Minerva temple and other magnificent public buildings, the Pantheon was the centrepiece. Founded by Augustus's general Marcus Agrippa in AD 17 as a 'temple of all the gods', it received its present-day appearance a hundred years later, under Hadrian. The building's astonishing state of preservation is due to its conversion to a Christian church in 608.

One of the most striking features of the Pantheon is the way it fuses the Greek *pronaos* (porch) of a temple with the Roman domed *rotunda*. The key to its harmony and striking simplicity is its dimensions. Inside, you discover that the diameter of the interior dome is exactly equal to the height of the building. It is a remarkable feat of Roman engineering – even the dome of St Peter's is smaller. The 6m- (20ft-) thick walls were constructed of concrete, tufa and pumice over a temporary wooden framework. The only source of light is a circular hole (or *oculus*) in the roof.

The terrace of one of the cafés in the fountain-splashed Piazza della Rotunda is the perfect place from which to marvel at this great treasure of Roman antiquity.

" *This open and secret temple [the Pantheon] was conceived as a sundial. The hours were to circle the centre of its carefully polished pavement, where the disk of the day was supposed to rest like a golden buckler; there the rain would make a limpid pool from which prayer could transpire like smoke toward the void where we place the gods.* "

**Marguerite Yourcenar, *Memoirs of Hadrian***

# Piazza di Spagna

*This colourful and spacious 'Spanish Square' of elegant russet, ochre, salmon- and apricot-coloured palazzi takes its name from the stolid Palazzo di Spagna in the south-west corner, built in the 17th century as the Spanish Embassy to the Holy See. It has long been one of Rome's most famous and popular spots, and is best known for its so-called 'Spanish Steps'.*

> *I have seen the ruins of Rome, the Vatican, St Peter's, and all the miracles of ancient and modern art contained in that majestic city. The impression of it exceeds anything I have ever experienced in my travels.*
>
> **Letter from Percy Bysshe Shelley to Thomas Love Peacock, December 1818**

In the 18th century, Piazza di Spagna became the favourite quarter of Rome for illustrious artists and Grand Tourists from all over Europe. Many made it their home, including Balzac, Goethe, Wagner, Liszt, Rubens, Elizabeth Browning, Berlioz, Byron, Tennyson and Shelley, and so many English milords that locals nicknamed the district *il ghetto de l'inglese* ('the English Ghetto'). Its most famous resident was John Keats, who died in the pink house at the foot of the Spanish Steps in February 1821, aged only 25. Since 1909 the Casa di Keats has been open to the public as a memorial to this great English Romantic poet and his compatriots Percy Bysshe Shelley and Lord Byron (*Piazza di Spagna 26; www.demon.co.uk/heritage/Keats.House.Rome; open: Mon–Fri 0900–1300 and 1500–1800 Apr–Sept, 1430–1730 Oct–Mar, also Sat 1100–1400 and 1500–1800 in summer; ££*).

## The Spanish Steps

The Scalinata di Trinità dei Monti, named after the church that perches at its summit, is the crowning glory of the piazza. An elegantly cascading rococo stairway of golden stone, it was financed by the French and designed by an Italian, but is still commonly known as the 'Spanish Steps'!

A popular meeting point for lovers and shoppers, and favourite hangout for youths, the 137 steps are crowded day and night, as people while away the hours chatting and watching the rest of Rome rush by at their feet.

At the foot of the steps, there is a charming fountain in the shape of a half-sunken barge ( *La Barcaccia*, 1629), wittily designed by Bernini's father, Pietro, to solve the problem of the low water level of the ancient aqueduct, *Acqua Vergine*, which originally fed the Pantheon and many of the fountains and baths of ancient Rome. It is said that his inspiration for the fountain was a massive flooding of the Tiber on Christmas Day in 1598, which stranded a similar barge on top of Pincio hill.

At the summit of the Spanish Steps, the twin-towered Trinità dei Monti ( *open: daily 1000–1230 and 1600–1800; £* ) is Rome's most photographed church. Inside, the colourful frescos of the transept by Raphael's star pupil Giulio Romano and the two fine paintings by Michelangelo's prodigy, Daniele da Volterra ( *Descent from the Cross* and *The Assumption* ), are worth a glimpse, but the main reason to visit the church is to admire the stupendous views over the rooftops of Rome from the entrance.

# Piazza Navona

*For centuries, the atmospheric pedestrian square of the Piazza Navona has been one of the main hubs of Roman social life. It occupies the site of an ancient sports stadium, the Circus of Domitian of AD 86, hence its unusually long, thin shape. Hidden beneath the foundations is seating for 30,000 spectators, and most streets leading into the piazza were once entrances into the stadium.*

For many hundreds of years following Rome's rebirth in the 15th century the piazza served as an important market-place. It also provided the backdrop for processions and sporting spectacles, including mock naval battles. It could be flooded by blocking the fountains' drains and, as recently as the 19th century, it was used in the coldest winters for skating.

In the 17th century, Piazza Navona was transformed into the glorious baroque square seen today, when Pamphili Pope Innocent X decided to embellish it in honour of his family. He commissioned the monumental **Fontana dei Quattro Fiumi** in the centre and the restoration of the two 16th-century fountains to the north and south, the **Fontana del Moro** and **Fontana del Nettuno**. Finally, he built the **Palazzo Pamphili** in the south-west corner of the square, decorating it in 1650 with a vast fresco of the Aeneid.

Today, life in the piazza revolves around its pricey open-air cafés. The ochre buildings provide the perfect backdrop for people-watching from early morning through to the small hours.

## Tip

*Piazza Navona is at its most colourful at the Christmas Befana market, named after the witch who gives children presents or coal depending on their behaviour. The square comes alive with sparkling stalls of toys, tinsel, cribs and even "coal" sweets. A real treat … especially for children!*

*Tourist information booth: Piazza delle Cinque Lune, just north of Piazza Navona. Tel: 06 68809240. Open: daily 0900–1800.*

# Fontana de Trevi (Trevi Fountain)

*Piazza di Trevi.*

Toss a coin over your shoulder into Rome's largest and most spectacular fountain to ensure your return to the Eternal City. Bring your camera too, as the confection of tritons, seahorses, rock pools and waves, wedged into a pocket-sized *piazzetta*, makes the Trevi Fountain irresistible.

The fountain is a **baroque extravaganza** of ancient sea gods and gushing water out of all proportion to the tiny piazza, at the meeting point of *tre vie* ('three streets'). It marks the site of one of Rome's earliest fountains, and was constructed in 1732–62, following the ancient Roman custom of decorating the spot where water emerged with a great fountain. The Trevi water is reputedly Rome's sweetest.

The **fountain** was designed by Nicola Salvi, using a wall of Palazzo Poli as a backdrop. Entire houses were torn down to make room for the monumental construction, which followed the popular **marine mythology** of the age: a massive figure of Neptune riding a sea-shell drawn by conch-blowing tritons and seahorses splashing their way out of the fountain. Two figures representing Health and Abundance look on from the side niches and the carved panels above depict the discovery of the *Acqua Vergine* in 19 BC, apparently revealed to Roman soldiers by a virgin.

Later architects added rows of seats from which to admire Rome's most sensational fountain. If it's too crowded by day, return at night when spotlights play magically on the newly cleaned marble and gushing water.

# Vatican City

*The world's smallest country, with its own stamps, currency, government, media, railway and police force, the Vatican boasts the world's largest church, piazza and museum. This 'City of Popes' is at the top of most visitors' 'must-see' lists as a destination of both religious and artistic pilgrimage.*

## Piazza San Pietro (St Peter's Square)

The semicircular colonnaded wings of this huge, theatrical square symbolise the outstretched, embracing arms of the Church. Built by Bernini in 1656 on the site of Nero's ancient circus (where many early Christians were martyred) for Pope Alexander VII, it took 11 years to complete. The square is adorned by two baroque fountains, 140 statues of saints and martyrs and a red granite obelisk brought from Egypt by Caligula in AD 37, topped by an iron cross containing a relic of the Holy Cross.

The piazza is a spacious meeting place for pilgrims. On Easter Sunday, 300,000 people cram into the square for the Pope's traditional open-air service.

*Tourist information office (Ufficio Informazioni Pellegrini e Turisti): on the south side of Piazza San Pietro. Tel: 06 69884466. Open: Mon–Sat 0830–1900.*

" *At Florence you think; at Venice you love; at Naples you look; at Rome you pray.* "
**Old Italian proverb**

" *You are Peter and on this rock I shall build my Church and I shall give you the keys to the Kingdom of Heaven.* "
**St Matthew's Gospel, 16.xvii**

# San Pietro in Vaticano

*Piazza San Pietro. Open: 0700–1900 (1800 in winter). Strict dress code.*
*£ (££ to climb the dome; open: 0800–1800 (1600 in winter)). Visits to the*
*necropolis under the basilica and St Peter's tomb by prior arrangement:*
*tel: 06 69885318.*

The first St Peter's was built by Constantine around AD 326 on the site where St Peter was buried following his crucifixion in AD 64. In the 16th century, Bramante was commissioned to design a completely new basilica. Its construction took over a hundred years: Michelangelo designed the lofty dome with help from Fontana and Porta, Carlo Maderno built the façade and Bernini constructed twin towers to frame the entrance.

The breathtaking interior, designed for grand papal processions and pilgrimage-sized congregations, is somewhat overwhelming. (The lengths of other basilicas – all much shorter than St Peter's – are marked along the floor of the nave!) Bernini's massive gilded bronze *baldacchino*, or altar canopy, rises six storeys over the high altar. The basilica's treasures include a 13th-century bronze statue of St Peter whose foot has been worn away by the touch of pilgrims, and Michelangelo's moving *Pietà*, completed when he was just 25.

# Castel Sant'Angelo

*Lungotevere Castello. Open: 0900–1900. Closed public holidays and the second*
*and fourth Tue of each month. ££.*

This bulky cylindrical fortress has been both a mighty military bastion and, linked to the papal apartments by a secret passageway (the Vatican Corridor), a palatial hideout for popes in troubled times.

199

The besieged popes still lived in great luxury. In the Papal Bathroom, every inch of wall and even the side of the marble bathtub is smothered in delicate designs. The water was heated by a log fire under a giant cauldron hidden behind the wall. The Vatican's precious papal jewels and crowns were once stored in the Room of the Secret Archives. The third floor of the castle boasts more luxurious apartments and the Loggia, which affords tremendous views in every direction.

# Musei Vaticani (Vatican Museums)

*It may seem ironic that the world's smallest country should contain the world's largest museum, but the Catholic Church has been enormously extravagant over the centuries, and great volumes of priceless art have been commissioned by its many popes. The Vatican's museums comprise mile upon mile of priceless collections, crammed into 1 400 rooms.*

Where to start? Be wary of trying to see everything. First-timers might like to concentrate simply on the Museo Pio-Clementino, the Raphael Rooms, the Pinacoteca Vaticana galleries and the Sistine Chapel. In getting to these, you will acquire a taste for other collections – Greek, Roman and Etruscan sculptures, modern religious art, books, maps, clocks, tapestries, gold jewellery and sumptuous papal apartments frescoed by the greatest artists of the times – as you wend your way through the vast labyrinth of corridors and galleries that were originally palaces built for Renaissance pontiffs.

## Museo Pio-Clementino

This museum boasts a staggering collection of ancient Greek and Roman art and antiquities, salvaged during the 16th century from ancient monuments ruthlessly dismantled to make way for Renaissance Rome. It includes the elegant *Apollo Belvedere* torso, which so influenced Michelangelo, and, most celebrated of all, the remarkable 1 BC *Laocoön* group, uncovered in 1506 on the Esquiline Hill, depicting the Trojan priest and his two sons fighting off the snakes sent by Athena to kill them.

# Pinacoteca Vaticana

The fifteen-roomed Picture Gallery is situated near the exit and often full of weary visitors, but it contains a remarkable collection of canvases spanning ten centuries. Among the most important exhibits are works by Giotto, Fra Angelico, Lippi, Bellini's *Pietà*, Leonardo's unfinished *St Jerome* in sombre sepia tones, Raphael's *Coronation of the Virgin* (one of his first works) and *Transfiguration* (his last great work), Veronese's moving *Sant'Elena*, Caravaggio's dramatic *Descent from the Cross* and Melozzo da Forli's ethereal frescos of *Musician Angels*.

# Stanze di Raffaelo

During the Renaissance, parts of the museums were decorated with sumptuous frescos, including the four Raphael Rooms, which contain the young artist's greatest works in Rome, commissioned by Pope Julius II.

Raphael's most noteworthy frescos, in the *Sala della Segnatura* (1509–11), show the epitome of his classical style, full of rich colours and with clever use of light and space, particularly apparent in the *Dispute over the Holy Sacrament*. The acclaimed *School of Athens* fresco opposite portrays ancient characters with the features of contemporary heroes – bearded Plato in the centre is Leonardo da Vinci, pensive Heraclites on the steps is Michelangelo, and to his right is Bramante, dressed as Euclid. Those in the *Stanza d'Elidoro* (1512–13) show the artist's development from High Renaissance art in *The Miracle of Bolseno* (over the window to the left) to a more powerful and realistic style in *The Liberation of St Peter*, where Pope Julius II is portrayed as the saint himself. These are some of the finest artworks in the museum.

> " *After a day of the papal renaissance and baroque, and of the great ancient walls of brick which being of brick often look as though they are not ruins but being built now by builders gone on strike – all one desires is a bidet of caffè granita [iced coffee] to bathe the feet in.* "

**William Sansom, *Grand Tour Today* (1968)**

201

# Cappella Sistina (Sistine Chapel)

*Nothing can prepare you for the visual impact of the recently restored Sistine Chapel, one of the most frequently visited sights in Rome, attracting over 20,000 visitors daily. On the ceiling of the chapel, Michelangelo (totally new to fresco techniques) laboured painstakingly for four years from 1508 to 1512 to create what is today considered the greatest painting ever produced.*

It is an astonishingly elaborate work based on Old Testament scenes, from the Creation to the Salvation of Noah. None is more famous than the *Creation of Adam* in the centre, with its celebrated outstretched fingers. Michelangelo began his oeuvre near the entrance and ended it over the altar. Benches are provided for viewing the ceiling from different perspectives. Remember to take binoculars and see whether you can spot the point (somewhere about midway) where experts agree that the great sculptor became more assured with his new painting techniques and started to produce bolder, more heroic and expressive figures. Around the walls, various biblical scenes have been added by other great masters of the Renaissance, including Botticelli, Signorelli, Ghirlandaio and Perugino.

The brilliant lapis-blue *Last Judgement* fresco on the altar wall was also painted by Michelangelo, 23 years after he finished the ceiling. Demonstrating his belief that suffering is a vital stage in the search for faith in God, it depicts the souls of the dead rising up to face the wrath of Jesus, with the good promoted to heaven and the damned cast into the abyss of hell. This harrowing subject, rarely used as an altar backdrop, was chosen by the Pope as a warning to Catholics to heed their faith despite the turmoil of the Reformation. Michelangelo's self-portrait can be spotted on the flayed skin held by the martyr St Bartholomew at Christ's feet.

# Other attractions

If you have time, try and fit in three other museums: the Egyptian Collection, the Etruscan Collection and the Gregoriano Profano Museum, which includes the Athlete mosaics from the Baths of Caracalla.

And as you go round, make sure you take a peek at the Vatican gardens through the windows. They cover over one-third of the Vatican's acreage, with woodland, fountains, Vatican Radio studios, a railway station and even a cabbage patch, essential fare for today's Polish Pope (*garden tours require advance reservation through the Tourist Information Office, tel: 06 69884466*).

*Città del Vaticano (entrance to the north in Viale Vaticano). Tel: 06 6983333. Open: Mon–Fri 0845–1545, Sat 0845–1245, 16 Mar–30 Oct. Also, for all other periods of the year, Mon–Sat and the last Sun of the month 0845–1345. Closed public and religious holidays and Sundays (except the last Sun of each month). £££ (free the last Sun of the month). Headset guides available at the museum entrance (££). To help control the flow of visitors, four colour-coded one-way paths guide them through the collections, varying in length from 90 minutes to five hours. All pass via the Sistine Chapel.*

" *In truth Rome was greater, and greater are its ruins than I imagined. I no longer wonder that the whole world was conquered by the city but that I was conquered so late.* "

**Petrarch, *c*1350**

" *Sauntering around the Vatican, I wilted from exhaustion, and when I got home, my legs felt as if they were made out of cotton.* "

**Anton Chekhov (1860–1904) in a letter to a friend in Moscow after his Vatican visit**

# Villa Borghese

## Gardens

*Porta Pinciana/Via Flaminia. Open: daily dawn–dusk. £.*

Rome's **largest central park** was laid out between 1613 and 1616 at the top end of Via Veneto just outside the Aurelian walls, as the grounds of the **Borghese family**'s summer retreat. Redesigned in the 18th century, following the fashion for 'English parkland', its woods and shaded walkways offer a cool retreat from the city centre.

The park is at its liveliest on Sunday mornings when Roman families stroll and play there, and couples go boating and sun-worshipping. With an aviary, racetrack (the Galoppatoio) and one of Rome's finest art museums, there is enough to keep the whole family amused for hours.

## Galleria e Museo Borghese

*Villa Borghese, Piazzale Scipione Borghese 5. Tel: 068417645. Open: Tue–Sun 0900–1900 Jun–Sept; Tue–Sat 0900–1700 Oct–May; Sun and holidays 0900– 1300. Closed Mon. £££.*

This handsome baroque villa was designed as a summer retreat for **Cardinal Scipione Borghese**, to house his outstanding art collection. He took full advantage of being the nephew of a pope by ruthlessly persuading owners to part with prized masterpieces, and even stole some paintings; **Raphael**'s *Deposition* was removed for him from the Baglioni family chapel in Perugia under cover of night.

**Napoleon** plundered the original collection, and many pieces went to the Louvre in Paris, but the remainder is generally considered, after the Vatican Museums, to represent Rome's finest classical and baroque collection.

The villa displays **sculptures** in the splendidly frescoed rooms of the lower floor (the *museo*), and all the major paintings are hung on the upper floor (the *galleria*). The sculptural *pièce de résistance* is Antonio **Canova**'s *Paolina Borghese* – Napoleon's sister, and Camillo Borghese's wife – depicted bare-breasted as a naked reclining Venus, with her right hand cleverly concealing her ear (her one imperfection!). Paolina, renowned for her flamboyance and her many lovers, was the subject of much scandal.

# Galleria Nazionale d'Arte Moderna e Contemporanea

*Viale delle Belle Arte 131. Tel: 06 322981. Open: Tue–Sat 0900–2200; Sun 0900–2000. Closed Mon. ££.*

Cesare Bazzini's dazzling white *belle-époque* palace is one of the few remaining buildings erected for the Rome International Exhibition of 1911. It houses Rome's main collection of **modern art** (from 1800 onwards), which makes a refreshing change from baroque and Renaissance.

# Villa Giulia – Museo Nazionale Etrusco

*Piazza di Villa Giulia 9. Tel: 06 3201951. Open: Tue–Sun 0900–1900. Closed Mon. ££.*

On the outskirts of Villa Borghese, the pretty 16th-century Villa Giulia houses a **world-famous collection** of Etruscan and other pre-Roman remains.

The villa, its fine gardens, pavilions and fountains, were designed for Pope Julius III by Michelangelo, Vasari and Vignola. Its façade, loggia and *nymphaeum* were frequently copied in later villas throughout Italy.

The villa is crammed with **Etruscan objects** – weapons, decorative vases, religious artefacts, bronze statuettes of warriors in full battle dress, jewellery, mirrors, combs and cooking utensils – from most of the major excavations in the region, bearing witness to the sophistication of this early civilisation.

# Around the forums, the Colosseum and the Capitoline Hill

## Eating and drinking

### Ai Tre Scalini
*Via SS Quattro 30. Tel: 06 7096309. Closed Mon. Reservations essential. £££.* One of the best restaurants in Rome, small and unpretentious, with inventive Roman cuisine, just two blocks east of the Colosseum.

### Caffè dello Studento
*Via delle Terme di Tito 94. No tel. Closed Sun. £.* This popular student hangout offers excellent value sandwiches, pizza slices, cheeseburgers, beers and coffee to eat on a sunny pavement terrace or to take away.

### Cavour 313
*Via Cavour 313. Tel: 06 6785496. Closed Sun. ££.* One of Rome's best-loved *enotece* (wine bars). Wash down typical Roman pub grub – savoury pies, *torta rustica* (quiche), pasta, pâtés, sausage and cheese platters – with wines of the region.

### Gelateria La Dolce Vita
*Via Cavour 306. No tel. £.* Treat the kids to an ice cream or a frozen yoghurt here, after a visit to the forum.

### Mario's
*Piazza del Grillo 9. Tel: 06 6793725. Closed Sun. ££.* Hidden up the hill behind the Imperial *fora*, this intimate restaurant serves such traditional local dishes as *spaghetti alla carbonara*, *saltimbocca* and *trippa alla romana* on a small, leafy terrace.

### Valentino
*Via Cavour 293. Tel: 06 4881303. Closed Fri. Reservation recommended. ££.* This tiny *trattoria* serves an excellent value *menu turistico* together with traditional Roman cuisine – *gnocchi* on Thursdays, tripe on Saturdays. Ideal for lunch.

## Shopping

Apart from a small morning fruit and vegetable market in **Via SS Quattro** ( *open: daily except Sun* ) and **La Voglia**, a delightful delicatessen at 295 Via Cavour, concentrate your shopping efforts on the area around Piazza Venezia and Via del Corso, where you'll find one of the city's largest **Benetton** stores.

# Around Piazza Navona

## Nightlife

Winebars ( *enotece* ) abound in this district, notably romantic albeit pricey **La Bevitoria** in Piazza Navona ( *closed Sun* ), **Il Piccolo** ( *Via del Governo Vecchio 74/75; closed lunchtimes* ) and **Cul de Sac** ( *Piazza Pasquino; closed Sun* ) with its list of over 1 400 different wines. For live music, try sophisticated piano bar **Tartarughino** ( *Via della Scrofa 1* ) or the **Jazz Café** ( *Piazza di Tor Sanguigna 12; open: daily from 2230* ).

## Eating and drinking

### Da Baffetto
*Via del Governo Vecchio 11. Tel: 06 6861617. Closed Sun and lunchtime. £.* You will almost certainly have to queue for a table at this small, no-frills pizzeria – the most famous in Rome – but the pizzas are well worth the wait.

### Papa Giovanni
*Via dei Sediari 4. Tel: 06 6865308. Closed Sun and Aug. Reservation essential. £££.* A classic Roman restaurant, serving traditional but refined Roman cuisine in an intimate setting.

### Tre Scalini
*Piazza Navona. Closed Wed. ££.* You haven't experienced Rome until you've had a generous scoop of the *tartufo* (truffle) ice cream here.

## Shopping

Head to **Via del Governo Vecchio** for fashions, **Via dell'Orso** for jewellery, **Via degli Orsini** for antique lamps, **Via della Scrofa** for delicatessens **Volpetti** ( *No 31/32* ) and **Antica Norcineria** ( *No 100* ), and the famous **Via del Coronari** for antiques. At the end of May and during October, Via dei Coronari holds its fair. The shops open late, the street is carpeted red and lined with candles, creating a truly magical atmosphere – ideal for an evening stroll.

### Ai Monasteri
*Piazza Cinque Lune 76.* Monastic products from around Italy – fruit liqueurs, herbal concoctions, holy chocolates, honey, soaps and essential oils – crammed into a church-like shop.

# Around the Pantheon and Piazza della Rotonda

## Eating and drinking
This is one of the most densely populated areas of Rome for cafés, bars and restaurants.

### Il Bacaro
*Via degli Spagnoli 27. Tel: 06 6864110. Closed Sun and lunchtimes in winter. ££.* A charming candlelit restaurant near the Pantheon, popular with the young set, especially in summer with its picturesque terrace.

### Caffè di Rienzo
*Piazza della Rotonda 9. Tel: 06 6869097. Closed Mon. ££.* Enjoy the speciality *granita di limone* (frozen, crushed lemon juice accompanied by a silver pitcher of water to adjust the sharpness) on a sunny terrace overlooking the Pantheon.

### Cíao
*Via del Corso/Via Convertite. No tel. £.* Italian fast food at its best – generous slices of take-away pizza at absurdly cheap prices, combined with a cheap, cheerful self-service restaurant at the back. Excellent value.

### Giolitti
*Via Uffici del Vicario 40. Tel: 06 6991243. Closed Mon. £.* This olde-worlde *gelateria*-cum-teashop boasts arguably the best ice cream in Rome, served in chocolate-rimmed cones, not to mention the moreish sundaes, cakes and pastries.

# Shopping

This district offers an excellent variety of shopping, from the inexpensive, mid-range clothes, shoes and accessories shops of **Via del Corso**, a street famed for its evening *passeggiata*, or strolling, to the tiny specialist boutiques near the Pantheon.

### Cartoleria Pantheon
*Via della Rotonda 15.* A tiny treasure trove of hand-made, marbled-paper items, from writing paper to beautiful leather-bound photo albums.

### Confetteria Moriondo e Gariglio
*Via del Pie'di Marmo 21/22.* On Valentine's Day and for Easter, Romans queue outside the city's only family-run chocolate confectioner's to have their special gifts sealed inside beautifully wrapped chocolate hearts and eggs.

### La Rinascente
*Via del Corso 189.* Rome's most upmarket department store, stocking designer and off-the-peg fashions for men and women, lingerie, costume jewellery and accessories.

# Around Piazza di Spagna

## Eating and drinking

### Ciampini
*Viale Trinità dei Monti. Tel: 06 6785678. ££.* The location of this café is more memorable than the food, with its sweeping views over the rooftops of Rome. Good for a light lunch.

### Margutta Vegetariano
*Via Margutta 118. Tel: 06 32650577. ££.* Rome's top vegetarian restaurant spoils customers for choice with its unusual dishes.

### Nino's
*Via Borgognona 11. Tel: 06 6786752. Closed Sun and Aug. ££–£££.* This popular, well-situated Tuscan *trattoria* near the Spanish Steps attracts the beautiful people of Rome.

## Shopping

This is Rome's most fashionable district. Italian flair is on show in the *haute-couture* boutiques and on the stylish customers of **Via Condotti** and its surrounding streets. Virtually every top Italian designer has an outlet here – **Gucci**, **Valentino**, **Armani**, **Ferragamo**, **Buccellati** and **Battistoni** in Via Condotti, **Fendi**, **Ferre** and **Laura Biagotti** in Via Borgognona, **Krizia**, **Dolce e Gabbana** and **Raphael Salato** in Piazza di Spagna and **Versace**, **Moschino**, **Cucci** and **Ungaro** in Via Bocca di Leone. **Pettocchi** (*Piazza di Spagna*) is jeweller to Italy's former royal family, rivalling **Bulgari** (*Via Condotti*).

## Tip

*Coffee drinking is something of a ritual in Rome. The drink is served in a variety of ways:* caffè *(a regular black espresso),* caffè doppio *(a double),* cappuccino *(half espresso, half frothy milk, topped with a sprinkling of cocoa),* caffè macchiato *(espresso with a drop of milk) and* caffè Hag *(decaffeinated). Try them all at* Sant'Eustachio *(* Piazza Sant'Eustachio 82; tel: 06 6861309; closed Mon *), the café that reputedly serves the best cup in town.*

# Trastevere

## Eating and drinking

### Il Forno Amico
*Piazza San Cosimato 53. No tel. Closed Sun. £.* Arrive around 1130 for *pizza bianco* – baked dough brushed with oil and sprinkled with salt and rosemary.

### Ivo a Trastevere
*Via di San Francesco Ripa 158. Tel: 06 5817082. Closed Tue and lunchtimes. £.* Ordinary-looking pizzeria serving some of the best pizzas in town.

## Nightlife

Trastevere has long been one of *the* spots for Roman nightlife, crammed with tiny, intimate bars and lively pulsating nightclubs, especially in the area around Piazza dei Ponziani.

### Stardust
*Via de'Renzi.* By day this cosy little bar serves delicious brunches. In the evenings it is jam-packed with locals, with live music sessions every Tuesday.

# The Vatican

## Eating and drinking

For the best selection of eateries in the area, steer clear of the overpriced restaurants on Via della Conciliazione and head to the Borgo just beyond.

### Alle Due Fontanelle
*Via Federico Cesi 23. Tel: 06 3612114. Closed Sun lunch. ££.* Basement fish restaurant serving such delectable dishes as fish soup *alla romana* (minimum four people), baked bass with oyster sauce and Sorrento-style anchovies.

### Caffè San Pietro
*Via della Conciliazione 40. Tel: 06 6864927. Closed Mon. £.* This espresso bar-cum-café has gained in notoriety since Ali Agca had a last cup of coffee here on the day when he tried to assassinate Pope John Paul II.

### Enoteca Costantini
*Piazza Cavour 16. Closed Sun. ££.* One of the best wine bars, with an impressive selection of wines from Italy and around the world.

## Shopping

Via Cola di Rienzo is the main shopping street near the Vatican. Try Furla (*No 226*) for classy handbags and Mondadori (*Nos 81–83*) for books and records. Romans consider Castroni (*No 196*) and Benedetto Franchi (*No 204*) to be top-notch delicatessens while tiny, family-run Tascioni (*No 211*) is *the* place to buy fresh pasta, with dozens of different types to choose from.

For ecclesiastical artefacts, concentrate on Via della Conciliazione. For religious Vatican souvenirs, try Savelli Religiosi (*Largo del Colonnato 5, opposite St Peter's Square*). For chalices, reliquaries and lay gifts in silver and glass, head to LMP at Via del Mascherino 16. If you miss the Vatican Museums, see the highlights in Edizioni Musei Vaticani (*Via di Porta Angelica 41*), a small shop selling quality reproductions.

# Aquatic Rome

*Rome is awash with **fountains** – over 4 000 in total – more than any other city in the world. Among these are some of the world's finest, the work of the greatest sculptors of the Renaissance and baroque period. Some are splashy, flamboyant displays, some are ornamental trickles, many are simply humble drinking fountains. You can drink the water from any of these fountains. It is still as 'clear, sweet and fresh' as it was in Petrarch's day, fed by mineral water running through the veins of the city in giant aqueducts, 11 of which date from classical times.*

## Papal splendour

The popes who restored these ancient aqueducts also adopted the emperors' custom of celebrating the spot where the water appears with a huge fountain or *mostra* ('show'). The most famous is the **Trevi Fountain**, immortalised by actress Anita Ekberg's late-night dip in Federico Fellini's film *La Dolce Vita*, an account of the decadence and exhibitionism of post-war Rome. Other grand papal *mostre* include the Paola Fountain on the Janiculum and the Moses Fountain on the Quirinal Hill.

## Piazza centrepieces

Nearly all Rome's great piazzas are graced with fountains. Piazza Navona has Rome's jewel of baroque sculpture, the **Fountain of the Four Rivers**. This dynamic *tour de force* of marble and rushing water, created by Bernini, was commissioned in 1651 by Pope Innocent X, who put extra tax on bread in order to finance the project. The imposing result symbolises the four corners of the world; the four

allegorical statues represent the Rivers Danube, Nile, Ganges and Plate. The centrepiece of Piazza Barberini is the Triton Fountain, created in 1637, and a favourite of the Romans – a joyful marine god rises triumphantly out of the sea, kneeling on two scallop shells held aloft by entwined dolphins, and blowing a high jet of water out of a conch shell. The sculptor also included the Barberini family's papal tiara, the keys of St Peter's and the distinctive Barberini coat of arms, with its three bees. Piazza della Repubblica's sensual Fountain of the Naiads caused a scandal when it was unveiled in 1901, revealing its nymphs in their rather saucy postures.

## Off the beaten track

Fountains of all shapes and sizes lie dotted about all over the city. Some are more unconventional than others. There's the Bee Fountain (in Piazza Barberini, with three giant bees representing the Barberini family), the Frog Fountain, the Eagle Fountain, the Tortoise Fountain (in Piazza Mattei, sculpted in a single night in 1585, although the bronze tortoises were added a century later), *Facchino* the 'talking fountain', a water-clock fountain on Pincio Hill, the modern Fountain of the Four Tiaras near St Peter's, the Navicella fountain, made from an ancient stone galley, *La Barcaccia*, a half-sunken barge at the foot of the Spanish Steps, and the giant grotesque *Mascherone* face in Via Giulia, which in its Renaissance heyday flowed with wine.

Rome would be impossible to imagine without its fountains. Along with the car horn and the raised voices of passionate locals, the gentle splashing of water is one of Rome's distinguishing sounds.

211

# Lazio

When in Rome, do as the Romans do and escape
into the refreshing countryside of Lazio, known
since ancient times as an extension of the
Eternal City. Mountains, volcanic lakes, olive

groves and vineyards are all woven into a rich tapestry, together with ancient villas, glorious water gardens and reminders of the forerunners of Roman civilisation, the proud Etruscans.

*Getting there: Rome is served by Leonardo da Vinci airport (information, tel: 06 65 951), more popularly known as Fiumicino, and Ciampino (information, tel: 06 794 941). There is a good bus service (COTRAL, head office: Via Volturno 65; tel: 06 575 31/freephone information: 800 431 784) from Rome to nearly all destinations in Lazio. For information on train services, tel: 166 105 050, 24 hrs daily (more expensive but English-speaking). Car drivers should be aware that Rome's Friday exodus and Sunday's return in the evenings can be especially frenetic – as well as usual rush hours.*

## (1) The abbeys of Lazio

The birthplace of St Benedict's Rule for monastic life at Montecassino, together with Subiaco where the saint founded the religious order and lived as a hermit in a cave, are both powerful reminders of the Benedictines.
**Pages 216–17**

## (2) Bomarzo

'Sacred wood' or 'monster park'? – for you to decide as you walk among scary stone monsters in this fantasy Renaissance theme park. **Page 218**

## (3) Cerveteri and Tarquinia

The ordered streets and grassy tumulus tombs of Cerveteri's city of the dead and the beautiful wall paintings of the tombs at Tarquinia are a superb legacy of the ancient Etruscans' extraordinary craftsmanship.
**Pages 218–19, 228–9**

## (4) Castelli Romani

The rich fertile volcanic soil here is good vine country and is the favourite out-of-town retreat for the Romans.
**Page 220**

## (5) Ostia Antica

The ancient Roman version of apartment blocks and a 20-person public loo are all part of one of Italy's best-preserved Roman towns.
**Pages 222–3**

## (6) Tivoli

Spectacular aquatronics, the remains of the Roman empire's greatest palace and dramatic waterfalls all make this the most popular day out from Rome.
**Pages 226–7**

# Abbeys

## Casamari

The region of Ciociaria is named after the *ciocie* bark sandals that were worn here long ago. Originally an 11th-century Benedictine abbey, **Casamari** was later taken over by the Cistercians who re-modelled it in 1203 along the lines of **Fossanova** (*see opposite*). It is a superb example of early Italian Gothic architecture with a rather solemn interior built to a Latin cruciform plan. The cloisters outside have a beautiful flower garden with a well at its centre and the chapterhouse is remarkable for its delicately ribbed vaulting.

*Getting there: 14km (9 miles) east of Frosinone in the southeast of Lazio, in the region of Ciociaria. Abbey church open: daily 0900–1230 and 1600–1830. Free.*

## Montecassino

Perched high on the Monte Cassino mountaintop, Montecassino was founded by **St Benedict** in 529. Based on chastity, obedience and poverty, together with intellectual study and manual labour, his **Rule** became the monastic code for the whole of western Europe. Since its foundation, the abbey has been destroyed several times, most dramatically during the Second World War, when it was taken by the Germans. After the protracted **Battle of Cassino** in May 1944, it was eventually bombed almost into oblivion; the adjoining cemeteries commemorate the 30,000 soldiers killed. Now faithfully rebuilt to the original plans, the abbey is fittingly austere yet the interior is richly decorated with marble, stucco, gilding and mosaics. Inside the chancel lies the marble tomb containing the remains of St Benedict.

### Tip

*The Roman **Campagna** – the plain between the sea and the Sabine mountains – was always a place for contemplation. It was once a wild area of grasses and malarial swamps, which are now, thankfully, extinct.*

*Getting there: about an hour by train southeast of Frosinone. Open: daily 0930–1230 and 1530–sunset. Free.*

# Fossanova

The abbey of Fossanova is the oldest of the Cistercian Order in Italy, dating from 1163. The Cistercians, a stricter form of the Benedictines, take their creed from St Bernard, whose values were based on austerity and self-sufficiency. In accordance with this, the austere abbey stands on a lonely site and, although extensively restored, is faithful to its 13th-century Burgundian-Gothic origins. There is a fine Gothic chapter house from where there is access to the guest house where the Dominican monk St Thomas Aquinas died in 1274.

*Getting there: southwest of Frosinone off the N156; bus from Frosinone to Priverno, from where the abbey is 5km (3 miles) south. Open: daily 0700–1200 and 1600–1930 in summer; 1500–1730 only in winter. Free.*

# Subiaco

Two monasteries survive here from the original twelve built by St Benedict and his twin sister, Santa Scolastica, at the end of the 5th century.

The extensively restored church dedicated to Santa Scolastica (*open: daily 0900–1230 and 1600–1900; free*), built around three delightful cloisters, still has its beautiful

original 11th-century campanile. Further up the road is a dramatic gorge on which is perched San Benedetto (*open: daily 0900–1230 and 1500–1800; free*), where two churches – one built on top of the other – are hewn into the rockface. The higher is richly decorated with 14th-century Sienese frescos, whilst the lower leads into the Sacro Speco, the cave where St Benedict lived for three years in self-imposed exile from decadent Rome.

*Getting there: about 15km (9 miles) northeast of Palestrina. By car, take the Frosinone road; bus from Rome or Tivoli.*

# Bomarzo

The Parco dei Mostri ('Monster Park') is a Renaissance theme park full of gruesome beasts, grotesque giants and scary sculptures – a nightmarish vision of surrealist Daliesque visions, where Dali himself did do some filming and contributed much to the marketing effort. Created by the hunchback Duke of Orsini in 1552 shortly after the death of his wife, it is uncertain whether the *Sacro Bosco* ('Sacred Wood') was intended as a tribute to her or to Ariosto's *Orlando Furioso*, the tale of Orlando's descent into madness.

Although unkempt and rather dilapidated, this allegorical 'theatre of the absurd' is one of northern Lazio's top tourist attractions – especially popular with children who delight in the bloodthirsty stone 'creatures' and love clambering over them. At the entrance, a giant warrior tearing a woodcutter apart sets the tone; screaming masks, elephantine elephants, nymphs, mermaids, giant wrestlers, ogres, dragons and unsettling, disorienting buildings complete the distorted picture. In all, it is a celebration of 16th-century Mannerism, the antidote to classical composition, where every rule is broken and sensationalism reigns.

*Getting there: 21km (13 miles) northeast of Viterbo on the S204. Nearest railway station is Attigliano-Bomarzo, followed by a 5-km (3-mile) walk; regular buses from Viterbo to Bomarzo, then a 10-minute walk. Parco dei Mostri (Sacro Bosco), Bomarzo. Tel: 0761 92 40 29. Open: daily 0800–1900 in summer; 0800–sunset in winter. £££.*

# Cerveteri

Ancient Cerveteri (*Caere*) was an important Etruscan centre in the 7th to 5th centuries BC. Today, it is known for its Necropoli della Banditaccia (*2km (1 mile) north of Cerveteri; Via delle Necropoli; tel: 06 994 00 01; open: Tue–Sun 0900–1900, closes 1600 during winter; ££*), the 'City of the Dead', laid out with streets, grass-covered tumuli and tombs. Excavation work began at the beginning of the 20th century, and only about 50 out of an estimated 5 000 tombs have been excavated, although many have been plundered. Most of the tombs date from the 7th century BC, and many are arranged like houses, with corridors, rooms and doors.

Men's funeral beds were adorned with a phallic column, while those of the women were decorated with a little canopy, showing the woman's role as guardian of the home. Show tombs open in random rotation; if possible, try to see the Tomba dei Rilievi, richly decorated with stucco reliefs of everyday Etruscan life, and the Tomba dei Letti Funebri, the 'Tomb of the Funeral Beds'. The beautifully crafted contents of the tombs included silver, gold, bronze and ceramics; the best of these are in the Vatican and Villa Giulia museums in Rome, but there is a collection of finds back in the town of Cerveteri at the Museo Nazionale di Cerveteri (*Piazza Santa Maria; tel: 06 994 13 54; open: Tue–Sun 0900–1900; free*).

*Getting there: 45km (28 miles) northwest of Rome. Tourist information: Piazza Risorgimento 19. Tel: 06 995 18 58. Closed Sun and Mon.*

219

## Etruscan tombs

*Giorgio Bassani's narrator in* Il Giardino dei Finzi-Contini *(1962) finds the Cerveteri Etruscans down to earth and very human in their desire to place in their tombs 'not only their dead, but everything that made life beautiful and desirable'. These sheltered, peaceful mounds are in sad contrast with the unknown fate of the bodies of the narrator's fellow deported Jews.*

# Castelli Romani/Frascati

*Descended from fortified castles of the Middle Ages, the 13 villages of the Castelli Romani ('Roman castles') were traditionally sited on the outer rims of extinct volcanic craters of the Albani Hills. The rich volcanic soil is ideal for vines and the cooler air makes the area a favourite country retreat for Roman city dwellers.*

Frascati is the most accessible of the Castelli Romani, well known for its crisp white wine. The lovely Villa Aldobrandini (*gardens only open: Mon–Fri 0900–1300 and 1500–1800 in summer; closes 1700 in winter; free permit from the tourist information office*), built in 1598, still belongs to the Aldobrandini family. Its terraced gardens are a delight, as is the view from the terrace at the front; on a clear day, you can see right across to Rome. The Pope's summer palace, Castel Gandolfo, is 9km (5½ miles) south of here. When he is in residence, normally from July until September, he gives an address from the balcony at midday on Sundays. Some 3km (2 miles) south of Frascati lies Grottaferrata, one of the most picturesque towns of the Castelli Romani, which also produces good wine. Worth a visit too is the 11th-century abbey, Abbazia di San Nilo (*open: daily 0600–1230 and 1530–1900, closes sunset in winter; free*). The chapel inside has lovely 13th-century mosaics and frescos by 17th-century Domenichino.

Nearby, to the southeast, is Lake Nemi, with the ruins of a temple to the goddess Diana beside the lake. Nemi is also known as the town of strawberries and every June celebrates its Sagra delle Fragole ('Strawberry Festival').

*Getting there: 20km (12 miles) southeast of Rome. Tourist information: Piazzale Marconi 1. Tel: 06 942 0331. Open: Tue–Fri 0800–1400 and 1600–1900; Mon and Sat am only; closes 1830 in winter.*

# Lake Bracciano

Bracciano covers an area of almost 58 square kilometres (22 square miles). The waters, famous for their fish, especially eels, fill the dramatic volcanic crater of Mount Sabatini. In the summer months there are boat trips and good swimming in the clear, clean waters. For the best views of the lake, visit the ramparts of Bracciano's splendid 15th-century castle, **Castello Orsini-Odelscalchi** ( *Via del Castello; tel: 06 998 043 48; open: Tue–Fri 1000–1900, weekends 0900–1230 and 1500–1930; ££* ). Inside, there are fine apartments, frescos and suits of clanking armour, and a charming central courtyard.

## Tip

*If you pine for wholefood (rather than lake fish) and good ethnic jewellery shops, visit the pretty village of* Calcata *, north of Trevignano, where everyone, including ageing hippies, congregates to enjoy fabulous views and great walks.*

South of the town of Bracciano is the pretty medieval town of **Anguillara**, whose name probably derives from *anguille*, or eels, the lake's speciality. A cluster of picturesque little streets lead to a rocky promontory that offers spectacular views.

*Getting there: 40km (25 miles) northwest of Rome. About 30 minutes by train from Rome. Tourist information: Via Claudia 72, Bracciano. Tel: 06 998 67 82.*

LAZIO

# Ostia Antica

*Ostia Antica takes its name from the Latin* ostium, *for 'mouth', reflecting its position at the mouth of the River Tiber. The community dates back to the 4th century BC, when it was a fishing village, before becoming the port of ancient Rome for 600 years. Its eventual decline was due to the curse of malaria and to silting up, and it sank under layers of sand and river mud.*

Protected by the muddy deposits, this is now the best-preserved Roman town after Pompeii, and offers a **fascinating insight** into the **everyday life** of sailors, merchants and slaves. Major excavations did not begin until the 20th century and it's estimated that a further third of the city remains uncovered. The expansive peaceful, grassy ruins cover a wide area, so comfortable shoes are essential for this visit to ancient Rome.

Access to the site is by the Porta Romana, which leads to the *Decumanus Maximus*, the main street, which always ran east to west in Roman towns. Of the **excavations** ( *Tue–Sun 0900–1900, 1700 in winter, last entry 1 hr before closing; admission also includes Ostiense archaeological museum, open: 0900–1400; £–££*), the focal point is the **Piazzale delle Corporazioni** ('Forum of the Corporations'). Here, under the portico, some 60 main shipping agents or corporations

maintained trading links with the Roman world; mosaics depict each particular trade – reindeer and elephants represent land transport, while other images symbolise ropemakers, cargo shippers and grain merchants. Remains of offices, shops and warehouses ( *horrea* ) still fringe this central square. In the *Horrea Epagathiana*, a large swastika is incorporated into the floor mosaic; the ancient symbol of the sun, it was also a lucky charm if the arms bent to the right, and the opposite if they bent to the left.

On one side of the square is the Theatre, now much restored and used for concerts and classical performances. Further along the *Decumanus Maximus* is the Casa di Diana, a block of flats dating from the 2nd century AD, where the rooftop provides wonderful views across the site. These four- or five-storey brick buildings, complete with shops on the ground floor and balconies above, have an internal courtyard, which to this day remains one of the features of Italian apartment blocks. Just opposite is the *Thermopilium*, a Roman bar with marble counter, wall paintings illustrating the menu and a garden (which would have had a fountain) at the back. Other highlights of this fascinating site include Ostia's largest baths complex, the Terme del Foro, a series of beautiful mosaic-floored baths. Alongside these is the public lavatory, the *forica*, which had 20 holes, a constant flow of water and a revolving door. Looking out towards the sea is the 4th-century Casa di Amore e Psiche ('House of Cupid and Psyche'), with remains of marble and mosaic floors and a lovely courtyard.

*Getting there: southwest of Rome. Take the 20-minute train ride from Piramide (Metro B); by car, the fast* autostrada, *Via del Mare, runs alongside the Via Ostiense. Tourist information: Viale dei Romagnoli 717, Ostia. Tel: 06 5635 8099.*

## Tip

*Not to be confused with Ostia Antica, the nearby Lido di Ostia is a very polluted seaside resort. The noisy, crowded beaches were the setting for film director Pier Paolo Pasolini's 1955 novel of post-war Rome,* Ragazzi di Vita. *Pasolini was murdered here in 1975, and a monument at Idroscalo, near the mouth of the Tiber, marks the spot.*

# Palazzo Farnese (Caprarola)

*One of Italy's grandest Mannerist villas, this palace looms dramatically at the top of the steep main street, dominating the little town of Caprarola. Originally built as a castle in 1520, it then became the home of Cardinal Alessandro Farnese, who commissioned the architect Vignola to transform it into a palace in 1559.*

**Vignola** was regarded as one of the most highly accomplished architects of the late Renaissance and he set about with great gusto to glorify his masters in this building. The grand spiral staircase, which the cardinal used to climb on his horse, leads up to an elegant courtyard from where you reach the **Piano Nobile**. Of the five floors of the palace, this is the only one open to the public; the others are at different stages of restoration. The tiers of thirty pairs of Doric columns are somewhat overbearing, but the beautiful **Sala del Mappamondo** is richly frescoed with maps of the then known world.

Outside, there are two gardens behind the huge park, including a summer house, the **Palazzina del Piacere**, and a 'secret garden' with grottoes, fake stalactites and grotesques – a reminder of Bomarzo (*see page 218*). It is perhaps no coincidence that one of the Bomarzo Orsinis was secretary to Alessandro Farnese.

*Getting there: north of Rome, 20km (12 miles) southeast of Viterbo. 45-minute bus service from Viterbo to Caprarola, then a 10-minute walk to the Palazzo. Tel: 0761 64 60 52. Open: Tue–Sun 0900–1830 mid-Apr–mid-Sept; 0900–1600 in winter (sometimes 1630). £. Guided tours available.*

# Ninfa/Sermoneta

The valley below Sermoneta was once the site of the medieval village of **Ninfa**, which was finally abandoned through the twin causes of warfare and malaria. Today it has been restored and is the home of exotic plants tumbling in disordered profusion around crumbling buildings. The glorious centrepiece is a stream said to be named after a nymph, who was so distraught at the loss of her lover that her cascades of tears formed the waters here. Romantic, heavily scented and magical, the **gardens** were laid out by the Caetani family in 1921. On the death in 1977 of Donna Lelia Caetani, the last of the family line, Ninfa was passed to the Caetani Foundation. Visiting birds are plentiful, as the area around is a **bird sanctuary** managed by the Foundation, LIPU (Italy's bird protection society) and the WWFN. Standing sentinel above these beautiful gardens is the pretty, medieval hilltop town of **Sermoneta**, with its tangle of cobbled streets and fairy-tale moated castle.

## Tip

*As only a limited number of visitors are allowed in to* Ninfa*, a booking through the* Caetani Administration *(*Via delle Botteghe Oscure 32, Rome; tel: 06 6880 3231*) is recommended.*

*Getting there: southeast of Rome, best accessed by car from the SS7 to Tor Tre Ponti, then by following signs to Latina Scalo/Ninfa (60km, or 37 miles); by train to Latina Scalo, then 9-km (5$^{1}/_{2}$-mile) taxi ride to Caetani Botanical Gardens. Tourist information: Via Duca del Mare 19, Latina Scalo. Tel: 0773 69 54 04 17. Open: 0900–1200 and 1500–1830 first Sat and Sun of each month Apr–Oct. ££–£££. Visitor numbers limited.*

# Tivoli

*Known as Tibur in antiquity, the hill town of Tivoli was always the playground of the rich, writers and poets, and nowadays is the most popular destination for day-trippers from Rome. For many, the Renaissance Villa d'Este is the top priority, but there is much more.*

It is not the villa itself but its gardens that make the 16th-century **Villa d'Este** (*Piazza Trento; tel: 0774 31 20 70; open: daily 0900–1900 in summer, Tue–Sun 0900–1600 in winter; ££*) so famous. Built in a relatively simple architectural style as a pleasure palace for Lucrezia Borgia's son, Cardinal Ippolito d'Este, in 1550, the villa has some fine, rather faded frescos. More exciting is the view from the window: elaborately terraced gardens stretching out in glorious symmetry and dozens of fountains. Pyramids of water splash along the splendid **Viale delle Cento Fontane** ('Avenue of a Hundred Fountains'), and in the upper garden do not miss

Bernini's shell-shaped **Fontana del Bicchierone**. To the left is the **Fontana Rometta** ('Little Rome Fountain') a miniature reproduction of the city's ancient buildings; below are the hydraulic organ fountain, the **Fontana dell'Organo** (sadly no longer operational), the **'Owl Fountain'**, which used to simulate birdsong, and the spectacular fountain of **Diana of Ephesus**, where water gushes from the goddess's countless breasts.

*Getting there: 32km (20 miles) east of Rome. By car on A24; by 50-minute COTRAL bus ride from Rome; or by train for Avezzano, stopping at Tivoli. Tourist information: Largo Garibaldi. Tel: 0774 33 45 22. Open: Tue–Fri 0900–1830; Sat and Mon 0900–1500.*

## Villa Gregoriana

Less theatrical, but more naturalistically dramatic, are the ravines and grand waterfalls at the Villa Gregoriana (*Piazza Massimo, Tivoli; open: daily 1000–1 hr before sunset; £* ). Throwing up rainbows and prisms of light, the River Aniene plunges in two waterfalls into a deeply cut gorge. The smaller fall, designed by Bernini, is at the narrow head of the gorge while the Grande Cascata ('Great Cascade') squeezes into the Siren's Cave before dramatically bursting forth from the rockface in Neptune's Cave.

# Villa Adriana

Here you can see the remains of Hadrian's Villa, originally built out of travertine and marble quarried at Tivoli, and the greatest Imperial palace of the Roman empire. Emperor Hadrian started work on his country retreat in AD 118, and aimed to re-create some of the wonders that he had seen around the world. In the Teatro Marittimo ('Naval Theatre'), Hadrian enjoyed contemplative moments in a little colonnaded palace set in the middle of a lagoon, accessible by an ingenious retractable bridge on rollers. The Canopo is a re-creation of the Egyptian town of Canope, with its Temple of Serapis, near Alexandria. Nearby, a museum contains finds from the on-going excavations (originally begun in 1870). The *terme*, or baths, were extraordinarily sophisticated, as was the private underground world, the Cryptoportici, a series of connecting subterranean passages for carts and horses as well as people. The villa was almost complete by AD 134; Hadrian died just four years later, but his legacy here is a superb model of the extraordinary capabilities and achievements of his life and times.

## Tip

*Villa Adriana originally covered a larger site than Imperial Rome, so do pace yourself. If you fancy walking to the bottom of the 60-m (197-ft) gorge at Villa Gregoriana, remember that it's a steep climb back – but worth every step!*

*Getting there: 5km (3 miles) west of Tivoli. Bus from Largo Garibaldi. Tel: 0774 53 02 03. Open: daily 0900–1 hr before sunset. ££.*

227

# Tarquinia

Founded around the 10th century BC, Tarquinia was a leading Etruscan city, probably the cultural and political capital of Etruria. Known to Dante and for centuries as Corneto (*Cornetium*), the old Etruscan name of Tarquinia was restored during the Fascist regime, when Mussolini wanted to glorify Italy's Italian origins.

Tarquinia's glory today lies in its remarkably vivid tomb paintings, the most famous in the country. The **Museo Nazionale Tarquiniense** (*Piazza Cavour; tel: 0766 85 63 84; open: Tue–Sun 0900–1900; ££*) has a superb collection of finds from the excavations of the **necropolis** (*see below*). The treasures include sarcophagi, fine Etruscan gold jewellery, painted ceramics and several reconstructed tombs with their original wall paintings. The highlight is the stunningly beautiful 4th-century BC sculpture of a pair of terracotta winged horses, glorious proof of the Etruscans' superb craftsmanship.

> *The women with the conical head-dress, how strangely they lean forward, with caresses we no longer know!*
>
> **D H Lawrence on one of the tomb paintings, *Etruscan Places* (1932)**

The maze of tombs at the **Necropoli Etrusca** (*2km (1 mile) southeast of the town; open: Tue–Sun 0900–1 hr before sunset; ££*), is concealed by a grassy hilltop. Since excavations first began, in the late 15th century, some 6 000 tombs have been uncovered – a small percentage of the estimated total of 100,000 that existed in the 10th century BC. *Tombaroli* (grave-robbers) are sadly all too common, so only about 15 of the tombs may be visited at one time, most of which date from the 6th–1st century BC.

After descending into the tombs, and becoming accustomed to the gloom, you'll see **wall paintings** that are still extraordinarily fresh. One underlying theme in all these tombs is the Etruscan belief that the life below could only be a splendid continuation of the good life on earth.

*Getting there: about 90km (56 miles) northwest of Rome. By car, autostrada for Civitavecchia, then the SS1; buses leave hourly from Rome; trains arrive at Tarquinia Lido, 3km (2 miles) from town centre (local buses). Tourist information: Piazza Cavour 1. Tel: 0766 85 63 84. Open: Mon–Sat 0800–1400.*

# Viterbo

Lazio's best-preserved medieval town has its origins in Etruscan times and, in the 13th century, briefly became the residence of the popes. Badly bombed during the Second World War, the new town is unremarkable, yet the seemingly austere medieval heart has some real treasures. Most picturesque is the **San Pellegrino** quarter, which reputedly has the finest collection of medieval buildings in Italy. It is often used as a film set and has some good antiques and craft shops among the lovely houses and fountain-splashed piazzas. The **Piazza San Lorenzo** is on the site of the former Etruscan acropolis and is now dominated by the 12th-century Duomo standing next to the 13th-century **Palazzo dei Papi** (*tel: 0761 34 11 24; open: Sat and Sun 1500–1800, Sun 0900–1200; £*). Built for the visiting popes, the *palazzo* has an especially beautiful early Gothic loggia.

*Getting there: 75km (46½ miles) north of Rome. By car, take the A1 and follow signs from Orte; the bus is quicker than the train from Rome. Tourist*

*information: Piazza San Carluccio 5. Tel: 0761 30 47 95. Open: Mon–Sat 0900–1300 and 1330–1530. Annual antiques show Oct/Nov.*

# Eating and drinking

## Cerveteri

### Sora Lella
*Piazza Alessandrina 1. Tel: 06 992
042 51. Closed Wed. ££.* Good pasta,
and regional dishes such as huntsman's
rabbit; extensive wine list, including
good local offerings.

## Frascati

### Cantina Comandini
*Via E Filiberto 1. Tel: 06 942 09 15.
Open: Mon–Sat. £.* This *cantina* is
one of several in town where you can
sample Frascati straight from the
barrel, generally agreed to be the
best way of drinking this crisp dry
white wine (which doesn't necessarily
travel too well).

### Enoteca Frascati
*Via Diaz 42. Tel: 06 941 74 49. Closed
Sun. £–££.* More than 400 wines are
featured in this wine bar, including, of
course, the wine of the bar's name and
other Castelli Romani wines. Good
light dishes too.

### Zarazà
*Viale Regina Margherita 21. Tel: 06
942 20 53. Closed Mon (and Sun in
winter). £–££.* One of many *osterie*
in the Castelli Romani, with good
regional specialities in a pleasantly
authentic atmosphere.

## Tarquinia

### Le Due Orfanelle
*Via Vicolo Breve 4. Tel: 0766 85
63 07. Closed Tue. £–££.* Good,
inexpensive food is served in this
friendly, traditional *trattoria*.

### Osteria Il Grottino
*Alberata Dante Alighieri 8. £.*
Atmospheric wine bar serving
wine straight from the barrel.

## Tivoli

The Villa Adriana is a great spot for a
picnic, especially as you may want to
take your time visiting this huge and
fascinating site.

### Adriano
*Via Villa Adriana 194 (close to Villa
Adriana). Tel: 0774 38 22 35. Closed
Sun eve. ££–£££.* Delicious pasta
made by hand on the premises and
scrumptious puddings together with
excellent service make this restaurant
very popular. Federico Fellini used to
be a regular.

### M31 pub
*Via della Missione 56/58. Tel: 0774
33 32 43. £.* Good sandwiches, pasta
dishes and very reasonably priced
drinks. Often has live music at night.

# Viterbo

### Caffè Schenardi
*Corso Italia 11. £–££.* Dating back to the 15th century, this institution has a wonderful art-deco interior and hosts regular art exhibitions.

### Enoteca La Torre
*Via della Torre 5. Closed Sun. ££.* Good wine bar that also features an olive oil and mineral water list together with good food.

### Zaffera
*Piazza San Carluccio 7. Tel: 0761 34 42 65. Closed Mon and Sun eve. ££.* Superb views from this lovely old restaurant which was once a monastery. Good regional dishes and an excellent choice of puddings and wines.

# Having a bath

*Terme Acque Albule, Bagni di Tivoli. 8km (5 miles) from Tivoli on the Via Tiburtina. ££.* Your nose will lead you to the sulphurous waters at these baths; their healing properties were described even by Virgil in the *Aeneid*. The entrance fee gives admission to swim in the sulphur springs, and massage, inhalation and mud treatments are also on offer as extras.

# The Etruscans

> *The Etruscans … were the people who occupied the middle of Italy in early Roman days, and whom the Romans, in their usual neighbourly fashion, wiped out entirely in order to make room for Rome with a very big R.*

**D H Lawrence, *Etruscan Places* (1932)**

*Lawrence obviously felt an empathy with the Etruscans, writing that he was 'instinctively attracted to them', as much for their joyous* celebration of life, *as for their superb* craftsmanship

Ancient Etruria consisted of **12 city-states** of which Tarquinia, sited on the crown of a sheer-sided hill, like the other Etruscan settlements, was the oldest and most important. They were a very cultured and artistic people, and more enigmatic than most. Their origins are still shrouded in mystery and their language is almost entirely lost. They were not Romans, nor Greek colonists, but there is evidence to suggest that they may have descended from a small group of Palestinian Phoenicians who arrived in Italy, bringing with them their knowledge of the east. Until the 5th century BC they held a dominant position in northern and central Italy, mostly living **between the**

**Arno and Tiber rivers**; the area was known to the ancient Romans as *Etrusci*, from which derives the name of the modern Italian region of **Tuscany**.

The superb **terracotta winged horses** found in the temple at Tarquinia are a glorious reminder of the artistry of the Etruscans. Their practice of building in wood means that little evidence of their achievement in construction remains, but the **tombs of Cerveteri and Tarquinia** still display exquisite frescos, vases, jewellery and sculptures, and the famous *She-Wolf* in Rome's Capitoline Museum is their work. The Etruscans were also skilled at **irrigation** and **land drainage** and intensively cultivated the fertile plains where they lived. After the demise of the Etruscan people, these plains became malarial mosquito-infested swamps.

The Etruscans believed that their good life would continue beyond the grave, and were devoted to the **cult of the after-life**. Their nobles were buried in great sarcophagi, while many others, including the slaves, were cremated and their remains placed in beautiful vases. How different their fate was from that of the Roman slaves, who were simply flung into huge pits outside the city.

" *Because a fool kills a nightingale with a stone, is he therefore greater than the little nightingale? Because the Roman took the life out of the Etruscan, was he therefore greater than the Etruscan? Not he!* "

**D H Lawrence, *Etruscan Places* (1932)**

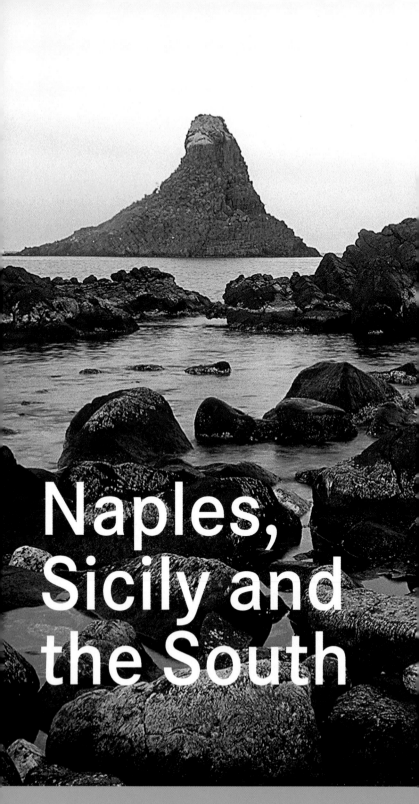

# Naples, Sicily and the South

The land of the midday sun, the 'Mezzogiorno', starts at the first petrol station south of Rome (or so the Romans will tell you). Sun-drenched, beautiful, barren, majestic, rich and yet achingly poor, the contrasts here are dramatic. The untamed landscapes of Abruzzo, the heel of the elegant Italian boot in Puglia, and the unique island of Sicily, with its active volcano, are matched only by Campania. The region of Vesuvius and of the glorious Bay of Naples, it was given the name Campania Felix, or 'Happy Country', by the Romans. Your happiness awaits.

235

# Naples, Sicily and the South

*Getting there: the main airport is Naples' Capodichino (tel: 081 789 6111), 5km (3 miles) north of the city. Other airports serving the south are Bari and Brindisi for Puglia, and Lamezia and Reggio di Calabria for the southwest of Italy. Sicily has its own two airports at Catania and Palermo.*

## (1) Alberobello

Truly unique as the capital of the little conical dwellings, the *trulli* – mysterious and magical in a lovely, picturesque setting. **Page 238**

## (2) Amalfi

The former great maritime power which gave its name to the most stunning coastline in Italy, the 'Costiera Amalfitana'. **Pages 238-9**

## (3) Capri

Known since antiquity as the pleasure island, with its glorious views and lush vegetation of lemon and orange groves. **Pages 240-1**

## (4) Lecce

At the tip of the heel of Italy's elegant boot shape, celebrated for its glorious 'Lecce baroque', it is known as the 'Florence of the South'. **Pages 244-5**

## (5) Naples

From the backstreets to the beauty of the Bay of Naples, this exuberant, passionate city is the heart of the southern 'Mezzogiorno'. It also has superb museums and is the birthplace of the pizza. **Pages 246-9**

## (6) Sicily

The largest island in the Mediterranean has its own fascinating culture, overseen by Europe's greatest volcano, the all-powerful Mount Etna. **Pages 252-5**

## Travel information

Naples' **Stazione Centrale** (*tel: 081 554 3188*) is the southern railway hub and regular trains from Rome terminate here. **National** and **international buses** arrive and depart from the Piazza Garibaldi in front of the station. SITA (*tel: 081 552 2176*) is the main bus service covering Bari, Lecce, Pompeii, the Amalfi coast and Salerno, amongst others. **Ferries** and **hydrofoils** serve Sorrento, Capri, Sicily and the Aeolian Islands and leave from either Stazione Marrittima or Stazione Mergellina. Contact **SNAV** (*tel: 081 761 2348*). Naples is on the **A1** (*Autostrada del Sole*) to Rome and Milan and the **A3** goes south to Reggio di Calabria. The standards of roads in the heart of the area vary greatly, and a **car** can be a trial in Naples and Bari, where parking and theft are major problems.

# Alberobello

The town of Alberobello has over a thousand *trulli* – curious beehive-shaped dwellings, standing against azure skies, whitewashed, with pinnacles of crosses and bizarre stone markers that are said to have magical significance. Some say they can be traced to the end of the 9th century, when the Byzantines conquered Puglia and Jewish and Middle Eastern communities settled here.

Another theory has it that the *trulli* were built as a tax dodge (a common Italian pastime). Made out of the local, calcerous stone, they were stacked without binding mortar, and could be classified as 'unfinished', and therefore exempt from Ferdinand I of Aragon's tax in the 15th century. Whatever their origins, they are unique, extremely functional, being warm in the winter and pleasantly cool in the baking Puglian summer, and picturesque, huddled together in the narrow streets of Alberobello. The oldest and most reliably dated is from 1559, but the majority date from the 18th and 19th centuries. The World Heritage Site, Aia Piccola ( *Via Duca degli Abruzzi* ) – *aia* means farmyard – is the oldest part, comprising about 400 *trulli* and looking like an old medieval village.

*Getting there: 50km (31 miles) south of Bari. By train on the FSE train line (Bari–Taranto); by car, take the coastal road S16 to Monopoli and follow signs to Alberobello. Tourist information: Piazza del Popolo. Tel: 080 721 1916/432 5171. Open: daily 1000–1300 and 1600–2000.*

# Amalfi

The famous Amalfi coast is the most beautiful in the whole country. Lying between the Gulf of Naples and Salerno, a mountainous ridge forms the dramatic backdrop to a glorious coastline that plunges precipitously into a deep blue sea. Towns and villages cling to terraced slopes, where oranges, lemons, vines and almond trees flourish among lush vegetation.

This stretch of coast takes its name from the town of Amalfi, which was founded in 840 and is Italy's oldest republic. It became a great maritime power in the 11th century and laid down the Tavole Amalfitane ('Amalfi Navigation Tables'), the world's oldest maritime code. Later claims to fame came in Edwardian times, when moneyed and aristocratic British travellers adopted it as their favoured winter retreat.

Today, it is extremely touristy, but its spectacular setting remains uncompromised. A climb up steep steps is rewarded with a commanding view from the Arab-Norman Duomo (*Piazza del Duomo; open: daily 0900–2000 in summer, reduced hours in winter; £*). The ornate façade was rebuilt in the 19th century but the interior is mainly baroque, with fine 12th- and 13th-century mosaics. Alongside, the 13th-century Chiostro del Paradiso, 'Cloister of Paradise', is a harmonious blend of Romanesque and Arab-influenced style.

*Getting there: east of Sorrento on the Costiera Amalfitana. By car, the drive along the corniche is scenic but hair-raising, with awkward narrow sections and sheer drops. Tourist information: Corso delle Repubbliche Marinare 19, Amalfi. Tel: 089 871 107. Open: Mon–Sat 0800–1400 and 1600–1900.*

239

# Bari

The capital of Puglia, Bari, was badly bombed during the Second World War, and has grown since the 1950s and 1960s into a rather disordered sprawl. However, it is definitely worth a linger and the best place to start is the old city, **Città Vecchia**. Little alleyways lead past balconies adorned with washing, while delicious aromas of oregano and garlic waft from doorways where people sit and chatter with southern passion. The 11th-century **Basilica di S Nicola Romanesque** ( *Piazza San Nicola; open: daily 0900–1300 and 1700–1900; free* ) is a splendid example of Puglian Romanesque architecture, containing the relics of St Nicholas. The imposing façade, made of white limestone, is flanked by two towers and on the north side, the **Porta dei Leoni** ('Lions' Door') is richly decorated with bas-reliefs and sculptures of chivalric scenes. On the outskirts of the old town, the imposing castle, **Castello Svevo** ( *open: daily 0900–1300 and 1530–1900; £* ), was built in 1233 over the foundations of earlier Norman and Byzantine buildings.

## Tip

*Bari*'s waterfront and old town are notorious places for theft and occasional muggings, especially after dark, so avoid these places at night.

*Getting there: trains (FS tel: 080 521 68 01) link with the main cities north and the southern cities of Puglia, including Lecce. Buses (SITA tel: 080 574 18 00) depart near the main train station; by car the autostrada A14 goes north to Foggia, south to Taranto. Ferries run from Bari to Croatia, Greece and Albania. Contact COTUP (tel: 080 521 2823). Tourist information: Piazza Aldo Moro 23a. Tel: 080 524 22 44. Open: Mon–Sat 0900–1300 and 1600–2000; reduced times in winter.*

# Capri

Capri has always been a pleasure island, known to the Romans as *Caprineum*, possibly because its outline resembles a reclining goat or perhaps because of the 'goatish' antics there of the emperor Tiberius. The island, gloriously situated at the mouth of the Gulf of Naples facing the Tyrrhenian Sea, remains a magnet for the rich and famous and for boatloads of tourists. One of the highlights is the **Grotta Azzura** ('Blue Cave') ( *trips depart from*

*Marina Grande; £££*), which seethes with boats virtually from dawn to dusk. The water inside the cave is an iridescent cobalt blue. Covering a huge area in the northeast of the island are the remains of Tiberius' **Villa Jovis** (*open: daily 0900–1hr before sunset, all year; £*), where the emperor pleasured himself during the last years of his life, from AD 26 to 37. At the back of the villa is the **Salto di Tiberio** ('Tiberius' Jump'), where Tiberius would watch his enemies being thrown into the sea. A 15-minute walk south leads to the **Arco Naturale**, a natural archway in the rock which provides a perfect balcony for superb views.

To get away from Capri's crowded, cosmopolitan main *piazzetta*, take the chairlift from **Piazza Anacapri** to the top of **Monte Solaro** at **Anacapri** (*open: daily 0900–1hr before sunset, Mar–Oct, reduced opening out of season; ££*). A leisurely ride passes over olive groves, drifts of bougainvillaea, lemon and orange trees, and, from the top, there is the best view of all of this beautiful pleasure island and its bay.

241

*Getting there: ferries and hydrofoils run regularly from Naples, Sorrento and towns on the Amalfi coast, all arriving at Marina Grande. Tourist information: Piazza Umberto. Tel: 081 837 0686. Open: Mon–Sat 0830–2030, Sun 0900–1300 and 1530–1900 in summer; weekends 0900–1500 in winter.*

# Caserta

Caserta's **Palazzo Reale** or **Reggia** ( *Viale Douhet; tel: 0823 32 14 00; open: Tue–Sat 0900–1400, Sun 0900–2200; ££; gardens until 1800 daily except Mon; £* ) and park were built from 1752 to 1774 for the Bourbon King Charles III. This is Italy's **largest royal palace**, designed by Luigi Vanvitelli to remind people of the French Sun King's Versailles, with more than 1 000 rooms, almost 100 staircases and 1 790 windows. It covers a vast area of 51,000 square metres (548,977 square feet). The sheer size is somewhat bewildering, but the grand staircase, **Scalone d'Onore**, leads to the more humanly proportioned **Royal Apartments**. There is also a theatre that is richly adorned with crystal, mirrors and tapestries; in 1780, English traveller and writer William Beckford attended a 'grand illumination' here, where 'six rows of boxes blazed with tapers', and 'vast numbers of ugly beings, in gold and silver raiment, [peeped] out.' More recently, on 29 April 1945, the German–Italian armistice was signed at the palace.

The 3-km (2-mile) long park and gardens are on a similarly grand scale, with lovely views from the terrace of the **Giardino Inglese** ('the English Garden'). A bus runs to the far end.

*Getting there: some 30km (19 miles) north of Naples. Accessible by CPTC buses from Naples; Reggia, on the main line between Rome and Naples, is the nearest railway station; by car take the A1 autostrada from Naples and follow signs to Caserta. Tourist information: Palazzo Reale. Tel: 0823 32 22 33/32 63 00 (same opening as the palace; see above).*

# L'Aquila

The medieval mountain town of L'Aquila ('The Eagle') is the capital of Abruzzo, for centuries ranking second only in importance in southern Italy to Naples. It was founded in 1242 by Emperor Frederick II, by the joining together of the citizens from the surrounding 99 villages and castles. The town's unusual origins are remembered in a 99-spouted fountain, the Fontana delle 99 Cannelle ( *Via San Iacopo* ), and the town-hall bell, which chimes 99 times at 9.09pm. However, many of the city's 99 original piazzas and churches have been destroyed by earthquake, most catastrophically in 1703.

Of the remaining churches, the region's most celebrated is the mosque-like, 13th-century Santa Maria di Collemaggio ( *Piazza di Collemaggio; open: daily 0900–1830; free* ). The sheer size of its pink and white stone façade is arresting. Inside is the tomb of S Pietro Celestino, previously an octogenarian hermit, who was crowned Pope, but forced to abdicate due to his 'unworldly' ways. The Museo Nazionale d'Abruzzo ( *Castello Cinquecentesco; tel: 0862 63 31; open: Tue–Sun 0900–1900, closed Sun pm, am only in winter; ££* ) is the region's most important museum. It famously contains the remains of a prehistoric mammoth found locally, as well as good examples of art from the region.

*Getting there: the train station (good connections to Pescara and Rome) is away from the centre, but accessible by bus; by car, the A24 connects the city with Rome. Tourist information: Via XX Settembre 8. Tel: 0862 223 06. Open: Mon–Sat 0800–1400 and 1530–1900; Sun 0930–1230; reduced hours in winter.*

## Tip

243

*Overlooking the town is the Gran Sasso massif, the highest peak in the Apennines at 2 914m (9 560ft). This is the best area south of the Alps for mountaineering and skiing.*

# Lecce

*Writer Giuseppe Cassieri wrote of southern Puglia, 'Here Italy ends. Or does it begin here?' Known to many as the 'Florence of the South', the lovely city of Lecce is celebrated for its voluptuously ornate and exuberant architecture, known as 'Lecce baroque'.*

Everywhere you go in Lecce you will be dazzled by the local yellow pinkish-tinged stone, uniquely malleable and carved to perfection by skilled architects. This was always a **city of migrants**, and Romans, Florentines, Genoese, Jews, Albanians and Greeks have all passed through here. By the beginning of the 17th century there were about 17,000 houses in Lecce, the result of frenzied building activity in the 15th and 16th centuries, when the city became an important **economic centre** of southern Italy and the Kingdom of Naples. The capital of the kingdom was governed by the Spaniards, and the earlier buildings display a decidedly Iberian imprint. The 17th century brought **stylistic independence** in the form of embellishments of flowers, human figures and animals, all lavishly interwoven, and thus the **Lecce baroque style** was developed.

The most perfect example is the **Basilica della Santa Croce** (*Piazza della Prefettura*), begun in 1549 and only completed 150 years later. The lower part is Renaissance, but the sumptuous decoration of the upper part of the

# Galatina

*The small, pretty town of Galatina (18km (11 miles) south of Lecce) is the centre of an important wine-growing region. The streets are almost awash with wine during the annual wine festival in August (information, tel: 0836 56 14 17). Galatina is also known for its connections with 'tarantism' – a form of hysteria known to afflict some women in the surrounding countryside. Known as the* tarantate, *they try to rid themselves of the 'poison' in their bodies (whether it be from a spider – hence the name – or, more likely, the result of some form of mental or physical repression) by frenzied dancing. On 29 June every year, the* tarantate *come to the tiny deconsecrated church of St Paul's at six o'clock in the morning to exorcise their energy and then go to the neighbouring St Peter's Church to be blessed. It is a private ceremony and there is still much shame attached to these poor women, whose external appearance reflects the deeper social problem of their state of mind.*

façade is attributed to Giuseppe Zimbalo, nicknamed 'Lo Zingarello' ('The Gipsy'). Grotesque human shapes and fantasy allegorical animals adorn the balconies, with 13 cherubs above on the carved balustrade, encircling the beautiful rose window.

A short walk west, the **Piazza del Duomo**, one of southern Italy's loveliest squares, is dominated by the **Duomo**. The cathedral, although founded in the 12th century, was entirely rebuilt by Lo Zingarello in the second half of the 17th century and its northern façade is characteristically ornate, topped by a huge 70-m (230-ft) high bell tower. At the heart of Lecce is its main square, **Piazza Sant'Oronzo**, dominated by the **Roman amphitheatre** (*open: Mon–Fri 1000–1300, weekends 1800–2100; £; guided tours also available*), which dates from the 2nd century AD. In the late 1930s, archaeologists discovered that the lower tier of seats remained mostly intact. After six years' restoration, it was reopened in the summer of 2000 as a concert venue.

*Getting there: in the southern tip of Puglia, linked directly by train to Bari, Brindisi, Naples, Rome and Bologna and, southwards, to Galatina, Otranto and Gallipoli. Regional buses connect to many towns on the Salentine peninsula; by car, about 40 minutes' drive south of Brindisi on the fast S379. Tourist information: Via Monte S Michele 20. Tel: 0832 31 41 17. Open: Mon–Fri 0900–1300 and 1700–1900.*

# Naples

*The beauty of the Bay of Naples, under the menacing presence of Mount Vesuvius, has inspired many to draw the contrast between the terrible and the sublime. Goethe concluded that, 'the Neapolitan would certainly be a different creature if he did not feel himself wedged between God and the Devil'.*

Perhaps this explains the exuberance of these people, who live in this passionate and unforgettable city at the heart of the 'Mezzogiorno'. Winding alleyways, peeling buildings, hanging washing, endless noise, traffic-choked streets and petty criminals are all alive and much in evidence. But alongside this nightmarish vision are countless **fabulous buildings**, colourful, bustling markets, beautiful people strutting and flirting on a continual stage set and, everywhere you go, reminders of the city that gave the world the wonderful gifts of the **authentic pizza** and the matchless **Sophia Loren**.

The old city, **Spaccanapoli** (meaning 'split Naples'), is at its most characterful around Via Benedetto Croce and Via Tribunali. Here, the streets are major tourist sites in themselves, but it is worth making a stop just off the western end of Via Tribunali at the **Cappella di Sansevero** (also known as the Cappella di Santa Maria della Pietà dei Sangro) ( *Via Francesco de Sanctis 19; tel: 081 551 14 15; open: Mon–Wed 1000–1700, Sat–Sun 1000–1330; £–££* ). This small 16th-century chapel also serves as a tomb for the Princes of Sangro di Sansevero, and its treasures are its superb sculptures. Sammartino's *The Dead Christ* is a work of extraordinary realism, the figure covered in a seemingly translucent shroud sculpted from a single piece of marble. On the left is Corradini's voluptuous *Pudicizia (Modesty)*, whose modesty is in fact barely concealed by a marble veil. Next to her is *Disillusionment*, a sad figure striving in vain to free himself from marble netting.

## Taste for pizza

*Travel guide writer Augustus Hare, in his* Cities of Southern Italy *(1883), wrote about how earlier travellers had described the simple joys of macaroni and oranges, but how now 'the horrible condiment called* pizza *(made of dough baked with garlic, rancid bacon and strong cheese) is esteemed a feast'.*

In the crypt are the gruesome results of some experiments of the 18th-century Prince Raimondo, who was responsible for the chapel and was also an **alchemist**. Behind glass are two cadavers of which only the inner organs and blood vessels remain, clinging to the skeletons. They are preserved in a mysterious potion developed by the prince, who was later excommunicated by the pope for his 'evil' practices.

*Getting there: city and suburban buses mostly stop at Piazza Garibaldi (SITA enquiries, tel: 081 552 2176); a small-scale underground and city buses, run by the ANM (Azienda Napoletana Mobilità), cover the city centre – tickets available from stations and* tabacchi; *the best advice on driving in Naples is – don't! Tourist information: Piazza del Gesù Nuovo. Tel: 081 551 27 01. Open: Mon–Sat 0900–1800; Sun 0900–1400. Also at Stazione Centrale. Tel: 081 268 779. Open: as above, but more erratically. Web site for Campania: www.regione.campania.it. Monthly magazine* Qui Napoli, *available at tourist offices, gives entertainment listings.*

# Naples: the cathedral and around

A short walk east of the Cappella di Sansevero brings you to the city's cathedral, which has a bizarre history. The **Duomo** (*Via Duomo 147; tel: 081 44 90 97; archaeological zone open: Mon–Sat 0900–1200 and 1630–1900, Sun am; £*) is dedicated to San Gennaro, the city's patron saint. It dates from the 13th century, but is built on the site of previous churches, including an original temple of Neptune. Legend has it that after San Gennaro's martyrdom in AD 305 just outside Naples, while his body was being brought back to the city, two phials of his congealed blood magically liquefied in the bishop's hands. The first chapel on the right in the cathedral houses the phials, together with the saint's skull. Three times a year the 'miracle' is re-enacted and it is possible to witness the liquefaction on the first Saturday in May, 19 September and 16 December (*arrive by 0700 at the latest for the Mass, which starts at 0900*). San Gennaro is traditionally regarded as the protector of Naples and, should his blood fail to liquefy, it is seen as a sign of immense bad luck. Curiously, of the few occasions when the blood did not liquefy in the last century, one was in 1944, after which Vesuvius erupted, and the other was in 1980, not long before the disastrous earthquake.

To the southwest is the imposing **Galleria Umberto I** (*Via Toledo; open: daily*), a glass-roofed shopping arcade built in 1887. It is reminiscent of the Galleria in Milan, but nowadays is rather run-down and even dangerous at night. The nearby **Teatro San Carlo** (*Piazza Trieste e Trento; box office, tel: 081 797 2331; opera season runs Dec–May; ballet and concerts Jun–Nov; open: for tours Sat and Sun 1400–1600; £–££*) is Italy's largest and oldest opera house, built for Charles of Bourbon in 1737. As well as its magnificently opulent interior, it has superb acoustics and is home to one of

# The cleaning-up of Naples?

*Mayor Antonio Bassolino, elected in 1993, has gone a long way to* clean up *the city and create traffic-free zones, but a car in the centre is still a liability. There is still a thriving market in* counterfeit goods, *and* drugs, *masterminded by the Camorra, the Neapolitan counterpart of the Mafia.* Hang on tight *to your valuables – especially at night.*

the oldest ballet schools in Europe. Walking north from here you will pass the Quartieri Spagnoli ( *Via Toledo to Via Chiaia* ), where the astoundingly narrow streets and laundry-draped windows match the stereotypical image of Naples. By day, it's highly evocative, but the liveliness and colour can turn into something much more sinister at night.

It would be sacrilegious not to visit Naples' Museo Archeologico Nazionale ( *Piazza Museo 19; tel: 081 44 01 66; open: 0900–1930, closed Tue; ££–£££* ), which contains the finest collection of mosaics and frescos in Europe. It is also the home of many of the best finds from Pompeii, of the fabulous Farnese collection from Campania and Lazio, and of the largest classical sculpture ever found, the Farnese Bull, which dates from around 200 BC. In April 2000 the 'secret cabinet' of erotic art from Pompeii and Herculaneum opened on the mezzanine floor ( *over-14s only; guided tours; be prepared to queue* ). The items on display are so-called 'disreputable monuments of pagan licentiousness', including amulets against impotence, mosaics, figures and paintings and a very graphic figure of Pan and a goat. It was prurient perhaps, but from Renaissance times collecting such obscene objects from the ancient world was a fashionable pastime.

249

# Pompeii

*The ruins of Pompeii provide modern-day visitors with a fascinating microcosm of Roman life, preserved by the very materials that destroyed it.*

At dawn on 24 August AD 79, **Mount Vesuvius** erupted in a fury of flames, sulphur and smouldering ash. Pumice stones rained from the sky and the dense fumes and smoke made a darkness blacker than any night. Two days later, when daylight returned, many of the bodies of the 2 000 who had perished lay embalmed, some still fully clothed. Although parts of the town were discovered in 1699, **excavations** did not begin until 1748, and they continue even now.

Pompeii's origins can be traced back to the 8th century BC, and by the time of the fateful eruption the city had a thriving population of 25,000 wealthy Romans. Living standards were high: there were artistic treasures, theatres, a market-place, wide streets (which still bear the imprint of chariots today), law courts and highly sophisticated baths. Evidence of a nutritious diet (much like the Mediterranean version today) has been found, and life after dark was lit by oil lamps.

From the western entrance, visitors arrive almost immediately at the **Forum**, encircled by temples to Jupiter, Apollo, Venus and Vespasian, and the **Basilica** (the law courts and exchange), Pompeii's largest building. Nearby, in the **Antiquarium**, are body casts taken from the volcanic ash, distorted into grotesque shapes as they were engulfed. North of here is Pompeii's best-preserved house, the **Casa dei Vettii**, the

home of two rich merchant brothers. Fine frescos, the remains of a lovely internal garden and a mural of the famous spectacularly endowed Priapus and other pieces of fairly explicit erotica are highlights. Just south is the **Casa del Poeta Tragica**

('House of the Tragic Poet'), with its famous *Cave Canem* ('Beware of the Dog') mosaic at the doorway. The house takes its name from mosaics of a theatrical production, now housed alongside many of Pompeii's finest treasures in the Naples Museum of Archaeology ( *see page 249* ).

Still *in situ* is the fine fresco covering the walls of the dining room at the Villa dei Misteri ( *outside the main site near to the Porta Ercolano* ). The scenes of initiation ceremonies into the cult of Dionysus (the Greek god of wine), including flagellation, sacrifices, bridal feasts and dancing, are vividly, sometimes disturbingly, portrayed.

Bathing was a highlight of Roman social activity and the Terme Stabiane baths are the oldest in Pompeii, dating back to the 2nd century BC. They are extraordinarily sophisticated, with changing rooms fitted with lockers, cold plunge pools and every variation in temperature, from the *frigidarium* to the piping-hot *caldarium*, via the *tepidarium*. The theatre was also of great importance and the Anfiteatro here dates back to 80 BC, the oldest-known Roman amphitheatre. On excessively hot days spectators were protected by a huge awning held up by wooden poles. You too will need protection here, so do bring a sun hat!

*Getting there: 30 minutes by bus south of Naples, or by train to the main Pompeii FS station. Tourist information: Via Sacra 1 (new Pompeii). Tel: 081 850 7255. Open: Mon–Sat 0900–1500. Site of Pompeii open: daily 0900–sunset; last admission 1 hr before sunset. Son et lumière June–Sept. Tel: 081 854 5111. ££.*

# Sicily

*According to Giuseppe Tomasi di Lampedusa, author of* The Leopard (Il Gattopardo) *(1958), for the Phoenicians*

*and Greeks, Sicily was the 'America of antiquity'. More recently, the Sicilian Tourist Board's advertising slogan has been 'Come and invade us – everyone else has!'. Colonists have always been attracted to this lovely island, the largest in the Mediterranean, lying in a convenient trading and warring position between Europe and Africa.*

The capital, **Palermo** (*tourist information: Piazza Castelnuovo 35; tel: 091 605 8111; open: Mon–Fri 0830–1400 and 1430–1800, Sat am*), is a potent mix of Oriental and European influences. Founded in the 6th century BC by the Phoenicians, the city is now the location for Sicily's parliament, in the **Palazzo dei Normanni** (*Piazza Indipendenza; tel: 091 705 4317; limited opening; £*). Named after the Normans who conquered the city in 1072, it was originally an Arab fortress. On the first floor, in the **Cappella Palatina** (*open: Mon–Fri 0900–1200 and 1500–1700, Sat 0900–1200, Sun 0900–1000 and 1200–1300; £*), glorious Byzantine mosaics virtually cover the chapel. They rank alongside those of Ravenna and Istanbul as Europe's very finest.

The city itself is exotic and chaotic – full of treasures alongside crumbling tenements, standing in a maze of vibrant back streets. But for the crumbliest of all, visit the catacombs west of Palermo, the **Catacombe dei Cappuccini** (*Via G Mosca-Via Pindemonte; tel: 091 21 21 17; £–££*). The sight of 8 000 corpses preserved from the 17th to 19th centuries, still dressed in their death-bed best, is certainly unusual and macabre, and an extraordinary showcase of the Capuchin skill and tradition of preserving their dead.

The sprawling suburbs south of Palermo are mitigated only by their setting, the lovely fertile plain of the poetically nicknamed **Conca d'Oro** ('Golden Basin'). However, the stunning 12th-century mosaic cycle and the lovely Norman cloister at the **Duomo** (*Piazza Vittorio Emanuele; tel: 091 640 24 24; open: daily; £*) at **Monreale** are worth the 8-km (5-mile) trip.

For the island's greatest archaeological sight, head south to the coast at **Agrigento** (*tourist information: Via Cesare Battisti 15; tel: 092 22 04 54; open: Mon–Sat 0900–1330 and 1700–1900*). Below the pretty medieval town is the Valle dei Templi ('Valley of the Temples'), whose highlight is the **Tempio della Concordia** (*eastern zone; free access*), dating from 430 BC. It is perfectly preserved and, with the other eight temples, amongst the finest classical Greek remains outside Greece.

Inland, 5km (3 miles) southwest of the town of Piazza Armerina is the **Villa Romana del Casale** (*Contrada Paratore, tel: 0935 68 00 36: open: daily 0900–1300 and 1500–1930; £*). The villa is a treasure trove of Roman mosaics, including, most famously, ten female athletes in bikinis!

## Tip

*La Vucciria market* **is a colourful symbol of Palermo, and the inspiration for the old saying,** 'Quando si asciugano le balage della Vucciria' *('When the paving stones of the Vucciria turn dry'). Simply translated, it means 'never', as the stones are always being washed down by the stallholders!*

*Getting there: Catania and Palermo are the island's two airports. Palermo's Punta Raisi is 31km (19 miles) west of the city (tel: 091 7020 111); Catania's Fontanarossa is 5km (3 miles) south of the city (tel: 095 73 02 66). Direct train services (tel: 091 6161 806) run from Rome, Naples, Milan and other capitals to Palermo, Catania and major towns (trains are transported by ferry from Villa S Giovanni on the mainland). Regular ferries cross the Straits of Messina from Villa S Giovanni (Tirrenia, tel: 091 33 33 00). Direct bus services run from Rome (Segesta and SAIS; contact Saistours in Rome, tel: 06 482 50 66).*

# Sicily: around the island

Birthplace of the great mathematician, Archimedes, and Europe's most powerful city from the 5th to the 3rd century BC, Siracusa (Syracuse) was also called 'the loveliest city in the world' by Cicero. The spectacular old town is on the peninsula of Ortygia (*tourist information: Via Maestranza 33; tel: 0931 46 42 55; open: Mon–Sat 0830–1400, Tue–Fri 1630–1930*). The Piazza del Duomo is adorned with baroque façades, overhanging balconies and lovely courtyards, and the town's most famous sight, the Duomo. Built on the site of the 5th-century BC Temple of Athena, the baroque 7th-century AD cathedral includes 12 of the temple's original columns.

At the waterfront is the symbol of Syracuse, the Fonte Aretusa (*Via Picherali*), where, according to legend, the nymph Arethusa was pursued by the river god Alpheus. As she fled towards the sea, Artemis changed her into a fountain so that she could reach Ortygia, whereupon Alpheus pulled her under the waves and 'mingled his waters with hers'. Now, at *passeggiata* time, it is *the* place for the gilded youth to see and be seen.

North lies Catania (*tourist information: Via Domenico Cimarosa 10; tel: 095 730 6233; open: daily 0700–2130 June–Sept, 0900–1300 and 1600–1900 Oct–May*), often referred to as 'Little Chicago' because of its high crime rate.

The Mafia headquarters have reportedly switched from Palermo to here, although the tentacles of the Mafia octopus (*la piovra*) cover the whole of Italy. Although there are some fine baroque buildings, the overall impression is rather grey and forbidding, dominated by towering Mount Etna. The volcano has frequently erupted, leaving some extraordinary lava relics and dark volcanic stone, yet 20 per cent of the population of Sicily live around Catania and on the flanks of Mount Etna. The fertile volcanic ash produces sun-drenched fruits and vines.

To visit Europe's highest, largest and most active volcano, go to Nicolosi (*tourist information: Via G Garibaldi 63; tel: 095 90 15 05; open: daily 0830–1300, also 1600–1930 in summer*), south of Etna. From there you can drive (or take the bus) to the Rifugio Sapienza on the mountainside, and then take the cablecar (*open: daily 0900–1530; £££*) part of the way up. A stiff walk through the eerie moonscape or, in summer, a 4WD vehicle (hefty tip extra) takes you to 3 000m (9 843ft). On a good (activity-free) day, mountain guides will escort you some way up through the rugged lava terrain to get as close as safely possible to the mouth of the volcano.

> " Straight ahead one sees the long ridge of Etna, to the left the coastline as far as Catania or even Siracusa, and the whole panorama is capped by the huge, fuming, fiery mountain, the look of which, tempered by distance and atmosphere, is, however, more friendly than forbidding. "
>
> **Goethe on Taormina's setting, *Italian Journey* (1786–8)**

To the north lie the grottoes, rocky coves, winding alleys and flower-filled balconies of the island's most popular resort, picturesque and historic Taormina (*tourist information: Palazzo Corvaja, Piazza S Caterina; tel: 0942 23243; open: Mon–Sat 0830–1400 and 1600–1900, also Sun 0900–1300 in summer*). It is perched on a terrace of Mount Tauro, from which the town takes its name. The Teatro Greco (*Via Teatro Greco; open: daily 0900–1 hr before sunset; £*), which has the most dramatic of locations, dates from the 3rd century BC. Originally a Greek theatre, it was transformed in the first century AD for gladiator spectacles.

255

# Eating and drinking

## Amalfi

### Gemma
*Via Fra Gerardo Sasso 9. Tel: 089 87 13 45. Closed Wed. ££–£££.* Near to the Duomo, this excellent *trattoria* serves one of the best fish soups in the whole of Campania. Another delicious speciality of the region is *melanzane al cioccolato* (aubergines with chocolate).

### La Marinella
*Via Lungomare dei Cavalieri di San Giovanni dei Gerusalemme 1. Tel: 089 87 10 43. Open: summer. Closed Fri. ££.* Superb views over the coast from this popular restaurant where fish is the speciality. Try the delicious regional dish *polpo al papacchio* (octopus with hot pepper).

## Capri

### Canzone del Mare
*A Marina Piccola. Tel: 081 837 7504. Closed eves in winter. £££.* Created by the 1930s singer, Gracie Fields, this restaurant's customers read like a celebrities' 'Who's Who', yet the location is still stunning and the food good.

### Giorgio
*Via Roma, 34. Tel: 081 837 0898. Closed Jan and Feb. £.* Superb Neapolitan pizzas and good wines at very reasonable prices – extraordinary on Capri, but true!

## Lecce

### Caffè Alvino
*Piazza Sant'Oronzo. Open: daily, but closes 1400–1700 for the siesta. £.* Overlooking the Roman amphitheatre, this is a lovely spot to enjoy a long, cooling drink or perhaps sample a *rustico*, a delicious local speciality of mozzarella cheese, with béchamel sauce and tomatoes wrapped in flaky pastry.

### Picton
*Via Idomeneo 14. Tel: 0832 33 23 83. Closed Mon. ££–£££.* Close to the church of Santa Croce, this elegant restaurant specialises in excellent local cuisine with an emphasis on light, seasonal dishes.

## Naples

### Chiacchierata
*Piazzetta Matilde Seroa 37. Tel: 081 41 14 65. Open: lunch and Fri eve. Closed Sun. ££.* A warm welcome awaits in this typical *trattoria* in the heart of the city. Good pasta and fresh seasonal vegetables and fish all feature.

### Gambrinus
*Via Chiaia 1/2. Open: daily. ££.* Founded in 1861, this elegant and best-known of Neapolitan cafés has outside tables in one of the city's most popular locations. Perfect for people-watching.

### Gelateria della Scimmia
*Piazza Carità 4. ££.* Delicious ice creams – some say the city's best.

### Da Michele
*Via Cesare Sersale 1–3 (just off Corso Umberto). Closed Sun. £–££.* Pizza delight – the traditional Neapolitan way with just *marinara* (tomato, oregano, olive oil and garlic) or *margherita* (mozzarella, tomato and basil).

Apart from pizza in Naples, try the delicious *sfogliatelle* (flaky pastry filled to brimming with ricotta cheese and candied peel).

## Sicily

### Leon d'Oro
*San Leone, Via Emporium 102, Agrigento. Tel: 0922 41 44 00. ££–£££. Closed Mon.* Specialises in regional dishes including excellent fish and good home-made pasta. An excellent

wine list is also offered, along with friendly impeccable service.

The best bars and cafés are in **Ortygia**, especially on the waterfront where there is a wonderful free fashion parade of the young and gorgeous. The **Bar Ortygia** at the Fonte Aretusa is very popular.

### Archimede
*Via Gemmellaro 8, Syracuse. Tel: 0931 69701. Closed Sun eve. ££–£££.* In the heart of Ortygia, this is one of the city's oldest *trattorie*, which specialises in excellent seafood. Very popular with the locals.

Palermo's **La Vucciria market**, off Via Roma, is a huge, sprawling affair with all kinds of food, including superb fish and other goodies. Open daily from 0800 to 2000 – keep your wits and your belongings about you!

### Antica Focacceria di San Francesco
*Via Paternostro 58, Palermo. £.* One of the city's oldest eateries, serving excellent snacks such as pizza *a taglio* (by the slice).

### Roney
*Via della Libertà 13, Palermo. ££.* Coffee and sublime pastries in this hugely fashionable *pasticceria*, arguably the city's best.

### Santandrea
*Piazza Sant'Andrea 4, Palermo. Tel: 091 33 49 99. Closed Tue. ££.* Close to La Vucciria market, this good-value *trattoria* serves good fresh fish and traditional dishes.

### Lorenzo
*Via Roma 12, Taormina. Tel: 0942 23480. Closed Wed and Sun lunch in summer. ££.* In a town noted for its expensive restaurants, this is a moderately priced excellent find. Classic good dishes, with a strong emphasis on seafood.

# Shopping

**Alberobello** and **Puglia** region generally: olives, olive oil, artichokes; Locorotondo wine; wood-carvings; paintings; mounted photographs.

**Amalfi**: ceramics; limoncello (delicious, very potent liquor made from lemons), local wine *Lacryma Christi*; paper – there are several paper mills and the main shops are located around the Piazza del Duomo.

**Capri**: hand-crafted goods include cord shoes, hand-woven silks, woollens, ceramics, coral and gold jewellery, straw hats and, of course, 'Capri pants'.

**Lecce**: the main feature of the **Lecce Fiera** (festival), which takes place between 13 and 24 December, is *pupi*, sacred images made of papier mâché. There are many shops in Lecce specialising in these figures, which are mostly religious, although a few are secular. Other good souvenirs include linen, lace and olive oil.

**Naples**: for gold, *capodimonte* porcelain, Christmas nativity scenes, head for the Scappanapoli area. The upmarket shops are behind Piazza del Plebiscito, from Piazza dei Martiri to Via Chiaia.

**Taormina**'s main pedestrianised street, Corso Umberto, has many exclusive boutiques and shops with prices to match.

# Under the volcano

*From mainland Europe's only active volcano, Vesuvius, to Sicily's highest, the very active Etna, Italy's volcanoes are powerful symbols of man's insignificance in the face of the power of nature.*

**Mount Vesuvius**, which means 'The Unextinguished', most famously erupted in AD 79, wiping out Pompeii, and continues to live up to its name. The most recent eruption was in 1944 but the slumbering giant continues to rumble, causing minor earthquakes; as recently as October 1999, there was a quake that measured 3.6 on the Richter scale. In the 19th century Charles Dickens was led up the volcano at night: 'There is something in the fire and roar, that generates an irresistible desire to get nearer to it … what with the flashing of the fire in our faces, and the shower of red-hot ashes that is raining down, and the choking smoke and sulphur … '. It is still possible to follow in Dickens' footsteps and take a guided walk to the summit.

The closest island to Sicily is the sulphuric **Vulcano**, whose name comes from Vulcan, the god of fire. Famous for its bubbling mud baths (excellent for the skin – remember to bring a peg for your nose!), it experienced its last major eruption in 1980. The regular eruptions on **Stromboli**, another Aeolian island a little further afield, are especially spectacular at night, viewed from the safe haven of a boat.

On the island of Sicily itself, although the Mafia may be invisible, you cannot escape the sight of the huge, black graceful cone of **Mount Etna**, towering at 3 300m (10,827ft). There are four craters, with frequent emissions of *lapilli* (fiery explosions) coming from the central one, but the locals will tell you that this is a 'kind' volcano with whom they can live comfortably. 'La Signora Etna' is hero-worshipped, given offerings and houses are blessed in order to escape her wrath. A cable-car, then a 4WD jeep take you to 3 000m

## Like a woman

*Mountain guide on Mount Etna, when asked why the volcano (* il vulcano, *masculine in Italian) is called 'she': 'Etna is like a beautiful woman – dangerous and mysterious.'*

(9 843ft), where you can walk on a moonscape of black rocks, passing the remains of ski lifts which have been taken out in the frequent fiery lava flows. People do ski here during the winter, seemingly oblivious to the might and power of the Sicilians' favourite volcano. As with Vesuvius, surely it is only a matter of time …

# Lifestyles

## Shopping, eating, children and nightlife in Italy

261

# Shopping

*From silks to ceramics, spices to marinated olives, immaculately cut clothes and the softest of leather goods, and much, much more, Italy is an earthly heaven for shopping. If there's one outstanding feature of the Italian way of shopping it is a quest for style and quality that affects everyone – from the very young to the very old.*

## Less is more

Italians tend to favour small, specialised shops over big department stores and shopping malls. Although over-zealous assistants will sometimes pounce, most will quite happily allow you to browse at leisure. In most cities, you'll find shops selling similar products – shoes or jewellery, for example – located in the same area. For a variety of items, such as toiletries, little general stores will often stock a small supply, or seek out one of the few department stores where you won't have to buy designer-brand shampoo, which you might have to do in the chemist (*farmacia*), for example. *Standa, Upim, Coin* and *Rinascente* are nationwide chains selling a variety of goods of reasonable quality, but the general rule is to visit specialist shops for the best products.

## Markets

Every town has at least one ritual weekly **market** where a huge variety of the freshest foods is

temptingly displayed. **Flea markets**, like Rome's famous *Porta Portese*, usually take place on a Sunday and are rich foraging grounds for everything from aristocrats' cast-offs to new leather jackets and jeans. Haggling is an accepted practice for everything sold in markets, except food. **Antique fairs** are held throughout the year everywhere in Italy. You might come across that bargain of the century, but do be wary of fakes; there is an especially active market in fake Etruscan vases and jewellery.

## Best buys

As well as designer clothes, design for the home is an art form in which the Italians excel. You may be sorely tempted by the beautiful furniture designed by such gurus of style as Cappellini, Matteograssi or Saporiti, but you'll find more affordable and transportable items in **Alessi**'s cutting-edge tableware range. His indispensable coffee pot and other stainless-steel pieces make great souvenirs, and can be found in good kitchen and household shops throughout the country.

Brilliantly coloured **ceramics**, or *faïence*, have been produced in **Faenza** in **Emilia-Romagna** since the 15th century. Also known as *majolica*, the brightly coloured ceramic plates, pasta dishes and other tableware are found in many shops in the south around **Amalfi**,

with the best buys coming from the factory at **Vietri**. Good ceramics can also be found in Friuli-Venezia Giulia, Puglia, Tuscany, Umbria, Sicily and **Venice**. The Venetian island of **Murano** is the centre of glass production; some pieces are amazingly 'overblown' but there are some beautiful, more subtle examples too. For **hand-made** and **marbled paper**, Venice and Florence are the main sources; Syracuse in Sicily is famous for **papyrus paper**, ancient Egyptian-style; Lecce is known for its exquisite **papier-mâché** figurines. For **wood-carvings**, **Puglia** in the south has some finely crafted sculptures as well as the northern regions of the **Aosta Valley** and **Trentino-Alto Adige**. In the mountain regions, you can buy a multi-spouted carved *grolla* bowl, from which you drink a warming alcoholic cup of friendship with flames literally licking round your lips!

## Design is all

Whether you're into the highest-quality leather, silk, linen, lace, kitten-soft woollens or even masks, Italy's range of luxury goods is irresistible. The best carnival masks come from **Venice** – after the city's long experience of the festival to end all others. The design capital is 'catwalk city' **Milan**, whose output in recent years has eclipsed that of the couture houses of Paris, but **Rome** is also a cradle of the best of Italian fashion. **Florence** is the leather capital and **Bologna** is also the home of **La Perla**, which creates

263

divinely gorgeous lingerie. In this country of *la bella figura*, a stylish tie from **Ermenegildo Zegna** or a little **Versace** creation that 'envelops the body like a magnificent painting' would be eternally memorable souvenirs. Although **Valentino** is arguably the highest-rated Italian couturier, the style of the much-lamented late **Gianni Versace** lives on in the outrageously vulgar, but glamorously sexy range now designed by his sister Donatella.

Luxury and quality do not come cheap, but the annual summer and winter *saldi*, or sales, offer excellent bargains. An increasing number of factory outlets now operate year-round, with savings of up to 70 per cent. **Naples** is the capital of fake designer goods – gloves, handbags, 'French' cognac, and so on – but you will be accosted by 'bag men' in many Italian cities, and there is also a special Wednesday market devoted to fakes in **Luino** on **Lake Maggiore**. Buyer beware!

# Food and wine

Pasta, olive oil, cheese and wine all travel well, as well as some of these local specialities:

Truffle oils from **Piedmont** and top-quality Barolo and Barbera red wines; gorgonzola cheese and *panettone*, the delicious fruit cake from **Lombardy**. Black spaghetti (coloured by squid ink), sparkling white *prosecco* wine, Valpolicella, Soave and Bardolino wines from the **Veneto**. *Risotto*, *polenta* (made from maize), *porcini* (dried wild mushrooms) and superb wines such as Teroldego of the **Trentino** area and *pesto* sauce from **Liguria**. *Salami, mortadella*, Parmesan cheese ( *parmigiano* ), Parma ham ( *prosciutto* ) and

balsamic vinegar from **Emilia-Romagna**. Red and white Chiantis, Montepulciano and sweet Vin Santo and delicious fruity and almondy *panforte* cake from **Tuscany**; olive oil and juniper berries from **Umbria**. *Pecorino* (sheeps') and *ricotta* cheese and the famous white wines of Frascati and Montefiascone from **Lazio**. *Mozzarella di bufala* (buffalo mozzarella cheese), *Lacryma Christi* wines and deliciously potent *limoncello* from **Campania** around the **Bay of Naples**. *Orecchiette* ('little ears') pasta, olive oil and Locorotondo wines from **Puglia**; couscous from **Sicily** and sweetly delicious Marsala wine.

## How to buy

While credit cards are common currency in larger establishments, Italy's cash society still prefers lire in all smaller shops – excluding the designer contingent. VAT (IVA in Italy, value added goods and services tax) is 19 per cent, refundable to non-EU residents for before-tax purchases of over L300.000 in one shop. Get your receipt and invoices stamped at customs at the airport, then send to the shop within 90 days of your arrival home, to claim your rebate. Some shops are members of the **Tax-Free Shopping System**, which allows you to redeem your rebate at airports' special tax-free counters.

# Eating out

*If imitation is the sincerest form of flattery, then Italian food is probably the world's best known and best loved. From pizza and pasta to* tiramisù *and cappuccino, few of us can have escaped the huge Italian influence on our daily life, but for the authentic versions of these – and so much more – you have to sample them in the country of their birth.*

There is really no such thing as 'Italian' food. What you'll eat here is a mixture of many different regional cuisines, from the robust sun-drenched flavours of the south to the highly prized truffles of Piedmont and Umbria, and the Austrian-influenced dishes in the far north. But, wherever you go in this beautiful country, everyone unites in the pleasures of the table – a joyous celebration of life itself.

## Regionality

The food of the south and **Campania** is famous for the classic *pizza napoletana* – the delicious wafer-thin pizza topped with garlic, tomatoes, basil and anchovies. The plump tomatoes, delicious seafood, freshest vegetables and fruity olive oil all contribute to the healthy 'Mediterranean diet' for which this region is so famous. Further south, in **Sicily**, there is a long tradition of delicious pastries, biscuits and the divine *cassata* – ice cream with ricotta cheese, pistachios and dried fruits. There has always been a friendly rivalry between Neapolitan and Sicilian

pastry chefs – it is a hard choice to make! More grapes and olives are produced in **Puglia** than in any other region in Italy; *orecchiette* ('little ears' pasta) are a delicious speciality here, too.

Pasta is the staple of any meal, listed on menus as *Il primo* (the first). At a conservative estimate, there are more than 350 different shapes. The rich flavours of **Lazio**, of which **Rome** is part, include the famous *spaghetti alla carbonara*, with bacon, cheese and eggs, or *alle vongole*, with clams. For authentic *tortellini*, the shape of which was reputedly inspired by Venus's navel, you need to travel to **Bologna** in **Emilia-Romagna**, the heartland of Italy's gastronomy. This is the area of the king of cheeses, *Parmesan*, and of *prosciutto* – succulent cured ham. Balsamic vinegar from **Modena** is a deliciously versatile seasoning that is at home on every table. The regions of **Tuscany**, **Umbria** and **Le Marche**

produce flavoursome and hearty cooking with top-quality pork, black truffles, wild mushrooms and especially game, as the Tuscans are passionate about hunting. The northern regions of **Veneto**, **Lombardy** and **Piedmont** are the country's main rice-growing areas and here you will find *risotto* – especially delicious when served with local wild mushrooms.

For true gourmets, Italy's highlight must be the 'white gold' of **Piedmont**. According to Antonio Carluccio, London restaurateur and author of *Carluccio's Complete Food*, 'Nothing compares with the white truffle from Alba. It has a far more concentrated flavour and aroma than the black variety.' A little of this hugely expensive delicacy goes a long way and it is often served as flavoursome shavings on top of a meat dish such as *carpaccio*.

267

# Choosing where to eat

In a nation so devoted to the pleasures of the table, the sheer choice of eateries can be bewildering. The golden rule is to try to avoid the touristy meccas with their set menus, and explore just a few streets away to find your own gourmet paradise. The *osteria* with less than luxurious surroundings and paper tablecloths will often serve some of the best food in town. There is an unwritten rule that the worse the murals on the walls, the better the food!

Restaurants are usually the most expensive option and in Rome and Milan fish restaurants are particularly popular. Frequently, the fish is sold by weight and on the menu you will see *SQ (secondo quantià)* or *PV (prezzo da vedere)*, indicating that the amount you pay depends on how much you eat. Although some Italians are now adapting to less lavish meals, you will still see people taking the traditional *antipasto* (hors-d'oeuvre), followed by the *primo* (the all-important pasta course) and *secondo* (fish, meat or vegetarian), and then cheese and/or *dolci* (puddings). If you miss out the pasta course you will be given a sad look, but ultimately the choice is yours! The *trattoria* is, in theory, a cheaper version of a restaurant; usually family-run, they specialise in fresh, seasonal produce of the region – the key to all good Italian food. Many *pizzerie* are open only in the evening, as the pizza is a very popular late-night snack for Italians.

## In vino veritas

Italy produces more wine than any other country most years, but the rich vineyards are by no means limited to 'Chiantishire'! Piedmont's powerful Barolo and Barbaresco are two of Italy's finest reds and in

Tuscany, *Vino Nobile* and Brunello are highly prized reds, as are Sassicaia and Tignanello. Modern techniques and a new breed of wine producers has revitalised some of the old familiar names, such as Valpolicella, Frascati, Chianti and Asti Spumante, who are shedding their raffia image. The poetically named *Lacryma Christi* ('Tears of Christ') is produced from vines growing in the rich volcanic soil near Mount Vesuvius. Puglia produces more wine than any other region. From the Veneto, a glass of crisp sparkling white *prosecco* wine is an excellent *aperitivo* (aperitif) or maybe a herby Campari with soda or a vermouth from its home town of Turin. There are some delicious liqueurs too, ranging from the potent *grappa*, distilled from grapes, to the sweet almond-flavoured *amaretto.* Around the Bay of Naples, lemons are plucked to make divine *limoncello* whose delicious fresh taste belies its potency!

## Table matters

In restaurants you will be offered the red or white house wine ( *vino da tavola* ), which has generally improved dramatically in recent years; if in doubt, stick to the reds or ask for the wine list. Don't be surprised if your order for a white coffee after meals is met with a quizzical look; the Italians find it difficult to understand why anyone would drink coffee with milk after lunchtime. Their caffeine fix is usually in the form of a strong *espresso* or even a *corretto* – the strongest black cut with a dash of *grappa*.

269

# Italy with children

*Picnics,* alfresco *dining, swimming, eating delicious ice cream, visiting theme parks and clambering over ruins are just some of the excitements awaiting children who visit Italy. The Italians are all too eager to clasp them to the bosom of their family and welcome them with open arms in all but the very smartest of restaurants.*

In the capital, **Rome**, the **Colosseum** (*see page 186*) will delight many older children, especially those who have seen the film *Gladiator*. There, they can visit the pens where gladiators and wild animals paced until they were winched up on special lifts to enter the fray. They can give the emperor's 'thumbs-up' signal, then have their picture taken alongside a thonged Roman

centurion. **Piazza Navona** is always entertaining, with its fountains and its comings-and-goings, and its wonderful *Befana* Christmas fair, throughout December. Encourage them to toss a coin into the **Trevi Fountain**, but don't let them take a dip, as this will incur a hefty fine! North of Rome is the Monster Park of **Bomarzo** (*see page 218*), a Renaissance theme park of fantasy creatures and monsters over which they can climb and clamber for many fun-filled hours.

**Pompeii** is sure to be another favourite for many older children (*see pages 250–1*), but do make sure that they (and you) are well protected from the sun's searing rays.

**Sicily** has a huge coastline and fabulous beaches as well as being the home of glorious *gelato* (ice cream) and delicious sweet pastries. **Taormina's Greek theatre** was the setting of gladiator fighting and is dramatically situated with Mount Etna in the distance. Near **Palermo** are the **Catacombe dei Cappuccini**

(Capuchin Catacombs), a series of dark subterranean corridors ( *see page 252* ), which are macabre but educational and also provide welcome relief from the hot sun.

In **Venice**, a trip along the Grand Canal will be a highlight (gondola optional, but ice cream obligatory!). All children enjoy watching the Moors strike the hours at the top of the **Torre dell'Orologio** clock tower, in **Piazza San Marco**, while the beach pleasures of the **Lido** are also close at hand.

On the Adriatic coast, at **Rimini,** there are wonderful stretches of sandy Blue Flag beaches, some 15km (9 miles) long. Rimini isn't all clubbing and partying, and offers a great family day out at the **Aquafàn** water park ( *see page 119* ).

In the north, near **Lake Garda**, Italy's most popular amusement park, **Gardaland** ( *Castelnuovo del Garda; tel: 045 644 9777; open: 0930–1830 Apr–June and Sept, 0900–2400 July and Aug, weekends 0930–1830 in Oct; £££* ) attracts some two million visitors a year. All kinds of rides and themed entertainment make this a great day out for children (and for big kids too).

# After dark

*Italians love to spend balmy nights* al fresco, *and the evening stroll, the* passeggiata, *is a wonderful stage on which to see, be seen and preen. Music lovers are in their element, with world-class opera and concerts. Nightlife tends to start very late on the club scene and, during the summer months, re-locates to outside venues where revellers dance under the stars until the sun comes up.*

## Classical music and theatre

Italy hosts some of the world's best concerts and festivals. The main concert season runs from October to June but during high summer many open-air concerts and festivals are staged in churches, *palazzi* and other lovely, atmospheric old buildings. In **Florence**, open-air recitals are held in the cloisters of **Badia Fiesolana** and in the **Boboli Gardens** in July and August, whilst the highlight of the Florentine musical calendar is the **Maggio Musicale Fiorentino** (international music festival) held in May and June at the **Teatro Comunale**. In **Turin** the famous international music festival **Settembre Musica** takes over the town from late August until the end of September. In Sicily, the outdoor **Greek theatre** at **Taormina** is the stunning setting for an annual festival of concerts, films and plays from July to mid-September.

Most **theatrical productions** are in Italian, but if your command of the language is good, there are wonderfully rich pickings. Check venues and times with the local information centre or local newspapers and listings magazines.

## Opera and ballet

**La Scala** in **Milan** is Italy's premier opera house ( *see page 38* ); the season begins on 7 December, the feast day of Milan's patron saint Sant'Ambrogio. Ballets and concerts are also held within these hallowed walls, which welcomes the country's most discerning and critical audiences. Second to La Scala, but the largest in Italy, is the **San Carlo opera house** in **Naples** ( *tel: 081 797 2111* ), where the opera season runs from December to May, and ballet and classical music from June to November. In **Rome**, the **Teatro**

**dell'Opera** ( *Piazza Gigli; tel: 06 4816 0255* ) has its opera season from December to June. Of the opera festivals, the biggest and best known is held from July to August at **Verona** in the city's huge outdoor Roman amphitheatre ( *tel: 045 801 5151* ). In **Pèsaro**, August is the time for the opera festival devoted to the composer, Giacchino Rossini, the town's most famous son. Near Viareggio on the Tuscan coast, an outdoor festival devoted to Giacomo Puccini is held at **Torre del Lago** from mid-July to mid-August ( *tel: 0584 359 322* ).

## Clubs and discos

The top cities for 'happenings' are Milan, with its discos and rock scene, Florence for its clubs, Rome for jazz and South American sounds and Naples for the blues, and stylish nightclubs for the well-heeled.

273

The club and disco capital of the coast is Rimini, which shares over 150 venues with Riccione. Discos are mainly for the gilded youth, while clubs attract an older, more sophisticated crowd and are more likely to play alternative style music. Both tend to be expensive and, for legal reasons, many require you to have a membership card ( *tessera* ), which you can buy at the door, and which entitles you to a 'free' drink.

In **Milan**, the hottest spots are in the canal district of the **Navigli**. Good jazz is on offer at the well-established **Le Scimmie** ( *Via Asciano Sforza 49* ), while at **Café Teatro Nobel** ( *Via A Sforza 81* ) there is also jazz and cabaret.

**Florence**'s **Taragua Club** ( *Via dell'Erta Canina 12* ) has a nightclub and Latin American disco and, for the young crowd, **Space Electronic** ( *Via Palazzuolo 37* ) is one of the most popular discos. **Rome**'s most happening scene is **Testaccio** – one of the city's most colourful and oldest quarters. The **Alibi** ( *Via di Monte Testaccio 40/47* ) is Rome's most famous gay club, which also becomes hetero in the summer. The ever-popular **Akab** ( *Via di Monte Testaccio 69* ) has R&B, soul, house and live acts too; prepare to queue.

Two of **Naples**' most elegant nightclubs are **La Mela** ( *Via dei Mille 50* ) and **Chez Moi** ( *Via del Parco Margherita 20* ).

As clubs tend to come and go very quickly, it is a good idea to check out the latest top spots in listings magazines, local newspapers or tourist information centres.

# Festivals

*The Italians love to celebrate: whether it's a tiny parish pump affair, a spectacular, showy festival, a religious celebration or a gourmet* festa *or* sagra*, there is one somewhere in the country for every day of the year and more – and everyone is warmly welcomed.*

Carnevale, meaning literally 'farewell to meat', is the period of ten days leading up to Lent, usually in February. It is celebrated most spectacularly in Venice in the famous masked festivities.

Spring is the time of rebirth and there are hundreds of festivities celebrating the new season's gastronomic delights, including asparagus and artichokes. During Holy Week, the Pope makes his Easter address from the Vatican and there are celebrations and processions from Palm Sunday to Easter Sunday countrywide. After the May Day celebrations, the Puglian town of Bari stages the great Feast of St Nicholas (7–9 May), when a statue of the city's saint is paraded through the streets and then taken out to sea.

Camogli (near Genoa) celebrates its Sagra del Pesce (fish festival) on the second Sunday in May with the world's largest frying pan of anchovies and sardines.

The Palio horse races take place in Siena on 2 July and 16 August.

The Umbria Jazz Festival, Perugia, is held throughout July.

The last week of August sees the great Ferrara Buskers Festival (in Emilia-Romagna).

The International Film Festival of Venice takes place at the Lido from late August to early September.

In Florence on 7 September, the Feast of the Rificolona (coloured paper lanterns) is celebrated with folklore and musical events.

The Miracle of San Gennaro is re-enacted in the liquefaction of the saint's blood at the Naples Duomo (19 September and 16 December).

The Fiera del Tartufo in Alba (Piedmont), on the first Sunday in October, celebrates the prized white truffle.

Wine festivals feature strongly at this time, especially in Trentino-Alto Adige and in Castelli Romani in Lazio.

Festa dei Popoli is a film festival throughout November and December, showing films in Florence in their original version (*v.o.*) for a change, with Italian subtitles.

In the run-up to Christmas there are many fairs, including Rome's La Befana, which is held in Piazza Navona. Naples also hosts a spectacular fair selling decorations and beautiful crib figures.

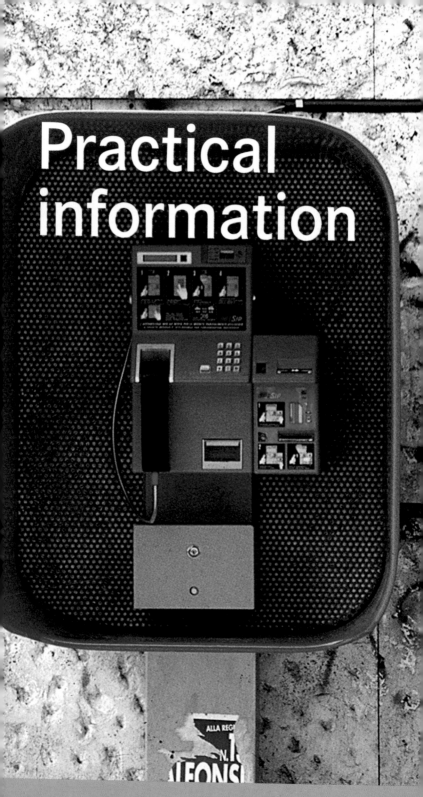

Practical
information

277

# Practical information

## Airports

Most airlines run direct flights to Italy but Milan and Rome are the only **intercontinental airports**. From Rome's Leonardo da Vinci airport (known locally as Fiumicino) there is a direct hourly train service which takes 30 minutes to the central rail station, Stazione Termini. The journey into central Rome is just over 35km (22 miles). If you decide to take a taxi, always look for the licensed taxis in their white or yellow livery. Unofficial touts are at best extortionate and at worst unsafe. From Rome's other airport, Ciampino, a bus takes you to the metro station Anagnina at the end of Metro A line from where the journey is another 25 minutes into the city centre; a taxi is an easier, but more expensive alternative. From Milan's intercontinental airport, Malpensa, a convenient Air Pullman bus goes to Stazione Centrale; the 50-km (31-mile) journey by taxi is extremely expensive. From Milan's other airport, Linate, it is just 8km (5 miles) to the centre on the ATM bus 73.

## Climate

Generally, Italy has **mild winters** and **hot summers** but, as with other aspects of the country, the weather can be unpredictable. In the northern Alps, Dolomites and the Apennines, winters are long and cold with shorter, although usually warm and bright, summers. The northern lakes enjoy a microclimate where even relatively severe winters seem to leave their citrus and olive groves intact. Milan is characterised by a heavy pall of fog during winter (and sometimes during summer due to its high atmospheric pollution); in general, winters are cold here and summers are humid and hot. In the region of Emilia-Romagna, similar conditions prevail, with thick blankets of winter fog and, again, hot, humid summers. Further south, summers start earlier and winters are shorter; the hot plains of southern Italy are only mildly tempered by breezes and can become scorching during the high season. If you're driving, **air conditioning** really is a necessity rather than a luxury.

# Currency

Italian currency is the **lira** (L) (plural lire, LL) in denominations from L50 to L500,000. The L50 and L100 coins come in two different sizes as new coinage is introduced. L200, L500 and L1 000 are coins, but L1 000 is also available in note form. On 1 January 1999, the **euro** became the official currency of Italy, but during the transitional period until 30 June 2002, lire notes and coins continue to be legal tender. Telephone tokens (*gettone*), worth L200, can also be used as cash. Legally, after any purchase or payment of bar/restaurant bill, you must be given a **full receipt** (*ricevuta*). If the finance police (*guardia di finanza*) find you without one within the first 100m (328ft) from the premises where you have made your purchase, you are liable to a fine, as is the owner of the premises. The idea is to try to clamp down on suppliers dodging tax, but there have been instances of unlucky travellers falling foul of the law!

Most banks, stations and airports have **cashpoint or ATM machines** (*Bancomat* in Italian) for withdrawing money on international credit and debit cards. (Remember your PIN number.) Credit cards are widely accepted in large shops in the bigger cities, but Italy remains essentially a cash society and, in more remote corners, local currency is a necessity. **Travellers' cheques** and currency can be exchanged in bureaux de change (*cambio*) but queues can be interminably long; you'll get a better exchange rate at banks showing the *cambio* sign, but opening hours are limited.

# Customs regulations

There are no exchange controls in Italy; however, if you exceed 20 million lire in any currency, you must declare it at the customs office. EU citizens are allowed to import duty-free up to 800 cigarettes/400 small cigars/200 cigars or 1kg of tobacco; 10 litres of spirits; 20 litres of fortified wines; 90 litres of wine (of which no more than 60 litres should be sparkling); and 110 litres of beer. Allowable duty-free imports for non-commercial use for US citizens are: 200 cigarettes or 100 small cigars; 50 cigars or 250g of tobacco; 2 litres of spirits; 2 litres of wine; 50cc of perfume; 500g of coffee. For more information on import regulations contact your local **HM Customs and Excise Advice Centre**, or, in the US, contact the **US Customs Service** ( *PO Box 7407, Washington DC; tel: 202 566 8195* ).

## Disabled travellers

Facilities in Italy for disabled travellers may be improving, but they are generally not exceptional. Wheelchair ramps are often available in galleries and museums, and there are reserved seats at the front of buses and trams, but these can be difficult to use in overcrowded conditions. Italians will generally be helpful and accommodating, especially if you phone in advance to alert the restaurant or hotel to your needs. Some more upmarket hotels may provide dedicated rooms for disabled guests. Should you need to bring a guide dog or hearing dog with you, contact your nearest embassy or consulate for details of the procedure.

The Italian association for the disabled is the **Associazione Italiana Assistenza Spastici** (AIAS) ( *Via S Barnaba 29, Milano; tel: 02 55 01 75 64, www.aias@mv.itline.it/* ).

## Electricity

The standard electric current is 220 volts AC for which British visitors need an adaptor plug and US visitors a voltage transformer. Most sockets have two, sometimes three, round pins.

## Entry formalities

A **valid passport** is necessary for all visitors to Italy. Neither EU citizens nor visitors from the US, Canada, Australia, New Zealand or South Africa need to have a visa for visits of up to three months. If you wish to stay longer you need to obtain a resident permit ( *permesso di soggiorno* ) from any police station ( *Questura* ). Check current **visa requirements** with the Italian consulate before departure if you plan to stay longer than three months. Within three days of arrival, all visitors to Italy must present their passport and register with the police – a formality normally taken care of by your hotel when you check in. If you are not staying in a hotel, you should register at the local police station.

## Health

No vaccinations are required for entry into Italy, unless you are coming from a known infected area. Do be sure to bring enough **prescription medicines** with you as brand names are frequently different and can lead to confusion in the pharmacies. The *farmacia* (pharmacy) is easily recognised

by a green cross and the pharmacist will be able to help with minor complaints and dispense a range of non-prescription drugs, including some antibiotics, or direct you to a doctor. For **emergency treatment**, go to the *Pronto Soccorso* (First Aid) at the nearest hospital. The most common minor medical crises in Italy arise from over-exposure to the sun, over-indulgence in food or wine and attack from biting insects such as mosquitoes. Generally, tap water is safe throughout the country, but signs saying *acqua non potabile* mean that the water is not drinkable.

## Information

General tourist information is available from the **Ente Nazionale per Il Turismo** (ENIT) ( *Via Marghera 2/6, Rome; tel: 06 497 1222, www.enit.it* ).

In the UK, contact **ENIT** at *1 Princes Street, London W1R 8AY; tel: 020 7408 1254.*

In the US, contact **ENIT** at *Suite 1565, 630 Fifth Avenue, New York, NY 10111; tel: 212 245 4822.*

Every major town has a local tourist information office, the **Azienda Provinciale per il Turismo** (APT), which gives useful information and maps.

## Insurance

Make sure you have adequate travel insurance, which gives the right level of medical cover. EU residents are nominally entitled to the same care as Italians, but UK citizens should be in possession of the **E111 form**, which should be filled in and stamped at the post office before departure. This will not provide for repatriation, but it does cover essential medical treatment, although you will have to pay a percentage of the cost of medicines and prescription charges. Doctors and hospitals often require immediate cash payment for their services. Keep all your receipts for medical expenses if you want to claim. If you are unlucky enough to have to spend time in an Italian hospital, don't worry – the exteriors may be rather grim, but their medical care is usually very good.

In cases of emergency call the Public Emergency Assistance number, **tel: 113** (24-hour service), **tel: 112** for the *Carabinieri* (police) immediate action service, or **tel: 118** for ambulances.

## Opening times

**Banks**: generally 0830–1330 Mon–Fri; some major branches also open 1500–1600.

**Bars and cafés**: mostly open from early morning (around 0600) until 0100 – but times vary dramatically, especially in the 'Mezzogiorno' (south) where the siesta is from around 1300 until around 1630. The sign *orario continuato* means continuous opening.

**Churches**: most open 0800–1200 and 1600–1800 daily, excluding services. Many close Sun pm.

**Museums**: many state-run museums close on Mon and Sun pm and at lunchtime from 1300 to 1600. Check beforehand to avoid disappointment.

**Post offices**: 0800 or 0900–1400 Mon–Sat; larger offices may be open from 0800 or 0900–1800 or 2000 Mon–Sat.

**Restaurants**: while many are open from 1230–1500 and 1930–2330, there are huge variations. Many close on Sun evening and all day Mon or on one other statutory closing day (*la chiusura settimanale*, or 'weekly closing'). Most also close for all or part of August.

**Shops**: generally 0830 or 0900–1300 and 1600–2000, Mon–Sat. Many close on Mon am and another half-day per week. Large department and city stores may stay open continuously from 0900–2000 but Sun and late-opening hours are still unusual.

**Tourist offices**: generally, the main APT offices are open 0900–1800 Mon–Sat; check under each town entry.

## Maps

**Italian State Tourist Board** (ENIT), *1 Princes Street, London W1R 8AY. Tel: 020 7408 1254; www.enit.it; www.italiantourism.com.*

The **Touring Club Italiano** (TCI) (*Corso d'Italia 10, 20139 Milan; tel: 02 85 26 72*) publishes a regional maps series.

**Michelin** (*38 Clarendon Road, Watford, Herts; tel: 01923 415000*) produces excellent maps and has created a helpful web site for motorists: *www.michelin-travel.com.*

**Stanfords** (*12–14 Long Acre, London WC2E 9LP; tel: 020 7836 1321*) is excellent for maps and travel guides.

# Public holidays

**1 January** New Year's Day
**6 January** Epiphany
**Easter Sunday**
**Easter Monday**
**25 April** Liberation Day (anniversary of the 1945 liberation)
**1 May** Labour Day (or May Day)
**15 August** Assumption or 'Ferragosto'
**1 November** All Saints' Day
**8 December** Immaculate Conception
**25 December** Christmas Day
**26 December** Day of St Stephen (Santo Stefano)

Each town also celebrates the feast day of its own patron saint.

# Reading

*History and Art*
*A History of Italian Renaissance Art* by F Hartt
*Lives of the Artists, Vols 1 and 2* by Giorgio Vasari
*The Civilisation of the Renaissance in Italy* by Jacob Burckhardt
*The Prince* by Niccolò Machiavelli
*The Book of the Courtier* by Baldassare Castiglione
*The Italians* by Luigi Barzini

*Travel and fiction*
*The Charterhouse of Parma: Rome, Naples and Florence* by Stendhal
*The Betrothed* by Alessandro Manzoni
*Accidental Death of an Anarchist* by Dario Fo
*Death in Venice* by Thomas Mann
*Remembrance of Things Past* by Marcel Proust
*The Name of the Rose* by Umberto Eco
*Pictures from Italy* by Charles Dickens
*Orlando Furioso (The Frenzy of Orlando)* by Ludovico Ariosto
*The Garden of the Finzi-Continis* by Giorgio Bassani
*The Divine Comedy* by Dante Alighieri
*The Decameron* by Giovanni Boccaccio
*The Woman of Rome* by Alberto Moravia
*Twilight in Italy, Sea and Sardinia* and *Etruscan Places*, all by D H Lawrence
*A Violent Life* by Pier Paolo Pasolini
*The Leopard* by Giuseppe Tomasi di Lampedusa

# Safety and security

Italy has been called a thieves' paradise and it is an unfortunate fact of life here, as in many countries. To foil the bagsnatchers, known as the *scippatori*, keep all your valuables and cash out of sight, preferably in a money belt. Never leave anything visible in a car and, when driving in busy cities, lock your doors to avoid snatch thieves when you are stuck in traffic or at lights.

Notorious black spots in city centres and the south are best avoided, especially at night: the golden rule is that there is more safety in numbers. If driving on remote roads, do not stop if you see someone trying to flag you down – it is often a ruse for robbery. If the worst should happen and you need to make a claim against your insurance, report the incident to the police within 24 hours, and keep a copy of your statement.

## Telephones

Public phones can be found on main squares, in bars and in *Centri Telefoni*, where you ring first and pay later (*scatti*). Most accept **phonecards** (*carte telefoniche*), which are available from tobacconists or post offices in L5 000, L10,000 or L15,000 denominations. Break off the small marked corner on the card before using it. A **token** (*gettone*) costs L200 and some phones accept coins of L100, L200 and L500. For charged directory enquiries, dial **12**.

## Time

Italy is on Central European Time (CET), **one hour ahead** of Greenwich Mean Time and **six hours ahead** of Eastern Standard Time.

## Tipping

Many restaurants include a service charge; otherwise around **10 per cent** of the bill will express appreciation of good service. In bars it is usual to leave any small change, and taxi drivers expect around 10 per cent. Service is included in hotel rates but porters, chambermaids and waiters should be tipped, assuming they have been helpful.

## Toilets

As there are not many public lavatories, the best option is to use the facilities in bars, restaurants and hotels or petrol stations. Standards vary dramatically and it may be wise to carry spare tissues with you. To avoid embarrassment, remember that Men is *Signori* and Women, *Signore*. Attendants expect a small tip.

# Index

# Editorial, design and production credits

**Project management:** Dial House Publishing Services

**Series editor:** Christopher Catling

**Copy editor:** Jane Franklin

**Proof-reader:** Gill Colver

**Series and cover design:** Trickett & Webb Limited

**Cover artwork:** Wenham Arts

**Text layout:** Wenham Arts

**Cartography:** Polly Senior Cartography

**Repro and image setting:** Z2 Repro, Thetford, Norfolk, UK

**Printed and bound by:** Artes Graficas ELKAR S. Coop., Bilbao, Spain

# Acknowledgements

We would like to thank John Heseltine for the photographs used in this book, to whom the copyright belongs, with the exception of the following:

**Christopher Catling:** pages 156 and 161B

**Adele Evans:** page 50

**Mike Gerrard:** pages 263 and 269

**Robert Harding Picture Library:** page 139

**Italian State Tourist Board:** pages 129 and 135

**Paul Murphy:** pages 69, 72 and 73

**Neil Setchfield:** pages 12, 13, 14, 48, 49, 128, 185, 186, 201, 203, 262, 267, 270, 271, 274, 276, 280, 281 and 284

**Spectrum Colour Library:** page 259.

Adele Evans would like to thank the following for their invaluable assistance:

The Emilia-Romagna Tourist Board
Go (British Airways' low-cost airline)
Regione Puglia Assessorato al turismo
Ryanair